Imaginative Sex

Imaginative Sex

John Norman

OPEN ROAD
INTEGRATED MEDIA
NEW YORK

978-1-4976-4481-6

This edition published in 2014 by Open Road Integrated Media, Inc.
345 Hudson Street
New York, NY 10014
www.openroadmedia.com

Contents

NO FANTASY, PLEASE, WE'RE AMERICANS

A Foreword by a Feminist
(Pat Califia, Only Briefly Tempted to Use a Pseudonym)

John Norman is a bad boy, okay? He's a sexist pig. And I own just about everything he's ever published; it's some of my most consistently rewarding jackoff material. So it's with great relish that I agreed to write a foreword to his opus *Imaginative Sex*, which is a sort of nonfiction companion to the series of science fiction novels he wrote about Gor, a world where Muscular Men Wield Swords and women have a lot of work to do—kneeling, fetching cups of wine, wearing skimpy outfits, listening to surprisingly pedantic lectures from their Warlord Masters about their True Feminine Slave Natures, and (oh yes) coming tons and tons.

It's very easy to pick apart the politics of the Gor series (and this book as well). Purchasing and reading Norman's work makes me feel like I'm doing something really naughty, like smuggling a barbecued pork sandwich into a vegetarian potluck. (But aren't you *supposed* to feel that way when you're reading erotic materials? It's delicious, that guilty feeling of doing what you want to do and really enjoy, rather than doing what you ought and should.)

Yes, the work is unrelievedly heterosexual. Gor contains no male or female homosexuality; men bond with one another by passing around their lovely Kajira. Norman posits a world in which biology is supposedly allowed to dictate the social and sexual roles which men and women will play—dominant and warlike, submissive and servile, respectively, in case you've been on some other planet yourself for the last three decades. I have been tempted more than once to staple together the pages of the Gor novels which lapse into diatribe. It's almost as bad as reading the Marquis de Sade. It's not that I mind a spot of philosophy now and then; but when it repeatedly interrupts the flow of the bondage and discipline—I mean, the flow of the narrative—a girl gets annoyed. But tops who write S/M literature have a tendency to top the reader—it just comes with the territory.

His consistent lack of political correctness has gotten Norman censored more than once. In the late '70s, a science fiction bookstore in the Bay Area refused to stock his titles because they were supposedly offensive to women. Not even members of the fledgling women's S/M community could get it together to protest. We were too deeply divided about his work ourselves, even though it was clear that the bondage, piercing, and occasional blows meted out by Norman's masters were troubling the staff at Another Change of Hobbit just as much as his espousal of sociobiology. There have been many other times when an antiporn, anti-S/M version of feminist sensibility was used to hamper the circulation of Norman's work.

I'd be happy to support Norman just to oppose this moral intrusion upon free expression of the human imagination. If J. G. Ballard can write about the erotic value of car crashes, surely Norman can be permitted the staff-and-frond brand on the thigh of a newly made slave and her tears at the humiliation of having her earlobes and septum pierced. But there's much more of merit in Norman's work than a mere opportunity to shout down the censors. He speaks for a portion of the S/M-D/S-fetish-leather community that suffers from a disproportionate amount of stigma.

Perhaps a little history is in order here. People who like to enact fantasies about dominance and submission have been creating a community and culture for three or four decades in this country. Gay leathermen have been the most successful at establishing publicly accessible institutions such as bars, sex clubs, and bathhouses where experienced practitioners can socialize or play, and novices can begin the process of being socialized into the leather community. Heterosexuals and leather dykes have been close behind, generating support groups, publications, parties, and other means of celebrating our sexuality and making contact with potential new community members. By creating slogans such as "Safe, Sane, and Consensual" and promulgating standards of emotionally and physically safe play, the S/M (or D/S) community has instilled a sense of pride and self-worth in its members. We've even begun to defend our legal rights—organizing politically to raise money to defend a couple in "the scene" who lost custody of their children, appeal the conviction of the Spanner defendants (who were jailed in England for consensual S/M activity) to the European Court, protest defamation and negative stereotypes of S/M in the mass media, and argue in court that our literature ought to be allowed to circulate freely across national boundaries.

Still, the S/M or D/S community remains deeply divided along lines of gender and sexual orientation. Each subgroup tends to prefer to devote most of its time and attention to itself, which makes sense, considering that the political act most frequently engaged in by kinky people is the simple matter of negotiating a scene. Most of our energy still goes into helping community members find one another for friendship, romance, and play. Prejudice against "the others" remains fairly strong in each subgroup. And there's one bunch of people that just about everybody (no matter how pervy) looks at askance—heterosexual male dominants and female submissives.

Just why this is, I am not certain. I suspect it has something to do with public relations. Power-exchange sex, often denigrated as merely a version of rape or some other form of violence against women, is regarded by antiporn feminists as the ultimate act of sexism and misogyny. If the couple in a scene consists of two women, two men, or a dominant woman and a submissive man, attempts to connect what's happening to rape or woman-hating are patently absurd. But if the fantasy Master is a man and the fantasy slave is a woman, an apologist for the leather community needs to demand much more of the audience he or she is trying to educate. It then becomes necessary to talk in more detail about concepts like consent, mutual pleasure, catharsis, the paradoxical nature of sex and power, the *real* equality of top and bottom which makes *pretended* inequality exciting, and a dozen other sophisticated factors.

That's why it's important for books like this one to be in print. *Imaginative Sex* was first published by DAW Books, Inc., in 1974. It did well enough to be kept in bookstores until recently, when (for reasons I am at a loss to explain) it became necessary for Masquerade to make it available once more. It was one of the first above-ground nonfiction books to offer a rationalization for dominant/submissive role-playing and some instructions about how to do it. Norman does not use terminology that is current in today's leather community (for the very simple reason that the jargon and conventions we take for granted had not been created when he wrote the book). So familiar concepts such as negotiation, safe words, limits, etc., are not to be found in these pages. But it is clear that he is describing activity between consenting adults which is intended to be mutually pleasurable, respectful, loving, and physically and emotionally safe. In Norman's work, the focus is on the pleasure of the female slave, much more so than on the gratification of her master. Her arousal is the centerpiece of his work: Without the consent implied by her sexual excitement, this whole worldview falls apart.

True, it's annoying to have to skip over the paragraphs about feminism and lesbianism. Unfortunately Norman connects the fantasy roles he prefers with evolution and biology. Evolution created man-the-hunter; therefore, it's normal and natural and good and right for men to be sexually aggressive and top their female partners. Men have testosterone; therefore, they are ordained by physiology to be masters. This results in the absurd notion that feminists and lesbians are women who have too many male hormones or not enough female hormones or both. Granted, in 1974, pro-pleasure feminism had not gotten much of a start, but it is still grating to see a movement that was mostly concerned with pay equity, protection from sexual violence, and sexual freedom become stereotyped as a man-hating effort to get rid of sex and romance and turn children over to the state to be raised.

But Norman is not the first person to look for a biological

explanation to justify his sexual preferences or politics. In *The Dialectic of Sex*, Shulamith Firestone argued that the technologically influenced evolution of human beings would eventually eliminate biological sex, reproduction, and childhood. Mary Jane Sherfey, author of *The Nature and Evolution of Female Sexuality*, posited a biological basis for the sexual superiority of the human female. In *The Descent of Woman*, Elaine Morgan constructed a biologically based alternative theory of human prehistory that accounted for a shift from matriarchal to patriarchal culture, as did Merlin Stone in *When God Was a Woman*. Gay activists as well as feminists have been eager to use biology, genetics, brain chemistry, and medical science to bolster their claims that sexual orientation is fixed, a part of nature, not susceptible to human control or change.

People make these ideological blunders not because they are evil or stupid (or not solely because they are evil or stupid). Such theories are infinitely appealing not only because they exonerate the individual from a charge of moral laxity or mental illness, but because *they mirror the way our sexual preferences feel*. What arouses each one of us, draws us to another person, or compels us to act out with that partner feels inbred, natural, involuntary. The process of creating a sex life or love life for oneself is at least as much about learning and teaching as it is about discovering one's secret, innate self; but it feels much more like the latter than the former.

Despite Norman's correlation of testosterone with dominance, if you look around the S/M community, you will see that male privilege and "male" hormones have mostly created men who want to grovel and submit to a strong, dangerous, powerful, free, and beautiful woman—not a bunch of Conanesque barbarian slave trainers. And recent studies suggest that it is the presence of estrogen, rather than testosterone, which makes both men and women aggressive. The whole attempt to blame social sex roles on "male" and "female" hormones is absurd anyway; we all need *both* sets of chemicals for our bodies to work properly. On some level, Norman seems to recognize that it just won't wash to try to equate being a top with maleness and being a bottom with femaleness because he includes several scenarios in this book in which the man adopts a submissive role.

I just can't see Norman as a thorough-going misogynist, despite his condemnation of crudely stereotyped "Women's Libbers." He obviously loves women a great deal. I can't imagine him actively working to deny us equal opportunity. His work is fiction; it's about fantasy, and not the allocation of salaries or education. As erotica, it's very effective. And this book is a potent source of sexual enhancement for couples who respond to Norman's particular type of fantasy matrix. *Imaginative Sex* could, however, be used by readers of any sexual orientation or gender. Norman is very good at pinpointing archetypal situations that are ideal for building the tension and polarization crucial to a good scene. It's fairly easy to adapt these scenarios to any S/M or D/S relationship. Both male and female submissives react to being pounced on, kidnapped, and "raped" (i.e., ravished in a thoroughly satisfying manner). A male slave being teased by a Mistress or a Master reveals his "true nature" just as a Kajira does—by becoming aroused when the habiliments of a slave are placed upon him, and he is "forced" to perform menial tasks and sexual service.

Imaginative Sex deals primarily with the psychological aspects of dominant/submissive role-playing. There's a little technical information in here about bondage and gags, but none about the full range of activity that many people in the leather community use to create intense sensations and emotional release. The "whippings" that Norman describes here do not involve the actual striking of flesh. The dominant partner is told to sharply clap his or her hands together, while the slave reacts as if being whipped. Norman suggests that any partner who really wants to be hit should be persuaded to seek medical attention. I'm not sure what a doctor is supposed to do about masochism that seeks a genuine physical expression, other than add to the amount of shame and confusion that is already way too common among caring, consensual masochists and sadists. Instead, I suggest you savor *Imaginative Sex* for its rich theatrical content, and consult another technical manual such as my own book *Sensuous Magic: A Guide for Adventurous Couples*, or Philip Miller and Molly

Devon's hilarious and sexy *Screw the Roses, Send Me the Thorns*. Many excellent "S/M 101" handbooks for beginners have been published in the last five years, and all are available from QSM, P. O. Box 880154, San Francisco, CA 94188, 1-800-537-5815, info@ qualitysm.com.

All of those quibbles and "yes-buts" aside, please do settle down and enjoy *Imaginative Sex*. It's a unique and wonderful book. Norman is, above all else, a thorough romantic. His work is an indictment of the industrial society we live in, a protest against the inhumane social forces that attempt to turn us all into identical and predictable units of production and consumption. Most people feel trapped, smothered, and humiliated by their jobs and assaulted by the urban environment. More than one person has probably carved out a little sanity for himself or herself by opening one of Norman's books and living vicariously, for a little while, on a clean and lovely planet where it is possible to be a hero or the dazzling object of his desire. A reader who takes the suggestions in *Imaginative Sex* to heart will be able to create a healing oasis of passion at home, with the person he or she loves best. Establishing that source of nourishment and renewal takes a great deal of trust and knowledge of oneself and one's partner. The relationship between the two of you and the secret truth you share can become a treasure that can't be bought or sold. The companion in such a journey is infinitely valuable, irreplaceable—the very antithesis of consumerist culture. Kinky people everywhere owe Masquerade Books a debt of gratitude for keeping in print this thoughtful and inspiring work by an elder of our community.

Imaginative Sex

I

IMAGINATIVE SEX: *The New Sexual Revolution*

The imagination has not yet been sexually liberated. Its liberation is the object of this book.

There are large numbers of people, perhaps millions of them, who will not be able to understand this book. It will doubtless seem strange to them, peculiar, incomprehensible. These will be individuals who are defective in imagination. Whether this incapacity on their part is congenital or the result of an oppressive, crippling conditioning is arguable. These two explanations are not incompatible.

We know that many human beings are defective in their grasp of spatial configurations, others lack sharp aptitudes in symbolic manipulation, others cannot, with a pencil, transfer an object in front of them to a sheet of paper; to some music is a mystery, save for the simplest of bangs and bumps. Some human beings have poor balance; others are color blind; some have slow reflexes; others seem incapable of understanding the plainest need signals of those about them, even perhaps their lovers. All of us, compared to what a human being might be, are multiply flawed with deficiencies. The capacity to use the imagination, one of the highest forms of intelligence, that of creative as opposed to dissective intelligence, is not an endowment bestowed in great quantity on human beings.

In the unusual dimensions and worlds of the imagination most of us are foreigners, flatworms stupidly crawling among stars. On the other hand, in each human being there are, however small or undeveloped, imaginative capacities, as there are capacities for speech, for thought and love. There would seem to be no reason then why almost all human beings, *qua* human being, might not be able to come to a greater or a lesser understanding of what this book is about. Some would understand more; some less; but all would, to one extent or another, comprehend it. Yet we know this will not be the case. Many human beings, even those with normal or above-normal imaginative endowments, will fail to comprehend, at least emotionally, what this book is about. I suspect that in their case the explanation is cultural, not congenital. They, like most of us, have been the objects of a pervasive conditioning process, universal, subtle and pernicious, which restricts the inventiveness of the human mind, the applications of the imagination, to certain approved projects and modes of experience.

It is, for example, acceptable to use the imagination, provided you do not use it too much, in the decoration of one's home; it is acceptable to use it, if not too wildly, in the naming of one's children; it is acceptable to use it in the writing of certain forms of approved fiction, etc. On the other hand, daring to apply this remarkable human capacity to sex is likely, at least initially, to jangle an entire warning system of negativities that has been, largely without our awareness, planted in our brains. Imagination should *not* be applied to sexual relationships, to improve and enhance them. It sounds quite stupid, because it is quite stupid, to say it that way, but that, in effect, is the message.

The human brain, and its inventive power, may be appropriately applied to building bridges and designing guidance systems for missiles, but it may not be appropriately applied to the intimate sexual relations between man and woman. Indeed, at such a thought, the imagination of an otherwise bright, promising individual may tighten into a knot of fumbling, frozen thumbs. You don't use intelligence in that business. Intelligence, inventiveness, creativity, imagination is for bridges and guidance systems, not people.

We have come a long way sexually in the last hundred years. Already we have discovered that a woman has a clitoris. There were many husbands a hundred years ago who were unaware of this. Already there is an open admission of the desirability of caressing a woman before penetrating her. One. even hears, in the more daringly avant circles, of fellatio-cunnilingus now recognized by even eminent psychiatrists, who have found out about it somewhere, as kind of nice. The fact that the very thought of this simple, pleasurable act still fills many people, men and women alike, with thrills of sexual horror, attractive and repulsive simultaneously, is an excellent indication that we are still in the bronze age of sex. It is probably still the case that most lovers, statistically, cannot bring themselves to practice fellatio-cunnilingus. Perhaps the bronze age is too advanced for us. Perhaps we are still wandering around looking at stones, wondering what they are for. At any rate, this book proposes a sexual revolution.

The expression "sexual revolution" is used already, but not too usefully. It seems generally to refer simply to the fact that young people are more public about what they are doing than we were. We bragged less. On the other hand, it may be that they are getting more sex than we did, and younger. That is quite possible, but it would be difficult to get reliable statistics on the matter.

Let us suppose that more people are getting more sex than used to be the case. Even so, that scarcely counts as a revolution. It counts rather as an increase in a certain form of activity. The agricultural revolution differs from the hunting phase of mankind in the sense that people started growing their food rather than chasing it. It was something different. The agricultural revolution is not constituted by the fact that there was an increase in the number of farms. If, on the other hand, "sexual revolution" means that the intellectuals began viewing sex as a natural, pleasurable function rather than a depravity or a disease, then that revolution took place in the generation before mine. On the other hand, I suppose "sexual revolution" might be applied to the phenomenon of large numbers of people catching on to what had been discovered in the generation before mine. In other words, sociologically, the modern sexual "revolution"

would simply be the more widespread acceptance of the genuine
intellectual revolution of two generations ago.

To me, the expression "revolution" is most felicitously
applied to the revolutionary conception, the revolutionary act,
the publication and defense of the transforming ideas, and
their acceptance by the intellectual elite, rather than to the
later derivative phenomenon, sociological changes brought
about by the percolating downward of these sexual theses
and commitments. Today's young did not invent their sexual
revolution. They are buying it. It was manufactured long ago.
The drug revolution, I gather, is their's. They are welcome to it.
We hope, however, for more from them.

It is now time, incidentally, for a new sexual revolution, not
in the sociological sense of mass acceptances of an idea, but in
the intellectual sense of the creating of new conceptions of and
modes of sex. In the intellectual sense of "revolution" it is now
time for a new sexual revolution. The sociological sense will
have to take its turn. The major sexual revolution, the honest
understanding of sex as a biological phenomenon, and not as a
legal, moral or theological problem, is now accomplished. Old
stains linger, but each generation begins anew, less disfigured
than the last.

The essence of the new sexual revolution, whatever its human
implications, is as simple as that of the old. The essence of the
old revolution was that sex was a natural biological phenomenon.
The essence of the new sexual revolution, that which I propose,
is as simple. It builds on the old. It accepts the thesis that sex is
a natural biological phenomenon. It then builds on this thesis by
taking note of the fact that this natural biological phenomenon
takes place *in a human being*. This, in itself, makes human sex
considerably different from animal sex.

Biology in an animal with an upper brain is not biology in an
animal without an upper brain. In one sense the codfish is much
better at sex than we are; in another sense he is an amateur.
Sex, once the constrictions of obsolete conditioning processes
are severed, is a dimension of human experience as open to, and
as inviting of, human imagination as any other.

Why should human thought not be used to enhance sex?

Why should sex not become fun, mentally as well as physically?

Why should not elemental sexual pleasure become transformed into psychosexual pleasure, the sexual pleasure of a creature with a complex brain and imagination?

We are now, still, in the hydraulic stage of sex, in which the potentialities of this glorious human capacity are seen largely in terms of manipulations and pushes and pulls.

It is my proposal, a radical one, that we get the whole human being involved in sex as well as a pair of complementary genitals. This is the sort of thing that everyone might be tempted to agree with, initially, or superficially, but also the sort of thing which, in practice, and emotionally, can be difficult to accept. Similarly, the husband, two generations ago, might have recognized intellectually that he and his wife were animals, but if she had been so unwise as to have crept to him in the middle of the night, whimpering, begging to be fucked, as it is permissible for a wife to do now, he would have been scandalized. They were animals, of course, but, but, but not really! It is our thesis, of course, that we are indeed animals, really, really, but that we are also much more, we are animals with brains, animals with intelligence and imagination, animals with the capacity to fantastically diversify and enhance our sexual experiences. Ways in which this may take place will be discussed in detail later.

It is generally my thesis then to insist on the importance of imagination in sex, to insist that the practice of sex, as performed among human beings, be accorded the same deliberate and playful application of fancy, imagination and intelligence as any other significant human activity.

Imagination is almost totally neglected in the area of sex. Indeed, it is even suspect.

To the repair of that tragedy this book is addressed.

Much in this book is new, but much is not. For example, I am certainly not the first to suggest the application of imagination and intelligence to sexual relationships. I am not the first to sense the exciting role which fantasy can play in intensifying and increasing and multiplying the gratifications of sexual congress. Others have, too, seen the importance of intelligence, of imagination and fantasy. Generally, however, they have feared to speak out plainly. I am sure that many couples, in the secrecy of their love, have practiced the sweet dramatic arts of which I shall write. That these arts should now be made manifest, and their legitimacy explained and argued, defended and set in a total human context, a scientific, psychological and personal context, is perhaps the most revolutionary thing in this book. The revolutionary act is to speak with clearness and in detail, to enunciate and explain imaginative sex with force and fullness.

We must now proceed to do so.

II

LOVE, HUNTERS AND EVOLUTION

By most people today the word 'sex' is still spelled with four letters. This is acceptable provided it is understood that four-letter words are often useful, juicy and expressive. It is not acceptable if such spellings continue to reflect shame syndromes and emotional cripplings.

An orgasm in the Nineteenth Century, which in some areas has lasted better than one hundred and seventy years as of this writing, was more than a breach of etiquette. It was taken as evidence of, and still is, in many quarters, or squares, moral defect. A woman who lay alone in her bed, lonely, wanting her husband to come home and touch her, was not a good woman. Ladies endured their husbands, and husbands, for the most part, endured being endured. A girl would have had to be a barmaid before she could admit to herself that she enjoyed a good fuck.

Those who did not endure being endured presumably sought other releases from sexual tension, doubtless most commonly masturbation and, less commonly, extramarital relations, commercial or otherwise. It seems likely that neither of these recourses was ideally satisfactory. There is, of course, more to be said for masturbation than is commonly said for it. For one thing, it has more dignity than being endured. It is less humiliating. The extramarital relation, on the other hand, owning deservedly higher status in the locker room, is hygienically and emotionally dangerous. Disease, even today, is a not inconsiderable risk, and there is nothing one-uppy or glorious in contracting it. It is not a badge of manhood but a misfortune. From an objective point of view doubtless the spirals of the Andromeda nebula and the spirals of the syphilis bacillus are equally glorious. But one would have to be a Spinoza to notice that the syphilis bacillus is a perfect syphilis bacillus. From the subjective point of view, which happens to be ours, among the many glories of the universe, the bacillus does not rank high. It is, of course, entitled to its own opinion. At any rate, there seems nothing desirable about being loaded with them. Emotionally, the commercial relation is generally impersonal and abortive. You must get out of bed and pull your pants on because the next fellow, on the other side of the door, is waiting. The girl who has collected your twenty dollars is not really in love with you. If you had not given her twenty dollars she might not even have permitted you to make love to her. Prostitution doesn't seem very rewarding to the customer. It is probably less rewarding to the salesperson. The twenty-dollar bill, or the fifty-dollar bill, is cheap. It has probably, in the long run, cost her more.

But why is there prostitution?

The most likely reasons, though not altogether sufficient, would be that the average wife is a bore and a crummy lay. This is not to suggest that the average husband is all that great. Perhaps he is why she is bored.

Affairs are delicious, and doubtless, once in a while, they are not altogether out of order, particularly in the unimaginative, dismal marriages that seem to be the statistical rule in our rather grim and loveless world. On the other hand, to put my cards on the table. I am rather stick-in-the-muddish, and am sold on the institution of marriage, as it might be if not as it is. This does not mean, of course, that I am opposed to having affairs. I am highly in favor of it. I am particularly in favor of having them with one's wife, but real affairs, not pretend affairs.

Later in this book I will explain the strategy of having an affair with one's wife.

Indeed, later in this book, I will describe and detail a remarkable variety of delicious love games and love episodes which a husband and wife might not only share, but which, ideally in my opinion, are to be shared by a husband and wife.

Other lovers are possibilities, particularly if both are unmarried, but the husband-and-wife relationship, the partnership of long standing, the durable and mutually respecting and understanding relationship, supplies, it seems, a desirable framework for these remarkable exploitations of human sexual capacity.

This is so particularly because most of these games require authentic affection and trust. One could not so reveal and trust oneself to a stranger. (Many of these games, of course, require each partner to *think* of the other as a stranger, to whom he, or she, is forced to reveal himself, or herself, whom he, or she, is forced, perhaps mistakenly, to trust.)

I have said that affection is needful. That is true. For these games, however, love is not needful. Rather it is one of the consequences of these games and episodes. These games can produce not simply pleasure, but love between a man and a woman. They twine together their bodies and minds and imaginations in so fantastically subtle and intimate a modality that trust, interdependence and full love is an almost inevitable result. Many people, of course, fear love, doubtless rightly, for love is a vast, tender, profound, binding instinct, which makes great differences in those lives it floods. The human being is both a single organism and a double organism. The human being consists either of a man or a woman, or the two in love. It is natural for the single organism in each of us to fight for its independence, its freedom to be self-seeking and selfish, and self-striving. But it is natural, too, for the single organism to desire its completion in the mated pair. The matter can be argued subtly but those who have been touched by love, usually briefly, have no doubt as to its superiority. Love, once tasted, is in no danger of ever again being regarded as inferior to egotism. Those who have tried both, and we have all tried the latter, would, were it possible, choose the former.

The games and episodes suggested in this book do not speak expressly of love, or seldom do so. Rather they seem to speak, often, of quite other relations, egotistical ones, exploitational ones, but, for subtle reasons, yet not incomprehensible reasons, love tends to be a natural consequence of their practice. That is perhaps because they *are* games, and are understood to be such. They bring men and women together sexually in ways that add light years of dimension to their sexual outlooks and understandings. They make them vitally interdependent on one another for incredible and fantastic excitements and pleasures. They unite a man and a woman in a complex, mentally-challenging relation in which the success of the game depends totally on the willingness, the eagerness and intelligence of both partners. These are games in which the woman, all of her, her mind, her imagination, her body, is fully and necessarily the equal of the male partner. If she is passive, if she does not understand, if she is puzzled, if she does not join fully, the games are impossible. Her ideas, her inventions, her imaginations are as needful and as important as those of the man. She is a stimulating and full participant or there is nothing. The natural outcome of these games, it seems to me, is love. Love, of course, sneaks up on the players. It need not be there at the beginning. The pay-off and the justification for the games is the profound pleasure they can produce. When two human beings, over a period of a year or two, or perhaps in some cases of only a few weeks, can give one another such exquisite and mind-expanding excitements, it is natural for them to grow terribly close and dependent on one another. Each becomes an intellectual, emotional and physical joy to the other. If this is not love, it is the bud of love. Perhaps some morning afterwards, over the coffee, as the husband and wife look upon another, he reaches forth. He touches her hand, gently, because he has an irresistible impulse to do so. She puts her lips to his hand. The petals have opened.

It must be understood, incidentally, that there is nothing wrong with a husband and a wife falling in love. Indeed, most husbands and wives fall in love, truly, only after marriage. Unfortunately, love is a fragile and delicate relationship. It is often evanescent, appearing and disappearing. It is, all things considered, more like a flower than a rock. It is very natural for it to fade but it is no less natural for it to reappear, fresher and deeper than before. In the years of marriage the relationship of two complex human beings is likely to undergo a variety of alterations and mutations. Sometimes, tragically, there is a growing apart, but if there is this growing apart, genuinely, then each plant, presumably, should take its own road, its own organic trajectory. Marriages held together by scotch tape, bandaids and paper clips, though they may last fifty years, are not good marriages. On the other hand, there is doubtless more separation and divorce and unhappiness than is necessary. I suspect, but do not know, that if more imagination entered into the marital relationship there would be a correspondent reduction in human misery, and, presumably, as a corollary, a reduction in the number of abandoned marriages. At any rate, it would be my recommendation to male readers that if you should find an intellectually and physically congenial woman who is eager to join with you in making your marriage an astonishing, surprising, unique, always different, always new relationship, do not let her go. Keep her locked up, selfishly, where she is yours, in the institution of marriage. She is a treasure. And similarly, it would be my recommendation to female readers that if you should find a man who eagerly joins with you to make your marriage a dramatic, startling, intimate affair, with its rich love secrets known only between you, cleave unto him, wench. His arms may be best for you. He is one man in a thousand.

The natural outcome of these games, it seems to me, is love. This assumes, of course, that there is initial and continuing affection and trust among partners. They are emotional dynamite, of course. For that reason they should not be played by individuals who either are not that fond of one another, do not have that much trust in one another or who, for one reason or another, should not fall in love. The ideal framework, it seems to me, for the practice of these love games is marriage. They can transform a marriage into an incredibly exciting, fantastic affair. Used outside of marriage, however, there is danger that they might precipitate emotional involvements which would then lead to marriage, regardless of the desirability of the particular marriage on independent grounds. These games can constitute a repair of marriage, an enhancement of marriage, a transformation of marriage. One must be careful that they do not constitute an inducement to marriage. Marriage is a complex human relationship which requires for its success, one supposes, more than exquisite mutual pleasures.

The reasons why these games can produce love are subtle,

but clear, once considered. The first reason is connected simply with pleasure, the second with human expression. When two people are responsible for producing inordinate mutual pleasure, it is natural for them to become deeply involved emotionally. Particularly is this the case when they realize that such a partner is almost unique. Such a partner is not simply another interchangeable unit, of which most of our marriages seem composed. Such a partner is a rarity. He, or she, is a jewel. The second reason is as honest as the first but, due to the lies we tell about ourselves, less likely to be accepted. It is that in all human beings there are exploitative elements, and elements of a desire to be the object of exploitation. In the crueler language of psychology in every human being there are certain sadistic elements and certain masochistic elements. These differ in amount and degree among human beings but they exist in all. Those with less of these elements are not, *ipso facto*, better than those with more. They may simply be more bland individuals, weaker, less alive, less deep. On the other hand, it is not the objective of these remarks either to commend or castigate these innate human tendencies. They are as natural as those of the cat and the wolf. The higher human being, if we must put people on ladders, is probably the deep, fierce, energetic individual, of high intelligence, who *controls* these powerful elements in himself. He rides mighty horses, but holds their reins in his hands. Morality for him is a victory, not the result of a slow metabolism. There is agreement that human beings should be kind, and moral and honest. There is also agreement that the human being is the sort of animal that often finds it hard to be these things. That he finds it hard to be these things is not the result presumably, of a prehistoric incident in a Middle Eastern garden, or of the temptation of devils. As Nietzsche recognized long ago, man does not need devils. He has his own. Man's defense against himself has been love and rationality. It is still the best we have. They are all he has to pit against himself.

Few people today think much about evolution, but it holds the key to why certain complex aggregations of molecules survive and others do not.

Love and rationality continue to exist because of their survival value. Presumably they, or their antecedents, occurred randomly in a population. Those who loved and cherished and protected tended to maintain their mating relationships and bring their progeny to maturity. The survival value of rationality needs no comment. It is doubtless what has brought us alive from the African plains. The taming of fire, the chipping of a knife, the construction of a wheel, the planting of barley, the catching of wild oxen, the making of laws, it is such things which distinguish us from the grosser brutes. We have an unusual brain. It thinks more deeply, more clearly, more frequently than those of our phylogenetic brethren. It can make an ax which will protect us from the cave bear; it can also construct a bomb with which we may destroy a planet, our own.

The survival value of a property, of course, is a function of its capacity to prolong the survival either of an individual or a group of individuals. There is a substantial correlation, of course, between these two capacities, but the capacities are not identical. The distinction may be clearly drawn in the context of an example. Let us suppose we have two individuals facing a danger. If each is courageous and loyal to the other, let us suppose the danger may be surmounted. Thus, courage and loyalty, in this context, have group survival value, and within the group, individual survival value. On the other hand, let us suppose that one individual turns and runs, and survives, and his fellow is slain. In this situation, courage and loyalty, on the part of the slain individual, did not have survival value. Cowardice on the part of the other did have survival value. He survived. Similarly let us suppose that a given group is attacked. Some refuse to fight, letting others be killed. This obviously has survival value for them. On the other hand, if everyone in the group took the same position, all might fail to survive. The survival value of traits is complex and context-related. A trait which might have negative survival value in one context, say, cowardice, might have positive survival value in another. Similarly a trait which might have positive survival value in one context, courage, might have negative survival value in another. The most courageous individuals, taking perhaps the most risks, might be the most killed.

Survival, essentially, is neutral with respect to what we think of as morality. In certain situations, probably the most selfish, avaricious, and cruel individuals would survive, those that are hardest and least sentimental; in other situations, perhaps such as that of our current world, such properties might be an invitation to extinction. The Bengal tiger has not survived because of his moral qualities. On the other hand, the Bengal tiger is not doing too well today. He might not survive at all if laws were not passed to protect him.

There is, of course, an institutional link between group survival and morality. If a group can trust its own members; if it can instill courage and kindliness and mutual sympathy among its members; if it can make of them moral individuals, at least toward one another, it is more likely to survive than a group which cannot do this. The greatest danger to a group, of course, is the loss of its final unities. An example is a democracy which permits controversy, but only within a mutually accepted context of rules. Without the final unity there is only the jungle. A group which thinks of itself as a whole, and works together, because of the efficiency of its effort, is more likely to be successful than another group, even one more morally oriented. Moralities may differ, though they do not differ as much as might be expected, either because of genetic code or institutionally necessary conditions, but there must be a morality, of one sort or another. Without the morality there is no tribe, no state, no world.

Now what of those elements in human beings, partly exploitative, partly sadistic, partly masochistic, which are a part of the human being?

These traits may at one time have had survival value. If not, they were perhaps concomitants of traits with survival value, exploitativeness perhaps with acquisitiveness, sadism with aggressiveness, masochism with submission to authority. Or, indeed, such traits might be, in effect, random traits with no essential connection whatsoever with survival. For example, blue eyes and blond hair are often genetically linked, but there is, presumably, no important survival value in this linkage. There might, of course, be a sexual value, aesthetically, in such a linkage. That is the second great dynamic of evolution, sexual selection. Perhaps individuals with such traits, women, were more often sought, captured or purchased.

It seems likely, though this is surely speculative, that what might be regarded as the "darker" elements of the human mind, its inclination to cruelty, and its willingness to inflict, and, in cases, its willingness to accept inflicted suffering, are indeed products of evolution, either in its simple survival aspect or in its more complex survival-cum-sexual aspects. If man had to fight for survival, had to hunt and hurt and make war, it seems likely that finding pleasure in such activities, and thus having a built-in reinforcement device, would be of survival value to him. If he did not enjoy stalking game and making the kill he would be less willing to hunt. Similarly, he may well have sought mates who were to him like game, sleek, beautiful and desirable, frightened of him, who could be caught and owned, and tamed, and who, in his snare, would writhe and cry out. Man, probably the sexual aggressor, has doubtless formed the biological character of woman, and, in so doing, through her, his own. I am assuming that a woman has a biological character. I am assuming she is not merely a hollow body, a *tabula rasa*, an emptiness, waiting to be filled with culture and molded by conditioning. It is true that a human being must be acculturated and is, in fact, subject to fantastic conditionings. It is my supposition, however, that there exists something which is conditioned, a body and a brain which is the result of several million years of survival-selected and sexually selected genetic transmissions. The "hollow body" theory does not seem plausible. On the other hand, even in our own century, we do not yet know what a woman is, or a man, or why.

We have already suggested a possible explanation for certain aggressive, exploitative, sadistic, cruel elements in man, an explanation connected with his evolutionary ascent as an ever more complex predator. We have similarly suggested that such an animal might tend to choose women who, at least in part, would be to him as object, as quarry, as game. Surely an ugly, large, dangerous, threatening woman would be less likely to be sought than one who was beautiful, smaller, less dangerous and less threatening. This is not to make a value judgment. There is probably much to be said for large, ugly, dangerous, threatening women. It is to observe that women, as sexually aggressive men have inadvertently bred them, are now seldom large, ugly, threatening or dangerous. They tend to be fantastically exciting, sexually desirable creatures. This is not just a coincidence. If men would tend to choose women who would be to them as game, they would be, in effect, breeding a certain amount of masochism into the human female. Simultaneously, of course, they would be breeding it into themselves.

All human beings possess both sadistic and masochistic traits. Sadism is probably somewhat more pronounced in men, and masochism in women. This is what would be expected. Masochism, of course, would have an independent role to play, of course, both in connection with survival and sexual selection in the following manner. A masochistic woman would tend to be more submissive to the authority of a male. Such a woman would tend to enjoy being dominated. Such a woman would tend to enjoy being commanded. Such a woman might find more pleasure in the performance of simple, trivial, servile, repetitive tasks than a less masochistic woman. She would not like them particularly on one level, but on another she would have less objection. They would be her lot. They would be properly hers to do because she was a woman. Men, the beasts, are the masters. Women are weaker than men. Thus it is on them that the necessary, undesirable work would be inflicted by the stronger animal. The woman who accepts this, who finds her pleasure in it, on some level, would presumably be the most often mated. Similarly, if a woman had a natural instinct to belong to a man, this would make the mating relationship biologically more secure. If the woman had been more independent, if she were inclined to wander off and do her own thing, the race would not have survived. The woman who remains at the fire, feeding it and nursing the children, chewing and scraping hides and fur, is the woman who is used in the firelit shadows, who is forced to do the work and bear the young. Accordingly, masochism would not only be the result of a sexual selection on the part of the male but connected intimately with the survival of family groupings. The result of these considerations is not to say that sadism or masochism is good or bad. They were probably, at a time, functional in evolution. They may be less functional now, but that does not mean they are less real. One thing that seems obvious is that sadism and masochism, for better or worse, are part of human beings. Statistically, men are probably somewhat more sadistic than women, and women are somewhat more masochistic than men. This is presumably a report of fact. Not a moral comment.

Incidentally, briefly, it might be mentioned that it is not clear that sadism and masochism do not still have survival and sexual aspects. For example, an energetic, aggressive male, one supposes, is somewhat more likely to have sadistic inclinations, whether indulged or not, than a less energetic, less aggressive male. Similarly, for better or for worse, a slightly masochistic woman makes an extremely desirable sexual partner. Instinctively she is felt by a male to be vulnerable, to be quarry, and this, for better or for worse, tends to arouse him and, simultaneously of course, improves his sexual performance.

But let us now consider certain conclusions, relevant to our project, which emerge from these remarks.

It seems true that human beings, for whatever reason, possess "darker" elements. It is true that there are exploitative elements in them, sadistic elements, masochistic elements. These are real, and they are *there*. It is naivety to deny them. It is also a bit stupid to deplore them. They are as natural to us as our skins and our prehensile hands, the motions of our blood and the circuits of our unusual brains. It is also obvious that whatever the results might be for the health of the single individual it is morally wrong to hurt, to truly hurt, human beings. We have in us then dark tendencies which may either be suppressed or expressed. It is perhaps not healthy to completely suppress these tendencies, but, on the other hand, it is surely wrong to express them in modalities which would increase the misery of the world. One cannot, if one is informed, deny that these things exist. Indeed, it may be that if one denies them they will have their say in more insidious ways, perhaps injuring health or erupting in disguise in the character of a persecuting moral righteousness.

How many of the nobler fanatics of our time, and previous times, have not claimed their cruelties as justices or dignities?

We have these elements in us.

Do we hurt people, or do we grit our teeth, and turn the acids inward?

The obvious solution seems to be to express these elements in a way that is both sane and healthy, that enhances life and produces pleasure. I do not speak of sublimation. I speak of the real thing. I speak of morally acceptable, gratifying, honest concessions to elements that are as much a part of us as our rationalities and our loves.

Is this possible?

III

MARRIAGE, SEX AND NORMALITY

Most romances, it seems, are exciting and delicious. Most marriages, it seems, are rather routine affairs, often founded on a genuine and deep affection, but mentally, sexually, largely uninteresting and boring. The average friendship and partnership aspects of marriage, so important, could obtain as well among two women or two men. Indeed, exclusive of the family relationship, two friends, or two roommates, if they cared for one another and were adequately efficient cooperants, would have functioning for them ninety-five percent of the average marriage. This does not say much for the average marriage.

A remarkable fact about marriage, seldom explicitly noted, is that it consists of one man and one woman. That is very sexy, to say the least. If there were another practical way to raise children marriage would probably be regarded as sinful. It would be worse than an affair because more prolonged; it would be worse than having a mistress, or such, because it would be so consolidated and secure. The married partners have even been so scornful of public opinion and propriety that they have actually contracted themselves, legally, one to the other, in their scandalous relationship. I once heard a cynic refer to marriage as legalized prostitution. Marriages might be more interesting if more wives took that definition seriously. How would the average wife react if she were to find two ten dollar bills pinned to her pillowcase one night? Would she be scandalized? Perhaps, but, it seems likely, deliciously so. Would she fuss, or weep?

Perhaps. Perhaps not. I expect she would be sexually excited. If she takes the twenty dollars, of course, she would have to understand that she is expected to behave accordingly. Indeed, if she wants another twenty sometime, she had better be a damn good lay. The central point of this paragraph is that marriage, whether intended to be or not, is a particularly sexy institution. What a fantastic opportunity for intricate and delightful sexual experiences is available in marriage. In marriage we have one man and one woman who have each other all to themselves and their pleasure. They are free in a socially accepted, if not approved, institution to contrive the most exquisite enjoyments for one another. The heights of their pleasures will be limited only by their own imagination. To be sure, the grim outside world, the society, will try to reach even into their home with its approvals and disapprovals, its permissions and prohibitions, its common-denominator definitions, its instructions for suitable, standard, repetitive, routine relations between men and women, its prescriptions for turning the intricate and stimulating joys of sex between individuals with *minds* and *imaginations* into, in time, a passive, too-familiar, boring congress of bodies, with little more to recommend it than a release from physiological tension and, perhaps, the assurance that one is a "good" person, i.e., a person who has conformed to standards set in eras of scientific ignorance by individuals who, tragically, feared and hated their bodies, and with the typical malice of such, through the control of education and by means of superstition, tried to preclude others from experiencing joys they had been compulsively driven to deny themselves. To a large extent the contagion of their loathings, centuries later, still infects and emotionally disfigures millions of human beings, depriving them of precious ecstasies, theirs by right of their intelligence and nature.

Less seriously, let us return to the thesis, but a true one, that marriage is an extremely sexy institution. There is no reason one should fail to take advantage of it. Humanly, it begs to be exploited. Marriage is filled with diamonds and glories. It is literally fantastic in what it could offer, in terms of what it could be. Before you read further, agree, tentatively, to put from your mind the familiar placidities of what marriage is supposed to be. Remember that it has been, in effect, defined by unmarried males, individuals who, for one reason or another, refused to love women and give them pleasure. Now, tentatively, agree to the possibility of your own redefining of marriage, what it could be. You must live it. It is up to you, not another, to decide what it shall be. You shall choose its nature. There are now, before you, thousands of possibilities, sunlit, numerous, astonishing. You must go slowly, you must think carefully. At this point, it is only necessary to be open, to try to be open.

Incidentally, society may have made a mistake. It has permitted marriage, probably because there was no practical social alternative. It surely recognizes the dangers of its construction. It tries to determine the nature of marriage, inside and out. It can, however, determine only the outside. It is up to you to determine the inside.

When you and your wife close the bedroom door you are alone with your love and your imaginations.

Before we enter into certain possibilities for deepening, intensifying, improving and transforming human sexual experience, a certain number of distinctions are in order, because words are likely to tumble us in one direction or another. The important thing, though difficult, is to try to think in terms of the world and what it is like, and what experiences are like. Concentrate on the nature of the experience; do not simply look for words to label it. What is going on in this book, in its stumbling way, is revolutionary, and the preprinted labels, with their value judgments saturated in the ink, are not helpful to achieving understanding.

First, let us think of the expression 'normal sex'. 'Normal' commonly has two uses, rather different. The expression can be used, rather neutrally, to designate a commonly encountered, statistically frequent form of behavior. For example, the normal sexual relation, in this sense, consists of a husband, tired from the efforts of the day, kissing his wife a bit, caressing her a little if he is really a terrific lover, and then, before she can be aroused to more than a friendly attitude, crawling on top of her, ejaculating, crawling out, washing, and going to sleep. It's no wonder that millions of women are of the opinion that sex is not all that great. For them it isn't. There are, apparently, literally millions of women who have never experienced orgasm. This is a tragedy of lost pleasure. Unless a woman has trained her body it will usually take her about a third of an hour to be readied for orgasm. The normal sexual relation lasts probably from between five to fifteen minutes. This should make clear one sense of 'normal'. In this sense, normal sex is obviously not very desirable. It is surely a flop for the girl and, for the man, it is hard to see how it could be more than masturbation with a clear conscience. On the other hand, 'normal' is often used, sometimes without notification, as a device for *commending* a certain form of behavior.

In the first sense 'normal' is primarily descriptive, reportive; in the second sense, it is primarily prescriptive, persuasive. That the same word is used in both senses is occasionally useful to the propagandist. For example, if the propagandist approves of mindless sex he will designate imaginative sex as not normal. In one sense, of course, it is not normal. Most people do not use their minds when engaging in sex. In the second sense, of course, the implication is that there is something iniquitous, unhealthy, undesirably deviant, sick, etc., about mentally enhancing sexual experience. There is no agreed-upon definition, incitally, in the psychological or psychoanalytic community on what constitutes mental health. It is not so much that they just do not know yet, as that any such definition would reflect a choice, a decision, on the part of the definers. It would, in effect, incorporate a value judgment.

There are some things on which all would presumably agree, of course. For example, if a form of behavior produced acute mental misery it would presumably be regarded as unhealthy. On the other hand, suppose that quite diverse behaviors could produce a feeling of well-being, release great energies, add stimulation to one's life, help one function enthusiastically in the world, etc. It is very clear that if the individual propounding the definition did not approve of certain of those behaviors, they would not be regarded as healthy, no matter what their results were. For example, if the individual approves of mindless sex, then imaginative sex is likely to be felt as inaesthetic or improper, and since it would be felt, by that individual, as inaesthetic or improper, he would, by a common, perhaps unconscious, subtrefuge, characterize it as sick or deviant. Usually when an individual says something is sick he means that he disapproves of it. If he meant something else, he would examine the behavior to see what its consequences in human life were. Was life made more joyous, more interesting, more worth excitingly living? But those are not the questions asked. Indeed, no questions are asked. Rather there is the automatism of reflex denigration.

It is indeed unfortunate that certain reputed social scientists confuse description and evaluation. It is an elementary fallacy. It is well for us to remember that the social and mental sciences are still in their infancy, and, indeed that, as yet, they are not genuinely sciences at all. It is likely that in the next century they will be. As of now they are handicapped by the complexity of their subject matter, their lack of scientific methodology and instrumentation, and the fact that, as of now, top minds are seldom attracted to the fields. That should change, however; perhaps it will change even within our lifetime. It is only in our time that *numerous* fine minds are entering biology. Perhaps the social sciences will be so fortunate in another generation or two. When *hard* facts can be established, when there is truly a readiness, scientific and emotional, for a form of truth, then top minds, sensing the possibilities, will gravitate toward the social sciences. They are now in the position that botany was in the Seventeenth Century. They are still observing the shapes of leaves and the coloration of petals.

At any rate, I take it that the evaluative use of 'normal' is now clear. In its evaluative role, as opposed to its value-free descriptive role, it expresses an individual's preferential dispositions. For example, I would commit the same fallacy if I said that imaginative sex was normal for human beings. That would be merely a way of my commending imaginative sex, of prescribing it, of saying that it fits my notion of what might be desirable for human beings. Now, I do, as a matter of fact, commend imaginative sex. I am less concerned in this book with prescribing it or with claiming that it is desirable for human beings. I am principally interested in explaining it.

It will not be necessary to prescribe imaginative sex to human beings. Once you understand it you will either prescribe it to yourselves or not. You will think about it and do what you want. That is the way it should be. Similarly, I am not concerned to claim that imaginative sex is desirable for human beings. I am surely convinced that it is desirable for many human beings, and that it could produce great pleasure in their lives. I also suspect, of course, that imaginative sex is not for all human beings, particularly as they have now been trained and developed.

One point of importance is that many human beings are extremely deficient in imagination. It is not likely that they will even understand imaginative sex. For them, mindless sex or reductive sex, physiological sex, is the best they can manage. This is tragic, but then some people can't draw and others can't carry a tune, and others are color blind. We all have limitations of one sort or another. It is perhaps part of being human.

Secondly, imaginative sex may not be good for certain individuals who have been thoroughly conditioned to negative attitudes toward sex. If one has a negative attitude toward sex to begin with, it is not unlikely that imaginative sex will seem unpleasant, frightening or strange. Further, even if such people should find imaginative sex attractive, it is not clear they should try it. If the imprinting of their antisexual conditioning is deep and efficient, presenting them with barriers they cannot break, then perhaps they should not try imaginative sex. They might find themselves the victims of conditioned guilt-reflexes or shame-reflexes. The result of the practice of imaginative sex is not supposed to be misery but delight and pleasure. It seems to me, of course, that imaginative sex might, in some cases, blast individuals out of their mental cages. Guilt and fear are excellent at locking doors, but pleasure and joy are not bad at opening them, either.

In short, I am not interested in claiming that imaginative sex is normal either in the descriptive or evaluative sense. I do think, of course, it can bring great happiness and pleasure to human beings. Also, our notions of "normality" change, and even descriptive normalities change. It is not impossible that in a liberated future where we have discovered not simply the genitals but also that we have minds, that what now seems so revolutionary, so peculiar and different, imaginative sex, may come to be a normal modality of human sexual experience, normal in both the descriptive and evaluative sense. That would indeed be a loving and beautiful future to envision.

In a discussion of "normality" I think it is worth a moment's attention to discuss what we might call square sex and Platonic sex. Platonic sex may be discussed briefly. It is sex with sex left out. The lover is primarily interested, if not totally interested, in the other's mind. Why he does not settle for reading a book is not clear. Sometimes carnal intrusions, like noticing that Belinda has a good ass, might be admitted but it must be clearly understood, at all times, even the moment of orgasm presumably, that it is the *higher* union, the meeting of minds, which is to be much preferred. It is common knowledge, however, particularly among those who have tried both, that it is not always the latter which is much preferred. Pure mind is pretty much of a bore. Few men have set themselves to seduce a computer, nor, I think, should they be advised to do so. Women are better than computers. The opposite pole of Platonic sex, and, in my opinion, only scarcely less dull, and similarly forbidding, is what one might call Miller sex, after the novelist Henry Miller. It is the suggestion, puzzling at having come from a creature as high on the phylogenetic ladder as Mr. Miller, that the best sex or the ideal sex is "pure cunt" sex. In short, sex is a sort of electric connection between two organs, with the people left out. This seems to be needlessly complicated masturbation. It is surely inferior to the wet dream for in the wet dream there is commonly supporting imagery. Indeed, I do not really wish to downgrade Mr. Miller's recommendation. It could well be that, sometime, for the charm and novelty of it, two individuals might wish to try "pure cunt" sex. I am not sure, however, how the woman tries it. It might be difficult for a woman to do even if she wished. "Pure cunt" sex, like most traditional sex, seems to be primarily for the man. The woman, perhaps startled out of her sleep, merely finds her ass grabbed, penetrated and fucked, all in forty or fifty seconds. She is like a female chimpanzee, caught by a dominant male, held and had in a matter of seconds. It seems to me that a woman might be interested in trying this once in a while, if only to find out what it is to be a female chimpanzee. On the other hand, there is little doubt that she will generally prefer to be a female human being. The experience, however zoologically interesting it is to her, is for her scarcely a sexual experience. It is interesting to note that "pure cunt" sex is, for most practical purposes, "normal" sex stripped of its frills, like paying token attention to your love partner; it is normal sex optimized; it is "normal" sex stream-lined, "normal" sex carried to its logical conclusion, reduced to its essentials. The major objection to Miller sex, as to Platonic sex, is that it replaces the natural love object, the human female, with something else, in one case a mind, in the other a portion of her anatomy. Both Platonic sex and Miller sex are forms of fetishism. What one wants, of course, is a whole human female, the unabridged edition, ass, mind, cunt, emotions, person. To take anything less is to be shortchanged.

It is not so much that Platonic sex and Miller sex are only parts of the story; it is rather that they are hopeless distortions of the story. It is not merely that they are incomplete; it is rather that they are stupid. Any male who has a chance at a whole woman and settles for less is a jerk. A woman is utterly marvelous and fantastic. She has a history, needs, inclinations, temptations, desires, feelings, thoughts; she is incredibly complex and sensitive; and you are going to have her, all of her; she has friends and enemies, and people who like her and people who do not; she can drive or she can't; she likes certain books or she doesn't; she has a favorite pair of shoes; she likes the feel of certain undergarments; she doesn't care for certain kinds of foods; you have been kind to her today or you have not; she has been kind to you today or she has not; and now you have her in your arms; she is stripped and completely open to you; no visual or tactual detriment is allowed to intervene between you; she is bare; her beauty is exposed to you, utterly. She is yours. What a magnificent creature! What a joy and glory to take her! What pleasure to have her! What an exquisite joy to make her cry out with happiness and yield to you. He who fucks less than such a creature is wasting his time. Together, two human beings, mentally and physically stimulating one another, you can create extraordinary and incomprehensibly delicious psychosexual experiences. This can be done by not fearing to bring the incomparable human imagination into your sexual relationships.

How to do this will shortly become clear.

I would now like to discuss, briefly, what we may call square sex.

Square sex in this century would have counted as quite trapezoidal in the Nineteenth Century. What will count as "square" sex in a hundred years is any computer's guess.

Square sex is the sort of thing that the polite psychiatrist will charge for for recommending to his clients. It is marriage-manual sex. The ideal sexual episode I gather, from a recent best seller by a now affluent psychiatrist, consists of three layers. Freudians are fond of layers, doubtless a Germanic heritage from the master. The first layer consists of twenty minutes of foreplay in which the male is encouraged to rub his partner's body in prescribed fashions; the second layer, commendably, consists of a bit of fellatio-cunnilingus; and the third layer consists of penetration and intercourse, normally ranging from fifty pumps in five minutes to one hundred pumps in ten. The concept seems very scientific, and might have done credit to Archimedes or Hiero of Syracuse. Sex tends to be seen in terms of erogenous zones, manipulations, applied pressures, and various principles of pneumatics and hydraulics. I have nothing against hydraulics. We are, as a matter of fact, complex physical systems. We are also, however, people. Square sex is a step on the road to human sex. It reminds us that we have bodies. On the other hand, few of us had forgotten that.

On the wilder borderlines of square sex, one is encouraged, for variety, to try new positions. Once again sex comes to be seen in terms of pulleys and levers. The knowledge that there could be a sexual position in which the female is not held under the male comes as quite a naughty shock to many people. Such people are improved by such shocks. The standard sexual position, woman under, of course, is not the easiest sexual position, nor does it provide maximum penetration. It is actually a rather difficult position, which accounts, doubtless, for many agonizing moments in young males who are making love to their first girl. One can sympathize with him because he has been conditioned to believe that is how it is done, and whereas it can be done that way, that is certainly not the easiest. That it becomes easy after practice and experience, of course, is not so much a reflection of its simplicity as of the value of practice and experience. The reason that the woman-under position is the standard sexual position is psychological, not physical. It deals with something very deep and basic, which is likely to be shocking to some women and offensive to others. The matter is species relative. In the spiders, for example, the female is large and dominant. In the humans, it is the male which is large and, unless crippled by conditioning, dominant. In our species it is the smaller, more sleek female who is natural quarry and game. This is standard among the primates. This does not mean that the female is passive. She, too, has needs. She often provokes the male to her hunt. The symbolic aspect of the standard sexual position is, upon reflection, devastatingly obvious. In it the female is permitted very little movement. In it she is most a prisoner. She has been caught. There is no escape for her. She lies there, on her back, pinned down by her captor, looking into his eyes, awaiting her rape. It is likely that the standard sexual position will remain standard.

These considerations also explain, incidentally, why aggressive women are fond of a sexual position in which the male lies upon his back and she kneels across his body. Thus she seems to be dominant. Her dominance, of course, is a pseudo-dominance. It is a dominance belied by her slighter body. In her heart she knows he could, if he wished, seize her and throw her to her back beneath him. This is, however, an interesting position, which can be quite enjoyable for both the male and female. It is particularly to be recommended to women who have a tendency to be too masochistic. It is good for their expansion and pride in themselves as persons. Too, many women find this position very exciting. One might add here that maximum penetration is effected in this position, and the possibility of pregnancy maximized. Accordingly, couples desiring conception might find it instrumentally useful as well as sexually stimulating. On the other hand, a man might not wish to impregnate his wife while lying in this position. When his child is conceived he might rather prefer that it is he who has her, rather than she who has him. We are all symbol-using animals. A man who loves his wife, of course, must be prepared to be had, as well as to have. He must be as willing to belong to her upon occasion as she is to belong to him.

Square sex then is the form of sex most recommended by current intellectuals with accepted psychiatric credentials. It is sex as practiced by educated, informed individuals. Those in the "know" do it this way, or ways. On the other hand, square sex, pleasant as it may be, great as it is, is still pretty much a matter of applied mechanics. There is a great deal more to sex, at least in possibility, than knowing the right places to rub. It is a bit too anatomical in its orientation. One could be quite adept in it without possessing an upper brain. If one has an upper brain, and human beings do, then presumably one might be tempted to use it.

I should now like to put in a good word for square sex, provided its corners are rounded slightly. The rounding of the corners, in this context, means such things as looking into your lover's eyes, and talking to her. She is a human being and can understand speech. She is not really a robot marked off into erogenous zones; she is a highly intelligent, sexually arousable wench. Words can be quite stimulating to a female. There is nothing surprising about this. Every man knows that he himself can be quite responsive sexually to verbal stimuli. How many men have had the delight of having their wife whisper to them in the middle of the night, in the darkness, "I want you to fuck me." When making love to his wife, it is not a bad idea to talk to her, at least until she starts to become lost in your touch and her sensations and only wants to hold on and feel. The talk, of course, is love talk. She is a woman and, accordingly, has beauties. These should be noted and commended, and touched and kissed. Too, you can speak of her of how you felt when you first saw her, and remind her of how she looked and dressed, and acted and held herself. You can speak, too, of other exquisite times you were together and made love. She must understand that she is desirable, and that you desire her, that she is exciting, and she excites you, and that you are going to have her.

This is square-sex-with-rounded-corners, intelligent, informed sex between two tender, intimately involved, loving persons. This can only be commended. This, if one likes, is a basic form of good sex. There is no reason it should ever be abandoned. It would be wrong to abandon it. Indeed, such sex might justifiably form the core of the sexual relationships of most individuals, and departures from it into imaginative sex would be just that, delightful side journeys into strange places, from which one could, delighted and refreshed, always return home to the intimate comfort of familiar lovings. Similarly, even if one should become enamoured of imaginative sex, one should be advised to continue the practice of basic sex. Reality and the sweet animal warmth of familiar lovings must never be rejected. In short, imaginative sex might function as a stimulating supplement to the standard sexual diet, or, if it becomes too exciting, and one becomes lost in feasts and banquets, one should never forget to return, with some regularity, to the common proteins of reality. The difficulty with basic sex, or "square-sex-with-rounded-corners," is that, great as it is, it tends to pale with repetition. Pretty soon you are saying the same things to your wife that you said last night, and the night before; pretty soon you are falling into a mechanical routine of predictable manipulations; pretty soon both of you know what's coming and, even though you love one another, sex, incredibly, begins not to mean that much between you. The exploratory glories of discovery and romance are behind you. Boredom yawns. The husband begins to notice the typists. The wife begins to read novels. If the husband and wife find it possible to take up imaginative sex he will presumably stop noticing the typists. They may be nice girls, and pretty, but to him, they will be dull, little more than bodies. And the wife may continue to read novels, but now in part to help her create her own, in her own life.

It is my suspicion that a whole human life requires elements of both reality and fantasy. We are fond of both rocks and flowers. We wish to have our feet on the ground but, too, sometimes, we like to play. The recommendations of square sex for the almost inevitable development of boredom in marriage are often trivial. For example, try a new position. The value of a new position, of course, is the accompanying mental stimulation. Physiologically the body is content with the old. Square sex is on to something here though, the need for mental stimulation, for difference. It is only that its concept of what is stimulating is simplistic. It is probably the case that making love on the floor at the foot of the bed would be even more stimulating. I would think so. Use of a different bed, or a different room, is probably more stimulating. Making love on the rug in the middle of the living room before the picture window with the drapes open at midnight would probably be even more stimulating. Square sex usually doesn't think in such terms. And never does it think in terms of the same people being different people, being new and fresh to one another, being related to one another in novel or bizarre, sexually charged situations. Let us suppose that the sleepy bites of lethargy have now begun to gnaw into a marriage. It is then time, if not before, for the couple to give some thought to imaginative sex. The justification of imaginative sex, like that of chess and music, is the joy and pleasure it gives. It can also, however, save marriages, provide a healthy release for the natural elements of hostility and aggression in human beings, and produce love. These are not inconsiderable accomplishments. On the other hand, its *raison d'être* is pleasure, simply that, exquisite and delightful psychosexual pleasure.

IV

SEX AND THE BRAIN

It is a clinically accepted fact that most impotence and frigidity are psychological in origin rather than physical. This is a somewhat misleading way to put the fact. Human beings are not divided up into mysterious minds and simplistic bodies. Once we get beyond broken legs the whole damned human being is pretty mysterious. We don't know much about them yet. As of now we havn't even figured out white rats. Psychological problems, on some level, it seems likely, are the results of certain neurological configurations. Misery can be programmed environmentally into people, and often is. One has certain sorts of compulsions or certain sorts of emotional responses probably both because one has a certain sort of brain and certain forms of stimuli have been applied to it. Dispositions to respond which are not useful to the organism are not hard to burn into the brain by conditioning processes. Similarly, incompatible responses can be programmed into human beings. This is cruel, but we do it all the time. We produce, by contrary programmings, contradictory tendencies to act. This often, then, produces indecision, doubt, agony, hesitation and neurosis. The sexual area, of course, is an unusually rich field for such conflicts because here the familial and societal conditionings are often at variance with natural tendencies which, of course, self-program affirmative responses, given certain behavioral acts. For example, receiving pleasure tends to reinforce a given response, say, touching the genitals. On the other hand, a societal prohibition, welded into the brain before the child has a chance to evaluate it, may indefinitely act to qualify and impair genital performance. It is no wonder some men have a hell of a time getting up a public erection, i.e., one before another person, a woman. Similarly it is no wonder some women have a hell of a time getting up a public orgasm, i.e., one before another person, a man.

There is a difference, of course, when the impotence or frigidity is the result of such programmings and not the result of injury or congenital defect in the involved organs. It is the latter cases, of injury or congenital defect, which constitute "physical" impotence. The former cases, results of the reception and processing of stimuli, are those which are often spoken of as "psychological." They are, of course, no less real. They are as real as nerve paths in the brain. Once this is understood the attitude that "psychological impotence" is somehow reprehensible, as if it were a moral or social fault, is seen to be uninformed. It can be as obdurate and vicious as a broken back or castration. On the other hand, it is also, like some forms of physical impotence, capable of dissolution. Habit patterns can be weakened and broken; new habits can overwhelm them.

Sex, perhaps surprisingly, is primarily centered in the brain. Theoretically, a disembodied brain, properly stimulated, could have sexual experiences. All feeling is located in the brain, though the sensation is extradited to the pertinent area of the body. It is important that it should be extradited, or felt, in the pertinent area. For example, if one's foot should be pressing on cactus, it is surely to the advantage of the organism that the pain is felt in the foot which is indeed pressing on the cactus and not, say, in the left hand. Feeling the pain in the foot we remove the foot from the source of injury. This may seem hard to understand but there is a fairly well known phenomenon which should make it clear. Amputees, often, continue to feel sensations "in the limb" which is missing. He feels pain "in his foot" though the foot is gone. Similarly, all sensation is brain centered. It is then extradited, by tactual illusion, to the "area of sensation." I mention this because it helps to understand the powerful role of the brain in the reception of, and control of, sensation. We feel not far from where we think. Indeed, in a sense, feeling is a form of thought, in the sense of constituting a *meaningful* conscious phenomenon. Confidence, mental attitude, are important. Mental context is important.

Without the brain there is no sex as we know it. This is one of the advantages, then, of imaginative sex. It recognizes the fantastic intricacy of the psychosexual apparatus and the interdependence of "mental" stimuli and "physical" performance. In enlisting the brain and thought, it is working not on something apart from sex but on the very home ground of sex. If the stimulation of the brain, if the efforts of the imagination, can produce better sex, this is not surprising. It is what one would expect. I am not entitled to, and I would not, propose imaginative sex as a therapy or cure for impotence or frigidity, but it seems to me not unlikely that it might have, relative to given individuals, efficacy in these respects. At any rate it would be worth a try. If it does not work, it is surely no worse off than other things which also to do not work. I would expect it, however, in some cases, to prove of value. On the other hand, even if it should remove blockages and lead to the pleasures of male and female orgasm, it is well to remember that that might well be no substitute for independent clinical inquiry and attention. If impotence and frigidity are not the disease but the symptom, imaginative sex would then only be effacing symptoms, leaving darker etiologies perhaps intact.

My point in this portion of our text is simple. I am not interested in being a quack, or claiming therapeutic efficacy or anything of that sort for imaginative sex. It would surely be no substitute for competent medical attention. On the other hand I do suspect that imaginative sex, in many cases, perhaps conjoined with other techniques, etc., would have definite therapeutic value. What value, if any, it might have, of course, would have to be scientifically established.

All I would like to claim for imaginative sex is that it is delightful and exciting, that it can be fun, that it can be, under appropriate circumstances, very pleasurable. Beyond this I would invite the medical community to consider its possible use in alleviating certain forms of psychosexual distress. Sexual excitement is often anterior to, and necessary for, adequate or superior sexual performance. If imaginative sex can produce these sexual excitements, if it can set the system in operation, that is surely of therapeutic relevance. Any dynamite powerful enough to blow apart walls is worth thinking about. On the other hand, imaginative sex, as I propose it in this book is intended only as what it seems to be, an art of erotic expression and pleasure. It needs no values beyond these, but if it should have them, then the more felicitous it is.

V

MARRIAGE AND THE VENTILATION OF EMOTION

I have suggested, and truthfully, that imaginative sex tends to deepen and consolidate marriages, and that it can produce not only intense emotional involvement, but love. I should like, however, here to note that it is also possible that it could bring about the termination of certain marriages. For example, if it becomes obvious to one partner or the other, or both, in the self-expressions of these games, that a truly deep-seated, ugly hostility, beyond the ordinary sorts of disgruntlements we all accrue with one another, is being expressed, that is a definite danger signal. If a man truly hates his wife, or she him, they should not be married. That marriage is a crime. If in the context of sex games not love and play, but genuine, deep cruelty or emotional antipathy is expressed, then this is symptomatic of a tragic relationship.

On the other hand, people who truly hate one another are not likely to engage in imaginative sex. If they do so, it might be merely to hurt or humiliate the other. That sort of thing is immediately recognizable. That is a perversion of the games. Hurting and humiliating human beings, genuinely and with malice, is morally wrong. This is very different from pretending to hurt and humiliate.

Drama can have cathartic effect, release emotion and enlarge one's energies and self-understanding. Reality, however, is quite a different matter. Trust and affection, as much or more than imagination, are essential for the games. Imaginative sex is only for individuals who truly care for one another. Indeed, these would be the only individuals who would be likely to so expose their egos and bodies to one another, to so put themselves at the mercy of the other. In short, if the self-expressions essential in these games reveal constant and vicious traits in the partners, then the partnership, presumably, should be terminated. No one wishes to live with an enemy. It is immoral to do so. If love games give individuals an avenue for revealing themselves to one another as authentic enemies, this should have value.

If you are married to someone who hates you, but, for social reasons, or because of his conditioning, conceals this, it is well for you to find it out. You can then look for someone who will love you, and so, too, can he or she. Frankly, however, if a husband and wife hate one another, they are not likely to need imaginative sex to find it out. They will know it already. Further, to some extent, we all build up hostilities toward those we most love. There is a difference, of course, between the natural irritations accrued in living together, and deep hatred. It is doubtless healthy, in a love context, to rid ourselves of certain accumulated emotions of resentment or aggression. We all accumulate these. It is then a question as to how they are to be ventilated. Normally we do so by screaming at one another and treating each other cruelly. It seems to me there are better ways, more satisfactory ways, better humored, more delightful ways.

Suppose, for example, your wife has dented the fender of your new car. Instead of screaming and yelling, or gritting one's teeth and telling her that everything is perfectly all right, you inform her, jocularly, that she will be punished that night. Then, that night, to your mutual delight, she is "punished," perhaps by some variant on the bitch game. In the morning you do not care if she dents the other fender. You have, symbolically, taken out your irritation, have taken it out on her ass, so to speak, and she, too, in the delights of the play feels that she has now "made it up," and knows, truthfully, that now things are all right again. There is no pretending at forgiveness. Forgiveness is irrelevant. The price has been paid. Accounts are square. He has, symbolically, taken it out of your hide, exactly as you felt he should.

Similarly, when a husband, unexpectedly, brings home

company for dinner, or in some other way springs an unpleasant surprise on his wife, she is surely entitled to a bit of vengeance. Why should she permit herself to be stepped on? She could cry and weep but that is not nearly as much fun as imaginative sex. "I'll get you later tonight," she smiles sweetly to him. She does, too. It is difficult to know whether to envy the husband or pity him. One thing is certain. When she is finished with him, she will be more than even.

VI

PRIVACY

You have a right to privacy.

The practice of imaginative sex does not require, any more than the practice of unimaginative sex, that you make your practice public, that you march forth with banners proclaiming your right to invent and participate in sex dramas. If you wish to do so, there is no moral reason you should not do so, but there are practical reasons. Most people will not understand imaginative sex. You will be in a minority, at least until the expansion of the general population's understanding and acceptance of these matters. You will be roughly in the position of an advocate of family planning in the Twelfth Century. You are well advised to keep your mouth shut and enjoy yourself. History has a way of taking care of itself. These ideas, like any good ideas, by hook or crook, will get around. No one ever need know that you and your wife have contrived sexual marvels for yourselves. To your business associates and neighbors, you may still seem the plain, serious, responsible, down-to-earth, commendably glum folks you always were. "Imaginative sex?" you ask. "What is it?" Indeed, one of the delicious aspects of imaginative sex is that it is your private secret with your wife; it is something that the world would be keenly interested to know but it is your own business, and your secret from them.

On the other hand, should you choose to waive your right to privacy, there could be a charm and openness in doing so. Perhaps it is healthier to do so. I do not really know. Consider the case of masturbation. All men masturbate, and there is nothing wrong with masturbation, but it is not exactly the sort of thing, in this time and place, that one goes about announcing publicly. Indeed, it might even be denied vehemently. If we were differently acculturated we might deny we had bowel movements. Masturbation, incidentally, is often superior to average man-woman sex. It is far inferior, of course, to a sexual experience with an eager, loving woman intent upon mutual delight. It runs a poor second to a sweet fuck with a live wench. It is a cookie as opposed to a banquet. There is nothing wrong with cookies; it is just that banquets are incomparably better.

At any rate, imaginative sex is not a social program which its practitioners are obliged to publicly espouse. They may do so, of course, at their option.

Who *does* imaginative sex?

We don't really know.

And it is not really any of our business.

VII

DISEASE

The practice of imaginative sex, because it brings partners together in exciting interdependences, into which strangers cannot intrude, tends to deepen and consolidate marriages. It is thus, for better or for worse, excellent for stabilizing and maintaining monogamous marriages. In short, anyone who is *really* in favor of monogamous *marriage*, and not merely monogamous economic and social arrangements, would be well advised to recommend and practice imaginative sex.

There is an interesting empirical corollary here, which may seem surprising but which, upon reflection, is obvious.

Monogamous marriage, by limiting sexual experiences to separate pairs of lovers, tends, through the simple device of sexual quarantine, to limit and reduce venereal disease. The chance to contract venereal disease increases geometrically with each new lover, because that lover, too, may have or have had lovers. Thus, interestingly, medically, monogamous marriage is the ideal sexual relation for minimizing venereal disease. If the man and wife are not infected to begin with and maintain the fidelity of their relation, they will never be infected. People do not pick up venereal disease from toilet seats. Accordingly, surprisingly, because of its effect in keeping husbands and wives fantastically engrossed in one another, and thus tending to make monogamous marriage an emotional necessity, imaginative sex, if generally practiced, would reduce considerably the venereal disease in the population. On the other hand, unfortunately, because of the unimaginative nature of most human beings and the crippling conditionings to which most of them have been subjected, imaginative sex is likely to be of little general consequence in reducing disease in the population, at least in this generation. Still, it is better than injections.

VIII

REQUIREMENTS FOR IMAGINATIVE SEX

In effect there are three requirements for Imaginative Sex, each of which has been previously mentioned. They are affection, trust and imagination.

One might add, however, a willingness to engage in imaginative sex and humor.

If one of the partners, or both, are for some emotional reason unable to participate in imaginative sex then, obviously, imaginative sex is not likely to be successful with that couple. Love games encourage, or require, that two fully play. If the wife, in her affection for her husband, merely cooperates, there is nothing of much interest. She will make him feel, implicitly and unintentionally, like some kind of nut. Similarly, if a husband, because he has an affection for his wife, humors her by strained and awkward pretenses, there will be little pleasure for either of them. Indeed, he will probably embarrass her and she will feel, inevitably, like some deviant or pervert. She is not, of course. She is just a human being who wants to bring her mind and her imagination into her sex life. That it doesn't belong there is preposterous. Sex is too important and pleasurable to be left to the glands. All human beings have sexual fantasies, and yet, amazingly, we are often reticent to communicate these to others. This is really a fantastic tribute to the efficacy of antisexual conditioning. One problem, of course, is that a fantasy which appeals to one individual may not appeal to another. It is then up to each individual, by imaginative techniques, to feel himself into the fantasy of the other. There is something there, presumably, or the other would not be attracted by the fantasy. Entering into the fantasy world of another human being can be a very stimulating and exciting experience. We do not know another person, really, until we know their fantasies. We add and subtract pretty much the same way, but our fantasies are branded with our own histories and individualities. They are precious and, in certain particulars, unique to us. A person who does not wish to know our fantasies does not really wish to know us; he may wish to deal with us, or use us, but he does not really wish to know us. Our secret self, grandiose, delightful, silly, happy, sentimental, reveals itself in our fantasies. They are probably pretty close to what we are; we are perhaps most what we would be; our dreams are significant components of our identity; are they not as intimate to us as our abstractions and behaviors?

For the true success of the games *both* partners must be imaginative; be stimulated by their common enterprise; both must really enjoy and contribute to their mutual inventions; both must be responsible for, and fully participate in, the creation of their mutual love fantasies. Love games require players. One man on a tennis court by himself is stupid.

A certain amount of patience, of course, is to be recommended. One partner, or perhaps both, may have to enter gently into these games, perhaps a bit at a time, tentatively, trying them out, seeing if, for him or her, they are pleasurable.

Indeed, it is doubtless desirable to begin with simplicities and build to complexities.

Invention breeds invention, and fantasy breeds fantasy. Like any other complex human activity, dramatized sexual fantasy requires, for expertise, practice and experience. Fortunately, however, gratification is available, or likely to be available, from the very beginning. From that point on it is merely the task to multiply, enhance, increase and diversify your psychosexual pleasures.

Lastly one might mention the desirability of a sense of humor. Life, when it is not tragic or boring, is often slightly ridiculous. There does seem to be something, innately, ridiculous about human beings. Perhaps only an extremely intelligent human being can be struck with how funny we really are. Entire populations of talking apes riding about in machines, competing for dollar bills, manufacturing problems for themselves, torturing themselves, being cruel to other talking apes, wearing hats and wrist watches, staring at colored screens for stimulation, their feet in socks and shoes, the whole panorama is dubious. To see the point just suppose chimpanzees happened to be where we are, and we, with our present intelligence, could observe them doing exactly the same things we do. It would really seem pretty stupid. Or much of it. But if there were underfed chimpanzees, or diseased chimpanzees, that would be tragic or sad, particularly if other members of the chimpanzee population had more than they needed to eat, or if, in the population in general, there were health and medical services which could help or cure the diseased, but these services were not universally available. On the other hand, let us suppose that these same bright, hairy primates, which look so strange to us, are capable of love, philosophy and music. They experience deep and profound emotions. They can be deeply and tragically injured. They can also know intellectual and physical joys, far beyond those of wolverines, flamingos and rabbits. I think then it would be seen that our chimpanzee population, funny as it is, is yet somehow dear and precious. It is not impossible to be both ridiculous and splendid. Don Quixote rides in all of us. It is easy to see how one might, with deeply mixed emotions, come to care for and love such animals.

Nietzsche said that life without music would be a mistake. Life without humor, love and tolerance might not be simply a mistake; it might be impossible.

There would seem to be two aspects in which humor would apply specifically to the practice of imaginative sex. First, it should be engaged in only with good humor. It is a form of *play*. If one believes that all play is silly, or a waste of time, one will probably not understand imaginative sex, or, surely, be much good at it. Imaginative sex is a form of human play. That must never be forgotten. It is *play*. Play can be taken seriously, of course. We all take our games seriously. Watch people play chess. Or basketball, or water polo. But it is *not reality*. It is, in the final analysis, only a form of play. Play, of course, can stimulate the mind, increase energies, and healthily ventilate, in a love context, bottled emotions and suppressed desires. Play is good for animals. All the higher animals play. Imaginative sex may be engaged in intricately and deeply, or simply and superficially, but it should always be engaged in delightedly and lightheartedly. It is supposed to be fun. If it isn't fun, it isn't imaginative sex. One can become lost in the delights of fantasies, but one must not stay lost. Reality comes first and last, if not in the middle.

Imaginative sex is not a substitute for reality; it is a refreshment for reality. Just as humor gives us a perspective for grappling with the world, so it gives us a perspective for grappling with the worlds of fantasy. Humor is a tool for survival, as much as the ax and fire. The world sets severe conditions on survival, and evolution is harsh. It is doubtless more than a coincidence that we are laughing animals. As soon as we begin to take ourselves too seriously we are on the way to insanity. Without humor there is only solemnity and madness. Secondly, humor is important in connection with imaginative sex because we need to be admissive of one another's mistakes or failures. Sometimes, in imaginative sex, it is possible to get involved in situations which are unintentionally hilarious, which do not work, which fail to "come off." These can be a source of fun as well as more successful exhibitions and performances. Like the bloopers cut out of television film they can be entertaining in themselves. A readiness to laugh at one's own failures or mistakes is an asset in imaginative sex, as it is in any complex human endeavor. It is impossible not, from time to time, to make mistakes. Mistakes are perfectly acceptable. It is not even as though everyone were going to know about them. The important thing to remember is that imaginative sex is not a serious business; it is supposed to be fun; it is supposed to be a delight.

IX

IMAGINATIVE TECHNIQUES

Role playing is fun. Almost any human being with imagination enjoys role playing. Some women are superb actresses; others are not. Some men are superb actors; others are not. Some men and women take to roles swiftly, imaginatively and creatively; others do not. Yet almost everyone enjoys playing, from time to time, that he is someone else, or that he is himself in some unusual and rather different context. It enriches our lives and is rich in gratification. Similarly, in our fantasies, role playing occurs. If we do not do this sort of thing overtly, as for example in theatrical work, or vicariously, in reading, we do so in our daydreams. Both men and women, of course, fantasize. Although there are no limits on imaginative sex, other than those consequent on the limitations of the imaginations of the participants, most sexual fantasy, in both men and women, has as its core, under thousands of variations, forced sexual congress, imbedded in a matrix of elements of dominance and submission.

As an example we might consider the extremely successful motion picture, *Planet of the Apes*, based on Pierre Bouille's novel of the same name. Aside from the considerable merits of the picture in a number of respects and on a number of levels, it was, subtly, an extremely sexy picture. It was so on the *mental* level, the fantasy level, where, perhaps surprisingly, the most dynamic and exciting sex originates. Glands and brain working together, stimulating one another, produce full human experiences which far outweigh the prosaic pleasures attendant merely on the proximities of bodies and the frictional stresses placed on surfaces. In the picture, doubtless a reflection of a fantasy of Mr. Bouille, human beings are reduced to the level of animals; they are hunted; they may be killed or caught. If they are killed, their carcases are tied like those of animals, upside down, to poles; if they are more fortunate animals, they may be merely caught; they may flee in terror, but, for some, there is no escape; they are even, in a brilliant fantasy stroke, netted; they are then bound and placed helpless, terrified, in crude, locked capture carts, as prizes; they are then taken to an animal holding area, where they are locked in cages; in Bouille's story, as opposed to the picture, they, being animals, are of course nude. Once they have been hunted and caught, of course, they are helpless animals at the mercy of their masters. In particular, they can be forced to mate. The hero, of course, a fully rational human being, mixed by accident with these fellow humans, and unable to make his rationality known, is wild with horror. A beautiful female, leashed, eating a fruit, is then led to his cage. She is locked within with him. She is his mate. This is a fantasy which appeals to both men and women. Doubtless the success of the picture was partly dependent on the force of this fantasy. The woman, of course, would like to choose into whose cage she is placed nude, to be this publicly behind the bars, on the straw spread over the wooden floor of the cage. Similarly, the man, though at the mercy of the rational creatures whose animal he is, may surely be allowed to hope that the mate selected for him will be as beautiful as that allotted to Mr. Heston.

This Bouille fantasy incorporates a number of elements indicative of the successful fantasy. It is detailed, and deliberate. It is carefully worked out. It gains a reality in virtue of the very multiplicity and obduracy of the detail which defines it. It is a congruent, appropriate, natural series of events in a congruent, appropriate, natural environment. It is a bizarre *real* happening in a bizarre *real* world. Furthermore, it incorporates hazard, capture, helplessness and forced sex.

The rape fantasy is the common sexual fantasy of both men and women. This being the case it is interesting that this common fantasy is so seldom acted out in love makings. It is delicious, or can be delicious, to do so. The fact, of course, that rape is a common sexual fantasy of women does not indicate that women, in any general sense, wish to be raped. They would surely, at the very least, wish to choose the time and the place, and the circumstances and the man. Rape, as a sociological reality, is commonly an ugly, brutal, unpleasant, sickening, horrifying, vicious act. It degrades the man and it doesn't do the woman much good either. Not only does she receive little or no pleasure, but the whole affair has no more intrinsic worth or dignity than a mugging. Further, sadly, she is likely to be brutalized and, at the least, intimidated. This is to take advantage of a weaker creature, who cannot adequately, in most cases, defend herself. The rapist, unless there are some extenuating factors, such as severe mental illness, scarcely comes up to scratch for a human being. To pick on a woman, because she is smaller and weaker, is much the same thing as to pick on a child or animal; or, it is much the same thing as a young man striking an old man; or a large, strong man beating a small, weak man; it is just something that it is not worthy to do. It is not that it need be a "sick" thing to do, though doubtless in some cases it is; it is rather that there is just no manhood in it.

On the other hand, regardless of the facts about rape in the real world, where it is usually a waste of time, it is clear that rape fantasies are extremely common in both men and women. This is not to be taken to prove that there is really no manhood in any man or that women are peculiarly degenerate creatures. Rather, the healthy man does, from time to time, want to rape; he is probably built that way; it is natural to be sexually eager to capture and use a beautiful woman; it is, I suppose, part of our animal heritage; similarly it is quite probable that it is part of our biogenetic heritage that a woman, on some level, desires her own capture and subjugation. This would be, it seems, a natural complementarity. If man's natural role is that of hunter and captor and woman's that of game and captive, our instinctual sexual fantasies would be precisely what they are. We are, of course, or should be, far from the jungle. Rape, real rape, even if we are naturally inclined to do it, is not to be done. Our rights to self-expression end where the other person's feelings begin.

Civilization, as Freud recognized, requires restraint. All things considered, civilization is better than the jungle, and it is a fragile and delicate set of relationships. We have lost it many times, and we must try not to do so again.

In short, a true man, one with normal aggressions and fully operating glands, presumably desires to rape, but also, having a hard-won manhood, does not in fact rape. This is not particularly because he does not wish to agitate the precinct detectives, but rather because, when the chips are down, if he really had the choice, he would not want to hurt or intimidate a woman. He might desire to do so, but, on the genuine level of his humanity, he just would refuse to do so. It is not a humanly good or worthy thing to do. From a woman's point of view a man who wishes to rape her but does not, because he gives her her due as a human being, is probably more interesting to her as a male than either one who does not wish to rape her, who does not find her worth the fantasy, or one who catches her by accident in a dark alley and does in fact penetrate her, ejaculate and dash off. The first man excites her; the second two, in their different ways, are bores.

The "rape thing," incidentally, is a motivating force in initial sexual contacts. The man *desires, wants to have*, the female. So he makes his advances. He approaches. Perhaps he spies on her. Perhaps he follows her. He sets himself where she happens to pass. He learns her habits, her clothing. He walks past her house at night, unknown to her. Where she is, she finds him, as though by accident. They meet, as though inadvertently. He finds it difficult to take his eyes from her. He gives her a lift in his car. She must lock the door. She must wear his seat belt. He is hunting her.

Any intelligent girl, from the first conversation, from the first telephone call, will catch the scent of the prowling male. It is then up to her whether she wishes to encourage or discourage her hunt. This puts her in a very difficult position because she is likely to have very mixed feelings not only about sex, which women tend, with some justification, to fear, for it is often exploitative of them, but about any given male. To begin with, most males will not be sexually interesting to her. She might *become* sexually interested in them, but, initially, she is not. That this is the case may reflect that she is the game, and not the hunter. It is natural that the impala is not much interested in the average lion; on the other hand, it is natural that the average lion, at least initially, is much less picky about impalas, that he is much more broad-minded, no pun intended. Further, even if the girl is sexually interested in the given man, as opposed to thinking that he is "nice," or something, she is likely to have ambiguous feelings toward him. He may appear to her both attractive and threatening. She may sense that he is intent upon her capture, and this, in itself, would be sufficient to initiate anxiety. She might fear the loss of her freedoms, of her potentialities for other activities and other human beings. It is no wonder that girls are often "teases." They are probably not so much teasing, as they do not know what to think; they are scared. They both want a man and fear him. There is justification for both attitudes.

When a man first becomes interested in a girl he seldom has her in mind as an object of matrimony. He is interested rather in her sexual capture. He sees her flanks move beneath her dress and he knows he wants to strip and fuck her. This is the most natural thing in the world. It speaks well for his vitality, his aggressiveness and his manhood. And, too, interestingly, what woman wants a man who does not have a powerful desire, a truly powerful desire, to remove her clothing and have sexual relations with her? She will fantasize it long before it happens. But the point here is that the man's initial motivations with respect to the female have less to do with matrimony and the qualities of her mind, which may be stimulating and considerable, than they have to do with her rape. Now it is quite true that as soon as he gets to know this woman, and learns her humanity and her mind, the primary center of his interests may shift, and doubtless should, from the crudities of rape, to the fantasies of delicious, willing conversation and love between them. He will probably still, and healthily, fantasize her rape, but the whole matter is now much more complex. She is now, to him, a real person, perplexing, challenging, delightful, complicated. Life is no longer simple. His fantasies may now even reveal her as the sexual aggressor, wanting him, begging for him. He wants her, but he wants her, too, to want him. Of her own will, she gives herself to him. Rape fantasies will now be subordinate, and appropriately, because it is pretty hard to think about raping someone you like. Rape is an aggressive act. She wouldn't like it. You would not want to hurt her. On the other hand, interestingly, she too has had, or is having, her rape fantasies. And the initial motivation for your pursuit of her was your desire for her sexual capture.

That rape remains in the background, though in a form which is desired by the female, is made clear when we consider the following situation. Let us suppose that we have a man and a woman who know one another, respect one another, care for one another and are involved romantically. Let us then suppose that one evening they are having supper in her apartment. She wears an evening gown, he a suit. It is an excellent supper. There has been gentle conversation. There is candlelight. Toward the end of the supper, she looks at the man. She does not touch him. "Rape me," she says. They would have a fantastic sexual experience. It would be quite different if she had said, "Make love to me." She is carried to the bedroom, stripped, thrown to the bed and used with a tender but uncompromising aggressiveness, patient and detailed, which leaves no doubt in her mind but what she is the object, dominated and commanded, of an incredible sexual desire. There are many ways to make love. All that is essential here is to recognize that this would be an unusually exciting experience for both partners. That it would be as exciting, or more exciting, than a love episode conducted in a more usual manner is of great importance. It says something about the rape fantasies of both partners. If the partners did not know one another or did not care for one another, presumably the experience would not be the delightful realization of a rape fantasy, but would have been merely a rape, and rapes, as we have suggested, are wastes of time. In this episode, however, the woman has invited the male, a startling, flattering welcome invitation to share her fantasy. She has yielded herself to him, deliciously, her lover, as his eager and willing rape victim. That the experience is as extraordinary as it is, speaks of the depth of their common fantasies.

We are now nearly ready to begin detailed sketches and suggestions for imaginative sex.

Imaginative sex, one supposes, could be any enhancement of sex beyond the sweet commonplaces of usual intercourse. For example, making love on the rug rather than on the bed would be imaginative sex. For some, something as simple as putting your wife in earrings and a necklace in bed, and otherwise nude, would be imaginative sex. For some, an enhancement of the ordinary beddingsdown would be as simple as to tell your wife to wear lipstick and perfume in bed. Such little things can make great psychological differences. Sex for the hippopotamus may be largely a matter of genital friction but good sex, for the human being, is likely to require, or at least be dynamically responsive to, psychological contexts and stimulations. Psychological factors are inordinately important in the male's attainment of erection and later ejaculation; similarly, they are inordinately important in the female's attainment of orgasm. It is a mistake to neglect them; and to maintain that is morally improper to enhance and cultivate them is not only pernicious but stupid. There is nothing wrong with wearing perfume in bed, even though, in fact, it might improve your husband's sexual performance.

Many of the sexual games and fantasies to be shortly discussed, of course, go well beyond the boldnesses of wearing earrings or perfume in bed.

Many of them trade heavily on common male/female fantasies, fantasies which are normally, for no good reason, kept concealed. If there are values in openness and self-expression, and it seems there are, then the acting out, in a protected love context, of certain fantasies might be excellent for mental health, the release of tension, the erasure of misplaced, conditioned guilts, if they exist, which can come with communication, and with the development of the mind and imagination through exciting, stimulating, challenging creative activities. The object, of course, of the games and love episodes is not mental health or development, but fun, enjoyment, delight, pleasure. There is nothing intrinsically worthwhile, it must be understood, about misery and boredom, self-denial and pain. It is morally acceptable for human beings to be happy, regardless of what we may have been conditioned to believe in this respect.

A moment must be taken now to consider love and sex. These are not, of course, the same thing. We are all aware of occasions when we want love and not sex. Similarly, we are all aware of occasions when we do not really want either. We want to do something else at the time. For example, we may wish to finish a problem or play chess. It is less clear that there are occasions when one wants *both* sex and love. One surely wants sex with a person whom one loves, and who loves you, but that is not precisely the same as wanting, simultaneously, sex and love. On the other hand, presumably there *are* occasions when one wants both sex and love simultaneously. When one senses the loneliness of the universe one might want both love and sex, the holding and the comforting; or, perhaps, when one intends to conceive a child, one might wish the two simultaneously. Let us distinguish between loving someone and, so to speak, having love with them. We all know individuals whom we love, but we are not always in a position where we are, so to speak, doing love with them, that is, exhibiting and feeling emotions of love. One can "do" love while doing sex, but it is doing two things at once. It is sometimes easier to "do" love when walking together with one's wife, holding her hand, talking to her, caring for her, than it is when approaching orgasm.

There is no doubt that neutral observers, without axes to grind, will admit that sex can interfere with love. It need not, but often it gets in the way. I myself, when I become sexually aroused, often find myself becoming sexually aggressive; I find myself wanting to dominate the woman, to drive her wild with pleasure, to possess her, to own her, to make her helplessly mine. *I want her. I want to have her.* These are not precisely the same emotions I feel when, perhaps afterwards, with great emotion and tenderness, I express my love for her. Love can lead to sex and sex can lead to love, and there can be sex simultaneously with love, but they are not the same thing.

It is my belief that the best sex occurs with an individual that one, in fact, loves. On the other hand, this is not to say that one is always well advised to try to perform sex and love simultaneously. Just as there are times when one wants love and not sex, so there are times when one is really more interested in sex than love. This does not mean one is simply, in some physiological sense, interested merely in the body of the woman. A foam-rubber dummy would not do, for example. It does mean that one sometimes wants sexual experiences which need not be explicit expressions of the great regard and tenderness in which the partners hold one another. Performing love and sex simultaneously can be done; it is, however, an achievement; it is a tricky triumph. Sometimes love gets in the way of sex, and sometimes sex gets in the way of love. It is hard to give a woman a smashing good fuck when one is gazing tenderly into her eyes and feeling that she is the most wonderful human being in the world. If you really love her, at such a moment, you might give her a great deal more pleasure, and make her much happier, by treating her less like your beloved spouse, which she is, and the mother of your children, which she is, and more like the terribly exciting, exquisite lay you find her to be. She is a marvelously desirable bitch and animal and she deserves the best you can give her.

Women wish to be loved, but they also wish to be physically attractive to men and to be the objects of strong sexual desire on the part of males. Give the female animal in your wife its due. Observe her sometime, perhaps in the kitchen, perhaps while reading in the living room, perhaps while she is shopping. Note how her body moves beneath its dress. Consider her ankles, her calves, the back of her knees, the thighs of her. Consider her hips, the sweet belly of her and the lovely vulnerabilities of her breasts, lovely and swelling, marking her, like other curvatures, even fully clothed, as female. Consider, too, the soft shoulders of her, her throat, the way the hair falls upon her neck. Consider, too, her carriage, and her head, and the expressions on her face, her eyes and her mouth. Look at her carefully, but rather as a stranger. See her as a woman, not known to you. Then, article by article, in your mind, remove her clothing, slowly, not hurrying, exquisitely revealing each marvelous inch of her. Only you then need to know that she is nude in the kitchen, that she reads naked, that she shops, with her metal shopping cart, considering cans of vegetables and reaching for boxes of cereal, without a stitch of clothing on her body. Consider her. She is your wife. Consider her carefully. Is such a woman not worth having? She is your wife, of course, but, considered objectively, is such a wench not well worth raping? I expect the answer is affirmative. You follow her home. She is yours to get.

Whereas imaginative sex, it seems, should be considered as any enhancement of sex beyond the sweet commonplaces of customary intercourse, it frequently reflects themes of deeply rooted male and female sexual fantasy. If there are common elements threading together many of these fantasies, they are those of capture and rape, or subjugation and sexual conquest, of dominance and submission, of the control, sexual and otherwise, of one human being by another. Those who are aware of the attractions of power will find these themes familiar. Similarly, the man who fantasizes rape and the woman who fantasizes herself as his sexually yielding, conquered victim will find them, in theme, not strange at all. In effect this is to say that the human being, given what he is, will comprehend the themes of these fantasies. His own fantasies, of course, may differ. What follows is intended neither as a catalog nor an exhaustive set of recipes for pleasure. We might take it, if we wished, as merely a graphic illustration of, and an introduction to, some of the possibilities of imaginative sex. I expect, of course, that they might serve, in certain cases, as suggestions for scenarios for fantasy, or, in a sense, as suggestions for recipes for pleasure. On the other hand, doubtless one's own recipes are always the best. They speak most deeply to us. We may have nourished and elaborated them since childhood. Some of the fantasies that follow will simply strike you as strange or funny. Some are, as a matter of fact, strange or funny. Others will strike different people different ways. The point is to get the point, to understand the nature of imaginative sex, the possible role of fantasy in increasing sexual pleasure. Fantasies which are astonishingly sexually provocative to one individual may not be to another. But most of us, I suppose, know or could invent fantasies which, relative to us, would be stimulative of incredible psychosexual pleasure. If we really do not know of any such fantasies, and cannot even think any up, which would appeal to us, then it seems imaginative sex is for others, not for us.

Perhaps a last suggestion is in order.

Generally these fantasies require, in play at least, that one sees the partner as someone who is new and different. They are the same, of course, but they are to be seen as new and different. One must, in some fantasies, for example, look upon one's wife as a stranger might look upon her, seeing her as a fresh, entirely different, unknown female, sexually desirable, little more, perhaps, at the moment, than an enticing, unexplored, provocative piece of ass. Sometimes this can be accomplished simply by looking at one's wife as she really is. Have you ever really looked at your wife? Have you ever paid her that much attention? Does she, for example, have a blemish on the sole of her left foot? If you truly knew her body, you would know. Do you truly remember, for example, how the small hairs grow on the back of her neck? At any rate, try to see her as a sexually stimulated stranger would see her. She will then seem more like game to you. And she, in her own mind, will feel more like prey. Similarly the wife must look at the husband differently, freshly. She has probably never looked upon him as a sexual animal before. He is one. See him so. What do you feel, as the female animal, as the object of his desire? Look at him. He wants you. Will he catch you? What will he do with you if he does?

There are various imaginative techniques which may be employed in these matters. One is to alter names. Sometimes the change of a name is an aid to the change of a personality. It helps to assume a new identity. If a wife's name is Jane, perhaps, in the context of a given game, she may be addressed as, and think of herself as, say, Linda or Marcia. Similarly, since Linda or Marcia are not Jane, they are someone else. Whom shall we invent her to be? Where was Linda born? What type of family does she come from? Where did she go to school? Did she go to college? If so, where? Did she get her degree? In what subject did she major? Was she a member of a sorority? If so, what sorority? Does she dress well? Is she sophisticated? Does she drink? If so, what is her favorite drink? Is she clever? Is she intelligent? How does she make her living? What are her attitudes on sex?

Does she have secret dreams? If she does, these should probably be the secret dreams of Jane, but, if they should, horrifyingly, come true, they must happen not to Jane, but Linda. Linda, for example, to her horror, may find herself sold in a slave market.

Time, and care, and detail, as well as imagination, will tend to produce excellent, coherent, reliably stimulatory fantasies. They may be retained indefinitely, used from time to time, and, on a continuing basis, elaborated or altered. A given couple may maintain several such fantasies. Supplementing each fantasy, of course, should be an entire civilization and background, an entire reality. Such realities might be our own world, supposed with certain changes, such as the institution of slavery, or they might be worlds of the past, such as that of ancient Rome, or exotic worlds of the present or future, for example, on distant planets. Do planets outside our solar system, for example, currently make slave raids on the planet Earth? Is the intelligence of such raiders so much above that of human beings that human females could be only sex slaves to them? Is there something about such aliens that makes them incredibly, irresistibly attractive to human females, that she has no choice but to yield to them with a totality of response she would not have dreamed possible? Similarly, perhaps the native females of the alien planet are frigid or "above sex," thus accounting for their males bringing human female sex slaves to their planet, to satisfy their "lower" needs. Such alien females, of course, would look with great jealousy on the helpless sex slaves of their males. They would treat them with great cruelty.

It is not a bad idea to keep notes. When a good idea occurs to the husband or wife, it should be added to the background of the world or the analysis of the characters they play. A book on each fantasy may be prepared. History is important, economics, social institutions, coinage, architecture, weaponry, cosmetics, customs, laws, ornaments, etc. Also, of great importance is what happens and to whom does it happen. Such a fantasy as we have just mentioned, of course, might begin with a capture on the planet Earth. It might also, of course, begin with the awakening of the captive female wearing odd chains in a strange cell. Or, perhaps, the male, too impatient for her body, slaps her awake in her bonds in his ship, enroute to his native world. Do it however it pleases you. Does she have to learn his language immediately? What will be the first words she is taught? That she is a sex animal? That she is a female slave? What pet name will he give her? What are the climates of the new world, its geography and weathers, its plants and animals, etc.? Are there gestures which she must learn to obey immediately, etc.? If she does not speak his language, after her first brutal usage, she would be presumably trained as an animal, by positive and negative reinforcement, struck when she failed to understand, rewarded when she did.

The construction of a world can be a creative delight. Consider our own world and the sorts of things, concrete and abstract, we find in it. How would these differ in the other world?

It is not important to have elaborate costumes and props. The imagination is important. Much, if not all, may be imagined. On the other hand, women can be marvelously inventive in these matters. The wife could create a costume, surprising the husband with it, which would drive him wild. Similarly with props. If she is an animal, perhaps she is not even clothed, but she would have to be identified someway. Does she wear a collar, or a band, or chain, locked on her ankle? Is she branded? A red magic marker makes a nice brand. Where is it placed on her body? What is the design of the brand? Does a virgin animal wear a different collar than one which is not a virgin, etc.? How many moons does the planet have? How long are its days and nights? Do people live on its surface or beneath its surface, or above its surface, on gravitationally suspended cities, each in its way an island prison. Or does she escape to the surface and attempt to flee? Is she captured there by another form of life? Or is she hunted with animals? If so, what are the animals like with which she is hunted? In Shakespearean theater a branch on the stage would make do for a forest. The imagination took up from there. Shakespeareans, on the other hand, were fond of costumes and props. Do as you please.

Once the character and the world, and the situation, begin to be developed, the next step, simultaneous with their continuing development, is working oneself into the role. One creates the role;

one studies it; one elaborates it; one works oneself into it. Here
the distinction between quality in actresses becomes important.
How would this particular woman, as she has been conceived,
with her antecedents and history, her accomplishments and
background, her prejudices, her preferences, her personality, *feel*
if these things were really happening to her? How would she act?
How would she behave? What would she think? What would
she say? You feel yourself deeply into the role, and then, as the
character, respond authentically and in detail to the situation
in which you find yourself. Much will occur quite naturally.
You are not "making it up"; you are reacting, perhaps in fear, in
horror, in misery, to what is occurring to you. You, in particular,
wish to repudiate the excitement which his touch generates in
you; you wish to fight him; to resist him, but you cannot do
so; you must, and cannot help yourself, respond to him with
the total surrender of a sex slave; in anguish, you know that he
scorns your helpless responses; he only respects his own frigid
women; but, still, you cannot help yielding to him, completely
and fantastically. You may, and should, if necessary, begin by
acting out this orgasm, or orgasms, but, if your lover is attentive
and he gives your body the time it needs, your acting will at
some point melt into the earthquakes of true orgasm, and you
will feel yourself, in the rich psychological matrix, shamefully
yielded to, exquisitely raped by, an uncompromising, dominant
male.

It is common knowledge that role playing is fun. Few people
suspect that it is this much fun.

Further remarks, explicatory of imaginative sex, may be
included in a specific discussion of various games and fantasies.

X

SENSUOUS FANTASIES:
Recipes of Pleasure

1. The Capture-in-the-Dark Fantasy.

This is a very simple fantasy, though it may be elaborated. It is also delightful. The room is utterly dark. You do not know the location of your wife, who is nude, in the room. You find her, capture her and take her to your bed. Then, over a period of an hour or so, you give her an exquisite raping, all in utter darkness.

Comment:

In the capture, there must presumably be struggle. On the other hand, it must be clearly understood that this is to be a lovers' wrestling, in which each, though exerting his strength against the other, is concerned that the other not be injured. In an actual rape, which is the last thing one is talking about here, it is extremely difficult, without beating her, to have intercourse with an unbound struggling woman. It can be done, I suppose, but the feat would seem to be more of an athletic than a sexual event. It is possible to intimidate rape victims into compliance. In such a case there is no struggle. It is also possible to beat the female. If she is half unconscious, or is sick, and can scarcely breathe from a blow to the stomach, she can't do much but lie there and wait to be fucked, and hope you will finish quickly and go away, so she can vomit and get up. Obviously, in a love rape, a fantasy between husband and wife, he neither wishes to intimidate her nor, obviously, to injure her or make her miserable. The love rapes of fantasy must be delicious for both; otherwise they are without point. If the wife doubts that her husband could really rape her, if he wished, she may be assured that he could, but she might not much care for it. Accordingly, the wife's struggle must not be motivated by the desire to see if he could *really* rape her. She must, and he, too, of course, play within the rules of the lovers' game. His greater strength, provided respect and love is maintained, leave no doubt as to the game's outcome. When she loses, they both win. There is no game, of course, if she gets clobbered in the head or he gets mashed in the testicles. That would be a bit like hitting the opposing pitcher with a baseball bat. In all love struggles, there must be delight. They are not real fights. Each, the lover of the other, must take care to avoid hurting the other; their second job, of course, is to see that each gets as much pleasure as the other can give. If the wife insists on seeing if the husband can really rape her, refraining, of course, from attempts to injure him, as he will refrain from attempts to subdue her by beating or intimidation, the husband has a simple strategy at his disposal. He turns her to her stomach, kneels across her body and, with a short cord, knots her hands behind her back. He then turns her to her back, and, a hand under the back of each knee, thrusts her back against the head of the bed or, if on a rug, against the wall. Then, let her struggle as much as she pleases. She has nowhere to go and she is confined. If she continues to struggle her movements will merely add to your pleasure. Unfortunately, of course, in this situation, she has presumably not been fully aroused, and you would be likely to ejaculate too quickly, thus robbing both of you of lengthy, pre-climaxing pleasures. This would be, except perhaps on occasion, a second-best continuation. It should serve to prove to the wife, of course, should she be in doubt, that her husband is fully capable of actually raping her, if and when he might please. She might then look upon him somewhat differently than she had before. That is the sort of man she lives with. Her position in the house as a vulnerable female is made more clear to her. Every woman likes a hint of danger; it is like perfume to a man. She will not think less of her husband, knowing he can rape her when he wants. She may even find it sexually stimulating. It doesn't hurt a wife's libido to understand that hubby may not be as harmless as she thought. A woman who is raped by her husband is likely to remember her rape long after she has forgotten more prosaic love makings.

Some further comment might be in order on the capture-in-the-dark fantasy.

Normally one will want adequate, if not strong, light in acting out fantasies. This is because the visual stimulation adds much to the joy of the fantasy, as it does to most love makings. In the capture-in-the-dark fantasy, however, we have the element of the hunt, for you do not know her location, and the delight of the catch, when you apprehend her. It appeals to the hunter in you and the quarry in her. Further, human beings have a fear, commonly, of the dark. In this case, the fears of being caught in the dark, rather than being a source of misery, are a source of stimulating excitement, for you know there is, truly, no danger. It is only delight, and sport. Similarly, the darkness, concealing the lovers from one another, makes it easier to suppose and fantasize that it is a delicious stranger whom you have caught and forced to your bed, and, for her, that it is an unknown, magnificent, mysterious male, who has captured you and will now force you, in the full perfections of your female reflexes, to respond to the enormities of his lust. He will have his way with you, and how, sweet wench!

Mechanics can vary endlessly in these fantasies. For example, the predator may or may not desire to bind his prey before he takes it to his bed, or den. He may force her to walk to the place of her rape, or he may carry her, and he might carry her in his arms, bound or unbound, or over his shoulder, bound or unbound. He may speak to her, or remain silent. She may plead with him, answered or not, or be taken in silence. If the woman wishes a gag, she should be gagged. An adequate gag consists of wadding and fastening. The wadding, commonly, consists of folded or crumpled cloth. It is held in the mouth by the fastening, which might be a handkerchief or tie; this is passed deeply between the teeth and knotted tightly behind the back of the neck. Tape might also be used, but then the entire mouth is covered. If tape is used a rubber ball may be forced into the mouth and taped within. The ball must not be tiny for fear of the danger of choking. Similarly it must, however, be large enough so that it fills the mouth and is difficult to eject. If the wife is not originally nude when captured, but wears, say, stockings, panties, garter belt and brassiere, she carries with her her own bonds and gag. Stockings are excellent for binding her, one for the hands, one for the feet. Her other garments are already removed. The garter belt is discarded; the panties serve as wadding; the brassiere fastens the wadding within her mouth. Then, secured, she is yours. Carry her to your bed.

At the bed, if you choose to unbind her and ungag her, you may or may not wish to secure her there, or, indeed, on the floor. A length of chain, with two padlocks, fastening her by the left ankle, or the throat, to the bed, might please her. If she does not wish to be secured, of course, then she should not be. All details of the fantasy must be mutually delicious.

Incidentally, in binding a woman or a man, such materials as silken cords, strips of cloth, neckties, etc. will probably be superior to rope. Rope does not hold as well, and, if rough rope, may scratch or irritate the skin. Rope, coarse rope, in my opinion, would detract from the pleasure. In binding, ankles and wrists are commonly crossed, looped about more than once with the binding device, and knotted. Confining the ankles or wrists in solid loops, fastened so that they cannot much give, is superior to looping each ankle or wrist separately. It is easier to free a single wrist, looped and tied separately to the other, than it is to free either wrist when both are bound in the same loops. This has primarily to do with angles and frictions. It is easier to pull an object straight through a ring, if one can do it at all, than it is to pull the object at an oblique angle through the ring. Each wrist of the captive prevents the other from aligning itself parallel to the loop. The captor forces the captive's body to work against him, in his own favor. Incidentally, one must be careful with bonds. A captive may be perfectly held without being tied particularly tightly. If he needs only a quarter of an inch to free himself and does not have it, he cannot free himself.

The bonds should be sufficiently tight that the captive knows himself helpless, but they should not be tight enough to pinch or mark the wrists, or slow the circulation. The captive is playing, as you are. Playing at suffering is one thing; suffering is quite something else; the one can be fun; the other is just painful. The little fellow who pretends he has been shot in the arm, in playing cowboys and Indians, does not really want to be shot in the arm. He is just playing. If the partner requests, at any point, seriously, to be untied or for the bonds to be loosened, immediately do so. If he begs, in play, that they be loosened, or removed, that may be a cue for you that they should be tightened, as though scornfully and callously. One thing to be particularly careful of is any fastening used on the throat. These must always be loose enough to insure free breathing and the individual must never be so situated that he might fall or roll in such a way as to inadvertently tighten such a fastening.

One simple way of bringing the captured woman to your bed is as follows. She is not bound or carried. She is pulled by the hair to her feet and then she is walked to the bed, bent over, her hair held at your waist. This makes a woman feel very much in a man's power. She is walked about the room a few times. Now her back and the back of her legs, and her hair, begin to hurt her somewhat. Also, she is humiliated, being led about as such a captive. Then, by the hair she is thrown across the bed.

Before we leave this particular fantasy, we might mention certain elaborations of it. These are variations on a theme.

Perhaps the female prowler in your room is a highly intelligent, sophisticated, sleek cat burglar, a debutante, the spoiled, beautiful daughter of a rich family, who steals for adventure. She gets more than she bargained for. She does not get your diamonds. Instead, you get her. She is stripped of her leotard or body suit and taken to your bed and raped. You are, of course, a handsome, wealthy, young bachelor, a connoisseur of wines, a collector of art, a yachtsman, a hunter, etc. Why not? You discover her identity, of course. That makes her capture more delicious. Further, she has in the past been rather haughty with you, treating you with a supercilious contempt. She is the sort of woman who had enjoyed putting men down. She had, we shall suppose, refused to speak with you; she had regarded herself as too good for you; she had refused all your advances, etc. She would never even give you a date. Now she is yours. In the morning, if you wish, you will turn her over to the police. On the other hand, let us suppose that you have the facilities to keep her, or that you have an island, a secret island, which you may reach with your yacht. You may then, if it pleases you, take her there, where she will serve you as a slave. Is she the only woman on the island, or does she find herself with others, similarly belonging to you? Fantasize with your delightful wife as you please. (I suspect she will wish to be the only wench on the island. Very well. Let us do it that way. You are now alone on your island, which is completely stocked, both for survival and love. On the sand she turns and faces you, tears in her eyes, her fists clenched, a thousand miles from anywhere, your beautiful captive. "What are you going to do with me?" she asks. You take her in your arms.)

Another variant on this fantasy reverses the roles, and has the man be the victim. In this case, perhaps the woman is large, strong and fierce, almost as though an alien creature. To his horror he finds himself overpowered, as easily as he might have overpowered an ordinary woman, and treated with the same lust and casualness that he might have inflicted on a woman in his position. Many fantasies have turnabout possibilities. Another variant here would be that the woman who overpowers him is brilliant in both mind and personal combat; she is, moreover, a marvelous, arrogant beauty. In spite of the fact that he is larger and stronger than she, she handles him swiftly and efficiently. To her he is simply a clumsy victim. He fears her for he knows that, as her beauty tortures and torments him, she can do with him as she pleases. He must obey her. She, like that of a dog, is his mistress.

2. The Aphrodisiac Fantasy.

The female is a sexually cold woman, captured, who hates you. She is forced to drink an aphrodisiac. You then wait. Soon, she begins to feel its effects. She insults you. She hates you, but, too, it is apparent that she will soon need you, desperately, sexually. She attempts to fight the effects of the aphrodisiac, both verbally and by body movements, trying to resist it. She is, of course, unable to do so.

Then she agrees, haughtily, condescendingly, to go to bed with you. You refuse. She is shocked. She had not counted on this. The drug continues to work in her system, relentlessly.

Soon she begs you to make love to her. Still, you refuse.

Then, desperately, she realizes she must provoke you sexually. She strips herself. She moves before you. She, at last, helpless in the piteous crisis of her need, kneels before you, her hair over your feet, pleading that you make love to her.

You give her permission to make love *to you*. She begins by kissing your feet, moving with her lips and touch lasciviously up your body, until she licks and kisses your genitals.

At this point you carry her to the bed, and there let her continue to attempt to please you sexually. When you are satisfied that the victim has suffered enough you turn her about and, to her joy, engage with her in mutual caressings, until together your needs are both satisfied.

Comment:

This requires an excellent female actress. The burden of the performance is on her.

Psychologically, incidentally, this is an excellent fantasy for the female in two respects. First, in feeling herself into the role, and imagining what it would be like to be overwhelmed by powerful sexual feelings, which are not answered by those of another, detailed awareness of the nature of her sexual arousal, in terms of sensation and desire, are required. To "fake" being aroused is to become, in part, through psychological gradients, aware of what it is to be aroused. It is paying attention to what it is to want a man. This is healthy for a woman who wants to enlarge and intensify her sexual appetites, bringing them more into the open, increasing their clarity. (Incidentally, if she *speaks* what is theoretically occurring in her body, this can be of importance to the male. Many men have very little notion of the sexual sensations, the inner life, of the female's body, either in arousal or orgasm. For example, does she feel a warmth in arousal? Are there sensations in her breasts, and along the sides of her body? What does a clitoral erection feel like? Are there incipient pelvic movements? Are there incipient vaginal contractions? What does it feel like to the woman when her sweet cunt loosens and becomes sweet with the oils that make penetration a delight, inviting it eagerly?) Too, of course, to pretend arousal can induce, through psychological techniques, arousal. It is hard to pretend you are sexually excited, particularly in a sexually exciting situation, without becoming sexually excited. A second psychological benefit for the woman is that it puts that beautiful thing, for at least once in her life, in a position that is only too painfully familiar to the male; that is, the position of the one who, though cruelly aroused, can be refused, repudiated and left unsatisfied. It would be well for her to have this painful and humiliating experience at least once in her life, even though in play. It is quite possible that it will make a better, more understanding, human being out of her.

For the male, of course, this can be a delightful fantasy. Here he, in a delicious turnabout, finds that it is he, and not she, who is in the position to either answer or not answer desperately aroused sexual needs. She, of course, cannot overpower him. She can only beg him to satisfy her needs. Here the male can sense the sexual power of a woman, in choosing to bestow or not bestow, her sexual favors. He can see her delight in teasing him, putting him aside, evading him, playing with him, making him squirm before her in his need. These are not pleasant gratifications, but they can be delicious to a woman. Now, in this fantasy, it is *she* who is put in the place of the male as their victim; it is he who can make her squirm, as women have made men squirm in the millions for thousands of years, perhaps since the abolition of capture as a mating institution. What man exists who would not, in the bottom of his heart, if only in a vengeance of his sex, relish the sight of a woman kneeling at his feet, begging *him* to make love *to her.*

Incidentally, actual aphrodisiacs are to be avoided. They are either useless or dangerous. The stimulations here must be mental, not chemical. Actual aphrodisiacs are *not* to be used. If one wishes to use an actual substance, a small bit of wine would be an idea. Women like wine; it is "sexy" to them; it relaxes them; it makes them glow; it lowers their inhibitions. Only a small bit of wine, however, perhaps an ounce or two, should be used. Being drunk does not improve sexual performance. Alcohol, chemically, is an anesthetic. Sex, particularly imaginative sex, calls for the brain in full swing. It wants the physical and intellectual powers at their top pitch. Similarly, it is not a good idea to have sexual relations when one is weary or sleepy. You would not wait until you were dozing before making love to a terrific date; in imaginative sex, your wife *is this terrific date*; accordingly, she gets the same treatment. Setting aside an hour or two in the morning or the afternoon is not a bad idea; then, the children may be in school, and the entire home will be at your disposal, increasing the range of your sexual activities considerably. If the daylight hours are not practical, and in many cases, they will not be, then the early evening is a good time. If your children are very young, you can make love shortly after they are asleep; if they are older, just tell them you wish to make love and lock the bedroom door; you can always see them for a snack before they go to bed. There is nothing wrong with children knowing that their parents love one another; they must be taught to respect their parents, just as all the books teach us to respect them; indeed, the children will probably have a much healthier attitude toward sex if they know that Mommy is happily being had by Daddy in the next room, and at length, than if Mommy and Daddy hide sex; we can tell children that sex is all right, but if we act like it isn't, why should they believe us? What we do means more than what we say. Today, our kids think they know more about sex than their parents; it is not necessary that we conspire to perpetuate their delusion. Privacy is important to good sex, but privacy doesn't require that sex be in engaged in only when our bodies are exhausted. Sex, being terrific, is worth being awake for. Believe me, when the young people realize that Mom and Pop are making out in the next room, they may be initially scandalized, but I expect, they will also be really proud of them. Why should Mom and Pop care what they think, any more than they care what Mom and Pop think? This is clobbering the young with their own generation gap. The young will also, rightly, be envious. They do not have anything so good going for them. The security and comfort of the bedroom in your own home beats the backseat of a Volkswagen, almost every time. Similarly Mom and Pop each have a real lover. This is something the young will probably not have until they have been married a year or two.

A last bit of embroidery on the aphrodisiac fantasy might be mentioned. After the woman has unequivocally yielded, passionately, putatively under the influence of the drug, you then inform her that she had been given only a placebo or "nothing" drug, that it had not been an aphrodisiac at all. Now the actress in your wife has a challenge. She, a "cold" woman, proud of her frigidity, has been tricked into revealing her true nature. She has been outwitted, tricked and forced to reveal herself as what she truly is, an incredibly passionate female. She can no longer lie. She lies nude and exposed to him, physically and psychologically. She has been truly *had*, both mentally and physically. The experience has shattered her. Not only her clothing is gone, but her dignity, and she has no excuses. She had prided herself on being "above sex." She now has been taught that, in reality, she is not whom she thought she was, but, rather, "that other sort of woman." She looks up at her lover, who has forced this insight upon her, humiliated, tears in her eyes, crushed. She puts her arms about his neck. "Kiss me again," she begs. She is now ready for another round.

Incidentally, it must be clearly understood that women are sexually terrific, and that they can produce more than one orgasm in a love making. Men who ejaculate in a physiologically normal fashion, unless long deprived of sex, will, usually, not be able to ejaculate again immediately. Thirty minutes or an hour might be required. In the meantime, of course, the woman may be carried through various orgasms. Under mechanical stimulation, such as a vibrator, a woman who has trained her body can enjoy an almost indefinite succession of greater and lesser orgasms, the limitations being those of time and stamina. There is no reason, incidentally, why the vibrator cannot be applied to her body by a male. This might fit in with a number of fantasies, particularly those which are exotic or futuristic. If the stimulation is manual, apparently some three or so orgasms, but good ones, would be a good batting average for a wench. I hope it does not follow from this that men are obsolete. There is, for example, no reason why manually and mechanically induced orgasms might not both figure in love. I'm told that a man is better than a vibrator, so this is good news for we men. We still have a chance. Women are certainly better than kleenex, too, of course. A word here might be inserted for those who might not have heard the news. For many women, if not most, the center of their sexual responsiveness seems to be the clitoris and not the vagina. Indeed, there is even speculation, incredibly, on whether or not there are vaginal orgasms. At any rate, regardless of these peculiar controversies, which would seem to be susceptible to simple and decisive empirical resolution, but apparently aren't, there is little doubt that the clitoris is of great importance. There is obviously a difference between little orgasms and large ones; the difference ranges from a delicious thrill of sensation to searing pelvic explosions; whether the former are to be identified as clitoral and the latter as vaginal, we may leave to sexologists; it is clear, of course, to all lovers, that the large, explosive orgasms may be clitorally induced, regardless of what we call them. It may be that there are intimate nerve linkages between these two areas and that excitations from one area can travel physiologically to another. At any rate, it is not my recommendation that the vagina be neglected, but that the clitoris not be. That the clitoris is extremely, if not exclusively important, is clear. Also, one hears much of erogenous zones. This is quite misleading. A woman can find it pleasant and sexually stimulating to be touched almost anywhere by a desired male. She may particularly like to have certain areas caressed, perhaps her flanks, perhaps her breasts, in which, psychologically, so much of the femaleness of her is invested, perhaps the interior of her thighs, the back of the knees, her calves, etc. But her pay-offs in orgasm are going to be centered in or near the clitoris. Her entire body should be kissed and caressed and loved, but she is not to be expected to explode into orgasm when her left shoulder is rubbed. Most erogenous zones, including the breasts, are not strictly erogenous at all, if we understand by 'erogenous' the areas of decisive sexual triggering. The clitoris, if not everything, is very important. It is the nub of an incredible web of sexually responsive tissue. It is like the tiny button which turns on the electricity for the entire system. It is unfortunate that some men do not know that women possess this feature. The clitoris, incidentally, should be the object of patient and lengthy loving. It is nothing to touch and kiss it for thirty minutes or more. Many women cannot attain orgasm until the clitoris has been loved for at least a third of an hour. Some women will respond more rapidly, some less rapidly. Also, in time, the responses of some women may become more dependable and rapid. It is my understanding that some women can enter into a series of orgasms within two minutes of the first stimulation. This is, however, extremely unusual, and, where it occurs, is presumably the result of a body honed to perfection by frequent masturbation. It must be further remembered that the clitoris, like the penis, and perhaps more so, is extremely sensitive and delicate. Women sometimes like a bit of roughness in sex, but they will not like it where the clitoris is concerned. Taking her by the arm and tossing her in bed is one thing; being ungentle to the clitoris is quite another. You would not like to have your penis pounded, for example. In masturbating, I understand, most women tend to apply pressure to the side of the clitoris, rather than the very sensitive tip. This is not a bad idea for the man either, at least much of the time. When he does touch the tip of the clitoris he should read the body of the woman to see if he is being too rough. He wants to maximize her pleasure. If he hurts her or makes her uncomfortable, he is not doing so. If in doubt, you can ask her, though this is rather clumsy. She, of course, should have no hesitation in telling you if you are hurting her or being too rough. But when the lovers are well familiar with one another's body and responses, discussions of these matters, exchanges of units of information, etc., will probably not be much necessary. Just as she must learn how to handle your penis to maximize your pleasure, so, too, you must learn how to handle her lovely clitoris, the key to her responses. Incidentally, one justification for the use of the tongue and lips on the clitoris is that, because of the wetness and delicacy of the tongue and lips, there is almost no danger of hurting her and, simultaneously, much likelihood of giving her delicate and exquisite pleasures. There are, also, of course, psychological gratifications in this for the woman. She is a female in what is, in fact, a male-dominated society. It is natural for her to build up resentments toward men, even if she likes them and is attracted to them, even if she loves them. Thus, holding a man's head, by the hair, between her legs, controlling him, while he kisses, and tongue caresses her for an hour or so, can be a marvelous experience for her. She can pull his lips and tongue to her clitoris, or force them away, as she wishes. There is also great pleasure, of course, not only in cunnilingus, but in fellatio, in which she, with lips and tongue, delights him, and, naturally, in fellatio-cunnilingus, in which both, simultaneously, in "69" fashion (ancient and revered *soixante-neuf*), delight the other. One difficulty here, of course, is the differentials in sexual responsiveness. The male will quite possibly be ready to ejaculate, whether he does or not, before the female is farther along than having a good time. If the female wishes a long love making, and wishes the male, eventually, to ejaculate within her, she must be careful how she applies fellatio. Once in a while, of course, she will presumably wish to give the male this pleasure, fully. More often, he will presumably wish to bring her to full orgasm, simply by kissing and tongue caressing. She, of course, has more orgasms to go, and bringing her to orgasm in this fashion does not preclude her having another, and another, later. One way of handling the differential responsiveness in fellatio-cunnilingus, of course, is to give the female this pleasure until she is on the brink of orgasm, and then adopt the 69 position; another, of course, is for the female to "take it easy" on the male, and back away when necessary, until both are ready. As a final word here, it might be pointed out that the objective is to give one another the maximum amount of pleasure of which each is capable. This does not mean that the orgasms of both partners need be achieved simultaneously. There is nothing wrong with achieving them simultaneously, but it is certainly not a necessary condition for good sex. For one thing, it limits the female, commonly, to one orgasm. Also, one of the most beautiful sights in the world is a woman you love in the throes of an orgasm which you have induced in her. If you are too busy with your own pleaures you will miss this incredible and marvelous sight. There are few things in the world which can so fill a man with a sense of power and joy as that of seeing a female, a beloved female, whom he has carefully prepared, yielding herself helplessly to him.

3. The Wife-as-Pickup Fantasy.

One picks up one's wife, as a casual lover, not much respected, and brings her home. She may also, of course, be taken to a hotel, or motel.

Comment:
   Most married men and married women have an interest in illicit sex. On the other hand, probably because they care for one another, they do not act on this interest. This fantasy then, and that of the type following, can be quite enjoyable.
   It is flattering to a female for a man to attempt to pick her up.
   Moreover, a husband is always driving about picking up his wife anyway. There is no reason he should not enjoy it. These pickups can be arranged on the phone. For example, perhaps the wife is downtown shopping. She can then tell her husband where she will be available. As she enters his car, only he and she need know she is not his wife, but only a casual pickup. If her arms are full of packages or if she has a grocery cart that must be loaded into the trunk of the car, take the packages or load the groceries, and then cruise around the block and pick her up, unencumbered, a minute or two later. She may be permitted to walk along the sidewalk, and you drive up and pull to the curb. Perhaps a look is enough. She hesitates. Then she enters your car. She has been "picked up." "What do you cost?" She tells you. She may also, of course, be picked up in a bar, near a restaurant, or anywhere. Perhaps you take her for a drink. Perhaps you buy her supper.
   You meet as strangers, testing one another, fencing with one

another. She may be a professional, or not. But she finds you attractive. She goes with you.

4. The Wife-as-Whore Fantasy.

You pay for your wife's services. Accordingly, you treat her as the whore she is. She, on the other hand, since she is being paid, must "put out" for you. She must be a real whore to you.

Comment:

There is a little bit of whore in every wife. If there weren't, she presumably would never have married you. Also, prostitution is a common fantasy with many women. Every woman is probably curious to know if she could make her living, and how successfully, by her body. Actual prostitution, with its haste, its degradation, its diseases, its commercialism, is doubtless an ugly and unfortunate business. On the other hand, as play, between loving partners, it can be very enjoyable.

A word of caution is in order. When, above, I say "treat her as the whore she is," that is meant in the context of the fantasy. First, you must not be, truly, callous with her, nor hurt her feelings. You are both playing. If you, truly, treat her callously, it will not be much fun for her. If you play "treating her callously" it can be delicious for her. Second, if she were a real whore, there is no excuse in the world for treating her callously. The real whore, not the wife playing a role, is a human being and deserves the same consideration and affection accorded to any other person. The real whore, if used, should be treated with affection and respect. She is a person, too, as much or more than you, who make use of her.

On the other hand, in the *fantasy*, the wife may be treated with a certain degree of objective bluntness. In particular, since you are paying for her, you want quality performance. If she wants her tricks to come back, if she wants to stay in business, she had better be good. Tell her what you want done, and how you want it done, if necessary. You are paying her. You make her work for you. Make her sweat a little to please you. Lay there and make her "put out."

The matter of payment is of interest.

It is my suggestion that she get real money. A couple of ten dollar bills, on the dresser, or even under her body where she can feel them, might be appropriate. She will not object, perhaps to your surprise, at earning the money for a new handbag in this fashion. Your wife is, after all, like any other woman, deliciously, part whore. She should certainly *not* be expected to return the money to you. Why should she? The poor wench has worked for it, and earned it.

A variant here is the "French Whore" fantasy. If the wife speaks French, so much the better. If not, it doesn't matter. In this version, she is paid in French money. (In this case you *will* probably wish to use the same currency again and again. If she feels gypped, of course, you can, later, give her the dollar equivalency. It is important to maintain good international relations. Probably, for this fantasy, the wife should see if she can locate some of that scandalously shocking, charming black lingerie. Garter belt, dark stockings, black choker, etc., are not inappropriate. You are familiar, doubtless, with the picture. I do not know if it is mythical or not. It can, however, whether corresponding to a reality or not, add to a delightfully stimulating fantasy. Even something like a French magazine opened on the dresser, or a French record on the record player, can add interesting and stimulating detail.

Another variant on the wife-as-whore fantasy is that in which the locale is somewhat more exotic. Perhaps the husband is in Port Said. He is a rough sailor, on leave from his ship. He wants a lay. What sort of woman is it who awaits him? The wife will contrive an answer for him. Does she wear a veil? Did she, below, on the first floor, belly dance for him while he ate, only then, when he signified his interest, to be sent upstairs by the proprietor of the establishment to wait for him? Is she a native woman, or is she a western woman, who, because of debts or known secrets, is at the mercy of the owner of the establishment? Is she a woman who has been conditioned to the mastery of men, or is she that western woman who, in fear of the power of the owner of the establishment, is forced to be more delightful and more servile than any native girl could dream of being?

As you can see there are many delicious variations on the wife-as-whore fantasy.

5. The Wife-as-Stripper Fantasy.

She removes her clothing, to the enhancement of music.

Comment:
   To see a woman remove her clothing is an exciting experience. To see her doing this, her body moving provocatively, to erotic music, is a treat and a delight. I gather that my appreciation of this sort of thing is not unique, as several fortunes have been made in this, and associated endeavors, and the practitioners of these arts have a loyal and devoted following. The problem with the professional strip tease, of course, is that it is a rather glumly commercial, if not cynical, exhibition and you don't get to grab the lovely lady afterward. It is indeed a *tease* and, in its way, accordingly, not a fulfilling and satisfying, but a frustrating experience. Imagine the pleasure of being treated, privately, to this performance by an excited, loving woman, who is eager that you make love to her. As her performance concludes, she dances, lovingly and aroused, to your arms.
   Man!
   The dancing, incidentally, may be subtle or not subtle. This is up to the two lovers. Tastes differ. My own feeling is that the more jarring bumps and grinds may be less appropriate in the bedroom than on the athletic field. Music can be reflected in a woman's beauty without turning it into a matter of cocktail shakers and tires blowing out. Some women can dance beautifully while scarcely moving. They have the music, however, burning in their body.
   Not all the clothing a woman commonly wears can be removed gracefully. A wrap-around skirt is more easily removed, for example, than panty hose. Hooks are more easily disengaged than buttons, etc. A G string, if improvised or purchased, is the last thing to be removed, etc. Details and planning in this matter are best left to the wife. She can startle you with her erotic inventiveness. There is no reason that the application

of her intelligence to her own sexiness need any longer be
limited to the selection of the right shade of eye shadow and the
appropriate matching accessories for a shopping ensemble.

If the wife wonders if her husband would appreciate this
particular experience, she might ask him. "Honey, would you
like to see me strip myself to music in front of you?" See what
he says.

There is nothing wrong, of course, if the husband, as the wife
approaches him, time after time, removes pieces of her clothing,
one by one, either from in front of her or behind her, as she
subtly moves, the music hot in her body. He may observe, until
she dances to him, or, if the lovers wish, he may participate, he
himself, article by article, stripping her.

6. The Wife-as-Belly-Dancer Fantasy.

A female, in exotic costume, belly dances before a male.

Comment:

Perhaps she should wear a veil, which is only torn aside when
she is thrown to her back on the bed, and the male presses his
lips to hers, his tongue moving between her teeth, forcing itself
into her mouth, touching and caressing her tongue. Probably,
too, she should still, at this time, be in armlets and bangles. If her
body is belled, so much the better, as the sound of these bells, as
she responds to you, can be highly stimulating. Presumably by
the time she is carried to the bed her other garments have been
removed, either by she herself or by you.

Next to making love or engaging in intercourse itself the
belly dance is one of the most sexually stimulating acts a human
female can perform. It is a fantastic invention. It fits somewhere
between fire and the wheel, probably. Before it the significance
of agriculture, also supposed to be an invention of women, seems
trivial. All human males owe a debt of gratitude to the sweet
wench, or wenches, who thought up this incredible delight.

It should be taught in girls' hygiene classes. Beside it, body
mechanics become irrelevant. Doubtless it belongs as a component
in any adequate course in sex education.

It is impossible for a female to learn to belly dance and still not know what being a female is all about.

It trains her body in the motions of love and makes her graceful, sensuous and beautiful. It makes her exotic, delicious, provocative, desirable. It drives men crazy with lust. If the wife, from time to time, would not mind driving her husband crazy with lust for her, belly dancing is something she might inquire into. Further, many women, themselves, have an interest in being desirable, beautiful and dangerously, deliciously erotic. They wish, sometimes, to be as stimulating and sexy as they can. And it is hard to be sexier than when belly dancing. It is an invention made to combine movement, music, beauty and sex. Barefoot, in bangles, vulnerable in the revealing costume of the belly dancer, almost any wife becomes an incredibly exciting sexual object. There are also, of course, all sorts of enriching sexual overtones involved in such a performance. It is almost as if she were a woman of another culture, conditioned to please the senses of men. Perhaps she *is* a woman of another culture, a culture in which women are permitted to be little more than the servants or slaves of males? Perhaps she is a western woman, a captive or slave in a harem or brothel, trained and forced to perform these dances, say, for customers, or for her master? Is she alone, or are there others, too? How does she compare with them? Is she beaten if she does not perform satisfactorily? Are gold coins thrown to her feet, which she must pick up and carry quickly to, say, her master?

If you happen to own an oriental rug, that, presumably, would be a desirable place for her to dance. If you do not, she will probably look good even on linoleum. To bring several bags of sand into the bedroom is to have several bags of sand in the bedroom, which is not desirable. At any rate, there are few objects as sexually stimulating as a woman clad in a revealing costume kneeling, or lying, or half lying on a rug. You will be lucky if you can get her as far as the bed.

My suspicion is that most women have belly dancing bred into their glands. On the other hand, lessons, in large cities, are available in this genre of the dance. If the husband proposes to go without his lunch for six months to pay for these lessons do not permit him to do so, as his nutrition will suffer. It would be better for him to give up cigarettes instead. This could be, incidentally, one of the more powerful motivations for giving up smoking. Even addicts will confess that sex is better than cigarettes. Moreover, there is little evidence that it is dangerous to your health. Indeed, the evidence seems to suggest that frequent and joyful sex is good for you. It is not unhealthy to use the human body. Those who have thought otherwise were mistaken.

7. The Earth-Females-as-Tribute Fantasy.

The Earth has been conquered by an alien planet, the population of which is, scientifically, far advanced beyond ours. Earthlings, and Earth governments, are terrified. The Earth is vulnerable, at the mercy of the aliens. If we do not cooperate with them, completely and perfectly, in all respects, selected cities will be randomly destroyed. Some have been destroyed already. If necessary, the Earth itself may be destroyed. The aliens do not wish to inhabit the planet Earth. They wish to use it primarily as a source for raw materials and females.

Each month one thousand of the most beautiful Earth females must be paid to the aliens as tribute, to insure our survival. All Earth women between the ages of seventeen and thirty-five must register, be tabulated and examined. The selection, processing and transportation of the monthly tribute is globally organized and systematic. Data processing machinery, computers, etc., are used. Our technology is applied to the selection of optimum tribute. One thousand women per month is, incidentally, not a large figure in a planet's population. We shall suppose, similarly, that the raw materials required by the aliens do not represent a considerable drain on Earth resources. Perhaps what they need is even renewable, as, for example, certain forms of wood products. Except for the monthly tributes and shipments, and the fact that the alien flag must be flown, with precedence, with national flags over public buildings, there is not a great deal of difference between the old Earth, free, filled with bickering nations, and the new Earth, helpless, not permitted war, a colony planet.

Life goes on much as it normally would.

Girls, of course, certain selected women, might now receive notifications to report for examination and assessment, for possible inclusion in tribute shipments. They would, in effect, be drafted for such shipments, much as, previously, men were drafted for service in the armed forces. The armed forces, of course, have disbanded. The aliens do not permit intraplanetary strife. They might, of course, wish at some time to draft Earthlings to fight as auxiliaries for them in other wars, interplanetary wars. They have not as yet done so, however. In drafting the girls for tribute, we might suppose that existing selective-service-system personnel and processing are used. It is merely turned to the acquisition of a new type of object.

The girls are examined with great care, both medically and psychologically. They are muchly tested. Only the most beautiful, most healthy, most intelligent, most sexually responsive, are selected.

The aliens get the best women of Earth.

These women do not return. It is not known to what purpose they are applied.

Comment:

The preceding material sets up a situation within which exciting fantasy can be created.

We shall suppose that "Linda" or "Marcia," or whomever your wife portrays, received her "notice."

The entire resources of her society are marshalled to see that she reports and, if qualified, takes her place in the tribute quota. Does she attempt to flee? What are her reactions? Was she content with the system, perhaps happy with it, because of the end of war, etc., until she discovered that it might be she herself who would pay this price? Does she wish that they would draft men instead, as before? Why do the aliens want *women*? If she tries to flee, do the special police used in such matters catch her and take her, in handcuffs, to the induction and examination station?

The husband acts a large number of male roles in this fantasy. He may be the policeman who captures her, and forces her to accompany him to the induction and examination station. He may be the examining physician, before whom she must strip herself and be medically assessed. He may be the examining psychologist. Perhaps horror at her fate is one of the properties which, for some reason, increases her desirability from the point of view of the aliens? Perhaps the police and physicians, etc. *are* aliens, conducting these matters to their own precise satisfaction? Perhaps the girl is strapped on a special examination table and electrodes are taped to her head and body, their inputs being fed to instruments with gauges and meters. Her clitoris is stroked and her responses, with scientific precision, are registered by needles on the gauges and meters. Linda, we shall suppose, is extremely sexually responsive. She is chosen, perhaps over other women, even more beautiful. How is she fed and restrained before shipment? How is she shipped? Is she drugged and crated? Are there special cells on the space ship that will transport her and others? What is her number? Is her number on a metal plate which is fastened about her neck by a chain? What happens to Linda on the ship? What happens to Linda when she arrives on the alien world?

8. The I-Am-Sold-in-a-Slave-Market Fantasy.

She is sold in a slave market.

Comment:

Most women are curious to know what their flesh would bring. They wonder what it would be like to be stripped and placed on a block for the examination of buyers. They wonder what it would be like to have men bidding for their body. What would they sell for? This fantasy gives them an opportunity to find out.

An obvious variant here is the beautiful female tourist who finds herself captured and placed in such a market. Another variant, interesting, is the beautiful female journalist who wishes to do an exposé of the slave trade. She bribes her way into a building in which such a market is located. She has her camera, her notebooks, etc. It will be a fantastic story. She intends to get a "scoop." She discovers, for example, that white women as well as black women are sold in such markets. Of course, she has been tricked. When she believes, in hiding, she has her pictures and her story, and is going to escape, she is, by prearranged signal, revealed to the buyers as a western intruder. With a whip she is driven to the block and, article by article, as the bids increase, stripped. Before she is sold she is forced to feel the lash, as a slave girl, and on the block, as a slave girl, is forced to dance for the men. She is then sold, and her buyer, binding and gagging her, takes her home.

Obviously, in the fantasy, the woman may not be struck with a whip. It would hurt her to do so. Acting, however, as though she is being beaten can be sexually stimulating to her. Really being beaten, besides being immoral, would just make her miserable. You wish to give her pleasure. Pain is not pleasure. If she should really desire you to hurt her, you should get her to a doctor. Assuming that a whip is not available, and there is no reason one should be available, the male may simply, sharply, clap his hands, and the woman reacts as though struck. The beating is completely symbolic, as it should be. Fantasy is fantasy. Moving her body *as though* it were under the whip of a man can give women pleasure; and, too, pretending to strike them, and seeing her react as if struck, can produce an incredible sense of dominance in a male. If she cannot see when your hands strike together the movement of her body, startled, will be extremely realistic. Your "blows" should be timed in such a way that different intervals obtain between them. She should not know when the "blow" is coming. She must wait for it, tense, frightened. Then, when it does fall, she reacts, startled, piteously, as though actually struck, as though feeling great pain.

One way of doing this is to tie her naked, on her stomach, on the bed, her wrists and ankles tied apart to the bed posts, a pillow inserted between her legs and under her body. This way, when she writhes, her clitoris is stimulated by the movements against the pillow. This combines the psychological gratification, common in female fantasies, of being completely at the mercy of a dominant male, with the intimate physiological stimulation of her clitoris, as though she were helpless to prevent it, two delights often combined in female sexual fantasy.

After the beating she is asked, "Do you beg to dance nude for the men?"

"Yes," she whispers, in agony, "—Master." As a "whipped woman" the word comes inadvertently, naturally, from her lips. The proud western woman is now a slave girl.

She dances, and is sold.

She brings an excellent price.

There are numbers of variations on this sort of fantasy. The husband, of course, plays all male roles. Perhaps she is kept for a time before she is sold. Her husband, of course, is her keeper. How is she restrained? Is she chained in her cell? Does he shackle her? What is she fed? Is she permitted to use her hands to feed herself? Must she kneel to eat out of a dish with her mouth, her hands tied behind her? Does the keeper feed her by hand? Does he throw her scraps of food, like a dog? Her husband, too, of course, is her auctioneer. Doubtless she is expected to perform well on the block. Doubtless she is expected to excite the interest of the buyers? Does her auctioneer, on the block, caress her clitoris, that the buyers may see that the slave is sexually responsive? And who, eventually, buys her, and takes her home? The husband again, lucky fellow. She will doubtless learn her slavery well at his hands.

The sales of women, of course, may be public or private. Perhaps she is privately exhibited only to certain selected buyers, perhaps one at a time? Perhaps each of these buyers is entitled to "try her out" to "see if she is any good." Perhaps the sale, public (in which there are many buyers) or private (in which there are few buyers, or only one) may be detailed and exquisite, or swift and rude. Which is more stimulating to your wife? To be sold before many men in almost a ritual of merchandising, or, say, at the other end of the scale, to be summarily disposed of for a quickly agreed-upon price to a single buyer? A "quick-sale" variant here, though not actually a "slave market" fantasy, is when the woman, nude, and bound hand and foot, is thrown to the feet of a prospective buyer to be assessed and bid upon. Perhaps he caresses her to note her responsiveness. Let us suppose she writhes helplessly, in an agony of shame and sexual stimulation, in her bonds. He buys her. She is then his slave.

9. The Rites-of-Submission Fantasy.

This fantasy begins on the game deck of a space liner. The wench is a young, beautifully assed, voluptuous, rich, arrogant, blond bitch. She wears, perhaps, large sun glasses, against the glare of the lights. She has on a terrific pair of blue shorts, and wears, too, a blue, cuffed, collared, mannish shirt, not unlike a workman's shirt. She is playing shuffleboard with a young, arrogant, suitably rich, suitably refined bore of an escort. Nearby, sitting, reading, is a large, gentle, studious appearing young man. He is diffident, and recognizes the social gap that separates him from his betters, such as the girl and her escort. In her movements, at one point, she trips over his feet, and is furious, and castigates him, for his clumsiness, etc. He apologizes, etc.

Later, as might be expected, for some reason, the space liner, in some catastrophe, deviates from course and, communications gone, drifts across space. It is lost, and there is no way of tracing it. Days later, following a series of explosions, compartment after compartment of the ship begins to depressurize, and the ship itself begins to break up. Survivors enter escape craft. The ship is abandoned. The region of space is uncharted. One escape craft, becoming separated from the others, after weeks, makes a crash landing on an unknown, but beautiful, lush planet. It is light years from known space lanes. It is unlikely that the small craft can be traced in the vastness of space. It is unlikely it could even be located, even had it not crashed through treelike growths, on the surface of the planet on which it has impacted. An adequate search, could it be conducted, would doubtless consume centuries. There are two individuals in the escape capsule. As the luck of fantasy would have it, you guessed it, the girl and studious young man.

She is miserable and frightened, of course. He, not having much else to do, sets about surviving. They make a camp on the shore of a sea, or large lagoon. He manages to make nets, fishing supplies, manages to get a fire going, sets snares for small animals, finds good water, builds a shelter, etc.

When the girl discovers they can live in this place, her responses become those of indignation and irritation, that she is "marooned" with such a person, a "nothing" person, a boor and clod, in her opinion; a fellow who does not even know how to dance, a fellow of no position, family or wealth; in her opinion, a real "jerk." She despises him and openly shows her contempt and scorn for him. She treats him, consistently, with contempt and cruelty.

True to his conditioning, he accepts this, acknowledging that she is better than he. He suffers in silence, not challenging her, obeying her when it does not prejudice their survival, trying to please her. The more he attempts to be pleasing the more she scorns him. He continues to do his work, and to keep them both alive, and tries to shut her cruelty and vehemence out of his mind.

In exploring the world on which they find themselves, if only to be away from her, he discovers a strange temple, on a mountain, reached by a tortuous trail. The temple is formed in the shape of a nude, prone female, lying on her back, over a gently rounded surface. The head is turned to one side. The arms are over the head, elbows bent; the knees, too, are bent. There is no mistaking the masonry; the wrists and ankles are fastened in great brick shackles.

He enters the temple. He cannot tell its age. Materials and decorations within seem as though new.

A sort of a story is told in mosaics in a series of large rooms within the temple.

In the first room are seen five large mosaics. In the first are represented three proud women, scorning the gifts and refusing the advances of three suitors. In the next the women are seen at play, tossing a ball among themselves. In the background, concealed by shrubbery, the three suitors can be detected. The third mosaic depicts the men leaping forth to seize the women and the women, startled. The fourth mosaic depicts the women being secured. One is already bound and gagged. One is being bound. One, held, is waiting to be bound. They are still fully clothed. The fifth mosaic shows the women, gagged, now in brief garments, chained as helpless prizes to the side of an open, round, strange air ship. It is manned, of course, by the three suitors.

Curious, the young man further explores the temple. The next six rooms present, in graphic illustration, an alien culture's procedure for the reduction of a proud woman to the status of a pleasure slave.

Each room contains a large, illustratory mosaic, and, when appropriate, the devices to signify and bring about the reduction.

The temple was apparently used, at least at one time, for the enslavement of women.

In the first room there is an illustration of a woman being stripped.

In the second room a long chain, with bolt-tightened wristlets, dangles from the ceiling. It may be raised and lowered by a windlass. There is, too, a rack of whips. The illustration shows a woman being beaten.

In the third room there are irons for branding, and braziers in which such irons may be heated. There is even fuel. The illustration, of course, is that of a girl being marked with a hot iron, being branded slave.

In the fourth room there are numerous slave collars, with keys. These are metal, and would fit closely, snugly about a woman's neck.

In the fifth room there is an illustration of a woman dancing naked before a warrior, with strange weapons. He is the same, of course, as he who was shown in the previous mosaics, stripping and beating her, and branding her, and fastening her in the collar.

In the sixth room, he is shown in representation as using her.

There are two other, smaller, last mosaics in the sixth room. In one the girl kneels at the warrior's feet, after his use of her. She holds his legs and looks up to his face. In her eyes, incredibly, shows love. The last mosaic shows the warrior leaving and the girl, naked, bearing a burden, following him.

The young man finds the temple fascinating. He wishes

to return immediately and inform the girl of this fantastic discovery. He is, of course, actually a highly intelligent person, a quiet, strong, usually gentlemanly person. He is well read, and he is stunned by his unusual, marvelous discovery. He has the scholar's joy in his find.

Bubbling over, enthusiastic, he returns to the camp, desiring to share his pleasure and happiness with the girl.

At the camp, however, she indicates no interest. He does not describe his find, only that he has discovered this strange temple, and wishes her to come with him to see it. If only because his discovery means much to him, she belittles it, and refuses to accompany him back to the temple. She "puts him down" by feigning boredom. She, instead, is going swimming. Already she is wearing a bikini-type swim suit, salvaged from the wreck of the escape craft.

She turns away from him, and prepares to go to the water.

In one searing instant a transformation comes over the young man. He is infuriated with her. She is a beautifully assed, arrogant, rich bitch. She has treated him like dirt. In that wild, reversing instant, he seems, in a blast of lightning, to rethink the relations between the sexes. The woman is weak. She has nothing protecting her but the artificialities of a conditioning which she herself, over generations, has contrived to weaken men and make them helpless and pliant to her will. It is as though antelopes would give laws to lions. The lion makes his own laws. Suddenly, in a great, liberating shattering of psychological shackles he sees her as a female, and a desirable one, his, if he should choose to take her. He is the male, the lion, and she, should he wish, his prey, the sleek, lovely haunched antelope. He recalls, too, that this culture, as exhibited in the great temple, ratified the slavery of the female. The culture was sophisticated. Could it have been right? Did they know more than his own sorry, complex culture, with all of its talk of equality, and all of its suffering and misery? Suddenly he is filled with a wild, predatory joy. He sees the girl, ass swinging, taunting him, walking toward the water. She knows he would never touch her. She can insolently, cruelly, flaunt her beauty before him, frustrating him, using it to insult his putative ineffectuality, his predictable and dependable weakness and agreeability.

He sees her ass, and decides that he will have it. She is utterly without protection. She believes herself, of course, completely safe, utterly secure. It would never even enter her mind that such a fool and bore as he would dare to even do so much as raise his voice to one such as she. She is now, of course, ignorant. She still thinks herself much above him. Little does she know that now, behind her, there stands a man freed of psychological shackles. She does not understand that she now has no more than the status of an attractive female animal before a large, strong, sex-starved, appetitious, predatory male. Did she know this she would scream for mercy. He looks after her. She has been arrogant and cruel to him. He will take his vengeance. He knows what he will do.

He laughs like a god, freed of chains.

She hesitates, but does not look back. Then, less certain of herself, she continues toward the water. Then, she stops again. She looks back. He regards her. She turns away, contemptuously again, and, once again her haughty, arrogant self, moves toward the water.

In an instant he is on her, felling her to her stomach on the sand, thrusting her head half under the sand. She lifts her head, gasping. Already, with his belt, her arms have been pinned to her side.

"What are you doing?" she screams.

"You are coming with me," he informs her.

By the hair, bent over, arms pinned to her side, he takes her to the temple.

There, of course, he puts her through the rites of submission. There he makes her his slave. He strips her. He fastens her in the bolt-tightened wristlets and, by the windlass, lifts her some inches from the floor. He then, savagely, lays the whip to her. He stops when she has been sufficiently beaten. She has cried out, unable to help herself, startling herself and him, from the depths of her female subconscious, "Please stop! Please stop, Master!" In the next room he fastens her securely. She lies there, waiting for the iron to heat. When the iron is hot, he brands her slave.

In the next room he puts her in a collar. In the next room he
forces her to dance for him. In the next room, repeatedly and at
length, he makes love to her. She responds to him as a slave girl
to her master. She is completely conquered. Their relationship is
completely transformed. She is to him now only a willing, eager,
loving, obedient slave. In the deep femaleness of her she has
been forced to recognize her natural master, man. When they
leave the temple, she walks behind him, a conquered, loving
slave girl behind her master.

Comment:
    A Rites-of-Submission Fantasy can be a powerful fantasy. It
is well to remember, of course, that it is only a fantasy. There is
something in a woman that wants to surrender itself to a strong,
desirable male. In a sense, sexually, a woman does frequently
wish to be dominated. The I-am-his-slave fantasy, so to speak, is
a common one for the female. It is, of course, only one side of the
complex, marvelous creatures that are women. There is also a side
that desires and deserves independence. Women are gloriously
complicated. They are part companion, part slave girl. A man is
very lucky to have both. If he has only one, I think he has been
short changed. Another obviously distorted fantasy element in
the preceding is the "rejection of psychological shackles" element.
That is a powerful element, and valuable *in fantasy*. On the other
hand, it is well to remind ourselves that restraints are a necessary
condition for civilization and an acceptable human existence as
we know it. They are necessary to protect us, the one from the
other. There is nothing wrong with conditioning *per se*, any
more than that there is something wrong with habits. Obviously
much depends on what the conditioning is; much depends on
what the habits are. Conditioning and habit, of course, must not
be blind; they must be recognized and rationally approved; we
must be the masters of our conditioning, and of our habits, not
vice-versa. It is sometimes hard to do this, of course. It is always
easier, for example, to break a conditioning pattern in one's
offspring than in one's self. This is how one generation helps the
next to free itself; that the more liberated generation does not
realize the debt owed to the liberating generation, which refused

to repeat their own conditioning patterns in them is an irony, one which may be placed to the ignorance of the young; when they are in their forties and fifties, they will realize what was done for them. One advantage of an open society, incidentally, is that one encounters alternative conditioning patterns, and must thus come to grips with alternative possibilities for the realization of humanity, and perhaps even find oneself forced to make a choice as to how one will select and realize the human potential in one's own self. An open society helps keep people on top of their own conditioning, which is where they belong. The value sets of many people, even in a free society, are nothing more than reflex spasms programmed into them. An open society, however, gives humanity a chance to find itself. This is also, incidentally, an argument for the retention of the family as a basic social unit. Millions of families provide millions of experimental laboratories in which different human possibilities can be protected and cherished, or invented and nurtured. Even if the great state nurseries and baby farms of the Utopians could provide emotional security, trust and love, intimate love, say, as between a mother and child, it seems unlikely they would do much for the nobility of human beings. They would, in effect, imprison humanity invisibly. We would become interchangeable units, all bent and twisted in the same planes. When the family is destroyed, the mass-produced human being will take its place. Mass-produced human beings are attractive only to those who expect to be their benevolent mass producers. Life is too short and too precious to waste it living out someone else's values. We must find our own. A natural concomitant, of course, of the attempt to maximize freedom and the opportunity for diverse realizations of the human potentiality is the commitment to tolerance and the respect for others. Their freedom ends where it bumps yours. As a judge once said, or something to this effect, the freedom to swing your arm stops where the other fellow's nose starts. Civilization is fragile, and depends on restraint, and, to a certain extent, on genuine frustration. It is, however, preferable to the jungle. We, on the other hand, retain something of the jungle in our blood. We are new to civilization, and have not quite caught the hang of it yet. We have surely bungled several civilizations,

and we may bungle the current one. Indeed, to those with
some awareness of history, there is much evidence that we are
well along in the process of doing so. Civilization, however, is
far better than the jungle. If it weren't, we would still be in
the jungle. If this civilization falls to the internal and external
barbarians, doubtless another will take its place, a stronger
one, one without the weaknesses of tolerance and freedom.
America, and the western world, may become, in retrospect, a
brief, bright moment in history, like Periclean Athens, the secret
memory of a few intellectuals who have managed to preserve
outlawed texts. Tolerance and freedom, of course, may not be
weaknesses but strengths. We are currently in the process of
finding out. But civilization, even a totalitarian civilization,
such as would be the *practical* implementation of Marx's naive
dreams in a technological century, would presumably be
preferable to hunting our food in the streets. Rational human
beings, statistically, will choose even a terrible civilization to the
law of the knife. Either hideous prong of totalitarianism, state
capitalism, as in "communist" countries, or fascism, would be
preferable to the horrors of murdering to eat. Accordingly, human
beings will, and doubtless should, choose civilization over the
jungle. The choice is not going to be between civilization and
the jungle but between competitive civilizations. On the other
hand, we carry the jungle about with us. In the fantasy which
we have delineated, certain concessions are made to the jungle
in us. This can be liberating and delicious. It expresses a side of
our personality, that of the hunter and predator. This is a side
which, in actual life, that we may live together as humans and
not animals, must be suppressed. In fantasy, however, it may
be joyously liberated. In fantasy we may laugh like gods freed
of their chains. It is good to do so. How many of us have ever
so laughed? In fantasy we may do *exactly* as we please. Who
can believe that it is not healthy and happy for a human being,
sometime, to do *exactly as he pleases*?

A few detailed notes may be in order on this recently
delineated fantasy.

There could be many different Rites-of-Submission fantasies.
There is no reason why the rites of submission employed need be

identical to these, either in number or nature. A superb source of ideas on such a matter would be one's wife. If she has not already engaged in fantasies of this sort, she will, probably, find them sexually stimulating and will be inventive in their elaboration. What, to *her*, would be a very sexy way of enslaving her? She is, after all, the one in this fantasy who is being enslaved. The more she has to say about it the more stimulating the fantasy is likely to be to her. For example, perhaps she will feel that she should be thrown a certain form of garment and be forced to put it on in your presence. It is the garment, of course, of a female slave. Perhaps a certain form of jewelry is placed on her body, slave jewelry, marking her as an owned woman. Perhaps she is forced to use a certain form of make-up which, between you, is agreed to be indicative of a slave female. Perhaps she feels she should be forced to kneel before you and kiss your feet as part of the ceremony, or, perhaps, put her hair or lips to your genitals. Almost certainly she may want certain words to be spoken, certain formulas of enslavement, spoken either by you or herself or, more likely, both. These may be simple.

Consider the following:

M: Do you wish to live?
W: Yes.
M: If you are to live, you will do so only as my slave.
  Do you understand?
W: Yes.
M: Do you beg to be my slave?
W: Yes, I beg to be your slave.
M: Say, "I will be your slave, Master."
W: I will be your slave, Master.
M: Say, "I am your slave, Master."
W: I am your slave, Master.

Perhaps at this point he fastens a certain form of earrings, or a collar, on her, something to mark her slave, that all may see and know. Perhaps he fastens bells on her left ankle.

His manner to her is now harsh.

M: Kiss my feet, Slave.
W: Yes, Master.

He then turns and leaves. She follows. If she wears bells, each of her movements, now those of a slave girl, is marked by the sound of the bells.

There are many possibilities. For example, what is her posture during the spoken portions of the rites of submission, etc.?

More particularly, with respect to specific elements mentioned in the sketched fantasy, the beating of the woman, of course, is symbolic. The sharp clapping of hands may serve, as in the slave-market fantasy, for the crack of the leather. She may, of course, without the clap of hands, merely move as though struck, when it seems appropriate to her to do so. You may simply say to her, "Your beating is now begun. React." You might later ask, "Have you been beaten enough?" "Yes, Yes, Master," she gasps. Her beating is then at an end. If later, of course, she should disobey or displease you, she may be beaten again. The whip is an important article in the instruction and management of the slave female. If she is not pleasing, she knows it may be used on her in an instant. No true master hesitates to use the lash on his beauties. It keeps perfect discipline among them. Too, it may be imagined that she is suspended off the ground. If she lies on the bed, hands over her head, belly down, wrists crossed, and doubtless bound, her body straight, toes pointed, this simulates the suspended position. Only the axis is different. Her ankles, if one wishes, may also be crossed and lashed together. Or, if one wishes, one may simply force her to kneel at the foot of the bed, tieing her lashed wrists to the bedpost. If she lies belly down on the bed, a pillow should be placed beneath her in such a way that her movements excite and caress her clitoris. If she kneels at the foot of the bed, the pillow, doubled over, is thrust tight between her legs. It may even be tied there. The whipping fantasy, incidentally, need not be elaborate. It may also be played unexpectedly. Perhaps she has said something you did not care for, or has not served you as completely and servilely as is her duty. Then a sudden hand clap or two might represent blows, from which she reels away, perhaps to kneel cowering in a corner or perhaps, prone, helpless and in disarray, to fall piteously to the rug, one of your slaves, a girl, at your feet. Will more blows fall? Perhaps, perhaps not. It is up to you. You do what you think necessary for her instruction. She must accept what you decide. She is your slave. When she is used in bed, perhaps bound there, hands over her head, watching you, she does not know whether she is to be beaten or caressed. Perhaps you do both, "beating her," and then, at length, using her. She yields as a slave, under whip and touch. Her ardor must be fantastic, she knows, even if feigned, or again the whip will give instruction, and well, to an inadequate, errant girl in the wishes of her master.

In the branding, similarly, of course, no injury is done to her. If desired, the body may be marked by something which can be later washed away. Lipstick is not good because it smears on the bed covers. A magic marker, a felt pen, might be used. Of course, it might be merely pretended that she is marked. With a finger you might trace a slave brand on her thigh, or wherever she is to be marked. A piece of metal, warmed or unwarmed, of course, may be used to simulate the pressing of the iron. If the metal is warmed it must not be hot enough, obviously, to cause her more than a slight discomfort. In particular she must not be, in fact, marked or scarred. If a piece of warmed metal is used try it out first on your own body to make sure that it will not hurt her. If it is too hot you can always, quickly, remove it from your body; if she is bound, she would not be able to do so.

The matter of collars is not difficult.

Many forms of jewelry worn by women about their necks, interestingly, are quite collarlike. Women know, on some level, that a collar on their throat is extremely sexually stimulating to a man. It speaks of her as slave, or bitch, or animal. It is a bold signal on her part that there is a female animal in her. Most men understand this, or, at least, sense it. When a woman wears a collar she is boldly issuing an invitation to her own hunt. A woman's own collar or choker may suffice for the collar. On the other hand, perhaps she should keep one or two collars for precisely such love games. They are then, for her and her husband, special collars. Animal collars, of course, are also good. There are many varieties of these, and some are excitingly attractive on the lovely

throat of a woman. Also, of course, here the female animality of
her literally screams itself at you. A short length of chain, too,
fastened with a small padlock, can also be delightful. When the
girl hears the snap of the lock she knows that she has been truly,
in fact, put in a collar. This can be very stimulating to her. She
cannot remove it. The chain and lock proclaim her bondage. The
male has done this to her. It is he who holds the key. It is he
whose animal she is.

10. The She-Is-Forced-to-Please-Him-as-a-Bound-Captive Fantasy.

The girl is forced to make love with her hands tied behind her
back.

Comment:

Most lovers, particularly women, do not even use their hands
well in making love. Some women seem to be of the opinion
that their portion in love making is limited to lying down and
waiting to be pleased. Both lovers, needless to say, can, and
should, be active. The hands of both are extremely important,
as well as the rest of their bodies. Beyond this, however, very
few lovers realize the value of the lips, tongue and teeth in
sexually stimulating the partner. One of the values of this
fantasy is that it forces the lover to rely heavily on these often
neglected or ignored instruments of love. Needless to say, the
"He-is-Forced-to-Please-Her-as-a-Bound-Captive Fantasy" would
be the complementary fantasy of this one. Whether the male or
the female is the captive, the captive must make love with his
hands bound behind him. This should teach him a great deal.
Let us suppose that the captive is, in this case, the woman. She
is, let us suppose, to be slain unless she makes superb love to
him. But she is bound! She feels helpless. She is thrown into
consternation. Then, wildly, she realizes she must try to please
him, and superbly, without the use of her hands. Otherwise she
dies. She crawls into his bed, hands bound, as he waits. With her
body, her breasts, her feet, her thighs, her sweet ass, her lovely
cunt, her beautiful lips and teeth and tongue she addresses

herself to his pleasure. After trying this fantasy once or twice the woman will have learned the fantastic potentialities of her body in making love, apart from the use of her small, delicate hands. After she has learned to do this well you can imagine how marvelous she will be when she has the use of her hands as well. What an incredible lover she will then be. This same fantasy, of course, like many, or most, of these fantasies can be used turnabout, with the male in the position of submission. Indeed, women may enjoy this when the male is bound. Having love made to them by a bound male can enhance their sense of power. Most women can use a bit of this. From time to time it is good for them to be dominant. It helps them to think better of themselves. It releases suppressed emotions and ventilates often-bottled hostility and aggression. It gives them more self-respect and helps them to be freer, happier human beings. There are pleasures in being the leader, the commander. These pleasures should be open to the woman as well as the man.

11. The Captured-by-Desert-Tribesmen Fantasy.

The girl is captured by desert tribesmen.

Comment:

The most successful fantasy of this type with which I am familiar was written by a woman, E. M. Hull. It was called *The Sheik*. It was not known, when it was published, that the author was a woman. It caused something of a stir when it leaked out. The movie, starring Rudolph Valentino, was a hit, and remains a delightful classic. Similarly, the sequel, *Son of the Sheik*, was popular, and that movie, too, is a classic. The books, in their time, were best sellers. The movies, even today, are joys. Doubtless much of the success of the movies is due to the remarkable performances of Mr. Valentino. For example, I have never seen another actor who, when he wishes, can express a man's *joy* in touching a woman as well as he. It has never even occurred, as far as I can tell, to most men that touching a woman is, or can be, a joyful experience. On the screen Valentino conveyed that women are marvelously desirable and beautiful creatures. Very few screen lovers convey anything of the simple *appreciation* of how fantastic women are. To be sure, Valentino could portray the looming, dark, male menace, dangerous, desirable, sensuous, intent upon her sexual subjugation, but, too, like perhaps no other actor, he could, when he wished, exhibit that he was almost uncontrollably thrilled and delighted to hold a woman in his arms. If that is flattery, it is flattery that will get a man just about anywhere. Women were not, to those of Valentino's generation, chicks and foxes and broads. His was a more romantic generation. Cloak swirling, on his Arabian stallion, he bore her with him, a captive, to his tent in the desert, there to be ravished at his leisure. Women, in his day, pale, proud and beautiful, were thought to be worthy prizes, worth capturing and carrying off. Today it is not clear that there is that much point in bothering. Even the sheik would not be tempted to carry off today's gum-chewing, pot-smoking chick. He would just feel stupid. She is fortunate, perhaps, that she is permitted to avail herself of public transportation. Hopefully, somewhere between the pale lady and the broad is something else, maybe a woman. Valentino, I would guess, in the *Sheik* and the *Son of the Sheik*, tended to *realize* the fantasy dream, or create something which could be accepted as an authentic fantasy dream, of many women. Not every movie of his is as popular as these two. *Blood and Sand*, for example, doubtless a better movie, is not as popular or as much shown. The success of these two movies is doubtless largely due to Mr. Valentino, but, I suspect, there is more involved. The fantasy plot, so superbly realized by Mr. Valentino, is powerful in its own right. I should like to think their success is not due simply to Mr. Valentino's presence in the films *per se* so much as it is also due, importantly, to his superb realization of the fantasy. His unusual and remarkable talents brought the fantasy to life, and brought it to life in pageantry and detail. Fantasy *and* Valentino is a potent combination. The books, as I mentioned, were best sellers, too. And the first book, of course, was published before the movie. The books turned on women all over the English-speaking world. It is extremely interesting and revealing that the author was a woman. That should shake up men a bit about what goes on in the pretty heads of lovely ladies. Surely it should make them seem more human, and more interesting. Further, it makes clear that the fantasies of men and women tend to be similar, save for the difference in perspective. Men often fantasize adventure, capture and rape, for instance; it is nice to know that women do, too. The men, in their fantasies, commonly do the capturing and raping; and the women, in their fantasies, commonly, by some coincidence, are the ones captured and raped. There is a set of congruent fantasies! All men and women have to do now is to put together their fantasies and get ready for a corking good time.

There are elements in the desert fantasy which make it interesting and attractive. Some of these might be noted. The desert, with its oases and caravans, and camel bells, and dancing girls, and striped tents, and palm trees, and bandits, etc., is a romantic locale. It beats downtown Chicago. Further, the position of the woman in Arabian culture, particularly in the past, is very low. Thus if an aristocratic English lady, for example, is captured, she would have very little going for her, which makes the fantasy better. She is to begin with only a female; further she is a captive; further she is to her captors a cultural "outsider"; they need have no respect for her; indeed, she is only a lovely infidel, white and beautiful, less than an animal, completely at their mercy; further, she is a woman of the enemy; and, thus, it is only to be expected that their hatred of the west, which threatens them and their way of life, and regards itself as superior to them, their rage and resentment, will be ventilated on her; they will see that they get much pleasure from her; they will make the west pay; she will stand proxy for the west; we may expect that she will be put to detailed and harsh use; further, she is their secret prisoner; no one knows her whereabouts; she cannot escape across the desert; she is helplessly theirs; the aristocratic, beautiful English lady, put in barbaric ornaments, dressed revealingly for the tactual and visual pleasures of her captors, can be in little doubt as to her new identity; she can now be bought and sold; she must be obedient; she must do whatever she is told; she is now only an educated, white slave girl, the property of barbarian Arab masters.

What happens to her, what is done to her, is up to the creators of the fantasy.

12. The Captured-by-Indians Fantasy.

She is captured by Indians.

Comment:

If the husband and wife enjoy horseback riding, some riding can help them get into the mood for this fantasy. They can plan it together, and play parts of it among themselves as they ride.

It also works well if the husband and wife are hikers or campers, where the openness of nature, with its felicitous air and stimulating scenery can provide an incomparable setting for the fantasy's enactment.

How many husbands have actually pursued their wife through a woods, or among hills, and have captured her? Girls love running from a man they would be delighted to be caught by. It seems to be in their blood both to flee and to yield deliciously, delightedly, when, inevitably, they fall prey. The chase is, probably for genetic reasons going back to evolutional selections, sexually stimulating to them; it is, of course, disappointing to them if, at its conclusion, they are not captured, and, uncompromisingly, sexually possessed by their captor. This all presupposes, of course, that she desires her capture. It is one thing to be chased by one whom one loves, in play, and quite another to be chased by some nut she has never seen before. The first is a delight for a woman; the second is only a misery. Interestingly, nature has not equipped her to outrun either.

If one wishes, the wife may be given a short headstart, say, some ten or fifteen minutes. The husband then trails her. This can be delightful, but it can also go wrong. There are ways of covering trails which would make it a chore for a bloodhound to follow one. If she doesn't leave a reasonable trail to follow they could both end up in the boondocks. This fantasy, incidentally, should not be enacted in nature if there is any danger of the partners becoming lost.

A tent, with its privacy, can serve well enough for a teepee. A small camp can serve well enough for the tiny camp of a brave with his capture, a caught white woman. Indians, of course, often found more of interest in white women than their hair. It was not unknown for them to be carried off and used as slaves. Their position in the Indian camp, of course, was miserable. They were lower than squaws and squaws hated them, and could beat them with sticks to make them do their work. In the teepee, of course, they were only a despised woman of another race, a female of the enemy. Further, of course, she stood outside the family and friendship ties of the camp. An Indian girl of one's own tribe would always be the daughter of another warrior, etc., and so, of course, could not be seen as pure female. The white captive, of course, could be so seen. What does the tribe care what he does to her? The more he abuses her and the more harshly he treats her, the more they will be pleased. Also, of course, we note, that Indians, even in their own communities, are not famous for chivalry to women, even their own. The lot of the white slave girl of an Indian master would not be an easy one. She would well learn what it would be to be a simple female at the mercy of men. She would learn it in the camp and, at night, she would learn it in the teepee of her master.

This fantasy, of course, need not be enacted outdoors. It, like any other, can be happily enacted in the bedroom. Indeed, it can be experimented with, and developed, in the bedroom and then, later, if the partners wish, taken outdoors. It may, of course, happily remain, too, in the bedroom, which can be, to the lovers, a thousand different worlds.

If horses, incidentally, are used, the woman should never be bound on the horse. The danger of a fall is too great. The same caution is lodged, incidentally, against even binding her ankles, with bonds passing under the horse's belly. In no fantasy should there be any risk of actual danger. Similarly, if the woman is bound, she should never be left unattended, even for a moment. In the open there can be various dangers, for example, from animals or snakes.

In the bedroom, of course, with you in the next room, the woman can always be "abandoned" for fifteen minutes or so, to permit her to struggle with her bonds, understand herself helpless and build up suspense. When you return to her then, you can pretend that she has been tied "for hours," helplessly, waiting for you to return to her, and have your will with her. During this time, these many hours, she has not known what her fate was to be. When you return to her, she is bound as perfectly, as securely, as when you left her. She looks at you with terror. She knows that she is yours. What will you do with her?

13. The Captured-by-Pirates Fantasy.

The girl is captured by pirates.

Comment:

This can be an enjoyable fantasy, rich in provocative and romantic elements. The pirates are strong, wild, colorful, dangerous men, without law save that imposed by their captain. If they are caught, they are hung. Accordingly, if, in the meantime, they rape and abuse a few wenches, their penalties are none the greater. The women, and this means ladies, are thus much alone with them. Their delicate, sweet pale flesh is thus completely at the mercy of the swarthy brutes. They will be forced to serve their captors well.

Their ship has been pursued for days; it has then been overtaken; there has been a naval engagement, with flags and cannon and splintering wood; their ship has been boarded, and taken; rough men, with cutlasses, order them from their cabin harshly to the deck; there, frightened in their long dresses, jewelry and elegant hairdos, they take their place with other captured treasure on the deck. Perhaps one challenges the captain, demanding their release. She is knocked to the deck as a common wench. Terrified, mouth bleeding, she shrinks back among the other cowering women. Their men have been killed or wounded. The killed and the wounded, alike, are thrown overboard. Sharks prowl the flanks of the ship. Captured men are, to the laughter of the pirates, now becoming ugly and drunk on rum, forced to walk the plank. Perhaps some of the captured men are given an opportunity to join the pirates, and do so. Perhaps no such choice is offered.

The pirates, led by their captain, now gather about the women, and the other treasure.

They are given a choice. If they are truly fine ladies, as they seem to be, or as they are pretending to be, they are to be treated with elegance and respect. They will be blindfolded, their hands will be tied behind their backs, and one by one, fully clothed, they will walk the plank, thence to plunge to the waiting sharks. If, on the other hand, they are not really fine ladies, and are only pretending to be such, and are truly, beneath their finery, only common sluts, they need not walk the plank. Let us suppose that one beauty, she who challenged the captain, chooses the plank. She is, accordingly, graciously escorted to the plank. There she sees the sharks twisting below, waiting. She begins to tremble. But she is blindfolded and bound, and, with cutlass points, and poles, thrust out on the plank. There she is ordered to walk. She begins to walk the plank. She does not know where its end is; it is narrow; it moves beneath her; she senses the water below; she knows the sharks are waiting. She cannot free her hands; she cannot see. "Walk!" she is commanded. She steps further forth. She hesitates. "Walk!" she is commanded. "No! No! No!" she weeps. "Don't kill me! I'm a slut! Only a slut!"

She is dragged back to the deck.

"Strip the sluts," orders the captain. The women are stripped on the deck. Their jewelry is taken. Their hair is unbound. The girl's hands, she who had challenged the captain and had begun to walk the plank, remain bound. Her blindfold is removed. She was perhaps of nobility. To the pirates she is only another wench and slut.

"Fire the ship," orders the captain.

The taken ship is set afire. The women, naked, in cargo nets with the other treasure, are swung to the deck of the pirate ship. The ropes tieing the ships together are cut, and the two ships drift apart, one burning and sinking, the other filled with the victorious pirates and their booty.

What will be the fate of the women? Will the captain reserve the proud girl to himself, or will he give her, with the others, to the crew? When he gets to his port, will he keep her, or will he sell her, with the others?

We may rest assured that the girl will be well used, and will serve her masters well.

If one happens to own a boat, even a small sail boat, that could provide a locus for this fantasy. In this fantasy, whether enacted on the water or not, much would be simply imagination. For example, two boats would not be involved, and there would be no cargo nets. Further, plank walking, even if the woman should only pretend to be bound, should not actually occur. It is simply too dangerous. The value of a boat, of course, is that it does take the fantasy on the water; it does ensure privacy; many women find boats sexy; and there is a sweet motion to intercourse, as one mixes one's love with the movements of the ship and the sea.

Incidentally, for my money, a woman should never be tied on a boat, particularly above deck. The risk of an emergency arising or an accident's occurring, while perhaps not high, is higher than I would permit anyone I loved to take.

In the safety and security of the bedroom, of course, it is a different matter. Obviously one does not need a ship for this fantasy. It is an excellent fantasy which, all things considered, is probably better in the bedroom than on a boat.

14. The Obnoxious-Woman-Shopper Fantasy.

An elegant, beautiful woman, unpleasant, cruel, hard-to-please, treats salesmen in, say, an Oriental rug department of a fashionable store, as dirt beneath her feet. They are supposed to smile, and please her and, no matter how cruel her remarks or how absurd or outrageous her demands, be cooperative and ingratiating. The customer is always right. The woman knows this power she has and she consciously and deliberately exploits it, to humiliate the salesmen and make them squirm. She is alone, near closing time, with a salesman in the Oriental rug department. He has shown her more than a hundred rugs. Yet she orders him about and makes new demands. It is not even of interest to her that the store is now closing. She is not yet finished with her shopping. What does she care if others should be delayed or inconvenienced. The salesman this time, however, does not seem disturbed at the delay. She suspects nothing. Suddenly, from behind, he gags her. He then throws her to the pile of rugs and binds her, hand and foot, tightly. He then rolls her inside one of the rugs. She lies there for hours. Late that night the rug, she within, helpless, is lifted and placed in a truck and transported to a wharf. There she is carried on board a cargo ship, bound for the Middle East. On the ship she is removed from the rug, stripped to brassiere and panties, and chained, wrists apart, to a steel wall with other women in a soundproof room. They are all white beauties, on their way to a slave market.

Comment:

I suppose every man has a woman or two he would like to put in such a situation, even if he would let her out of it later. Part of being a man is being frustrated, and no one is better at frustrating a man and making him angry than a woman. What man has not known a lovely, unpleasant bitchy woman he would not enjoy owning? What man would not enjoy reducing some woman, who has given him a hard time, to slavery? And if it should be he who turns out to be her master, so much the better.

It is hard to be both uppity and a slave girl. You now own her. She must now, with all her intelligence and might, strive to please you. Doubtless it will not be easy to please you. Doubtless you will make her, the haughty bitch, sweat and squirm to do so. Then, of course, later you conquer her sexually, and she becomes your helpless and obedient love slave.

15. The Virginity-as-an-Offering-to-Rude-Gods Fantasy.

A beautiful virgin is caught and stripped by the celebrants of a strange rite.

She is chained naked, limbs apart, on a stone altar. There is music, costume, ceremony, the chants of the celebrants, the responses of the faithful. She looks up. A great stone statue of a god of phallic triumph looks down upon her helpless, chained body. In the background, in the torchlit room, on either side are statues of other rude gods in this strange pagan pantheon.

Gradually the pagan priests, by caressing her, arouse her to sexual paroxysm on the altar. She writhes helplessly in her chains. At the wild climax of the ceremony, one of the pagan priests, either himself or with an instrument, deflowers her.
Comment:

Women tend to fantasize this sort of thing rather well. It is, in fact, a feminine fantasy that will strike a responsive chord in many women. This recommends it, of course. Any fantasy that a woman, intuitively and immediately, can feel in her blood is likely to be capable of delicious enactment for her. For some women it might provide an attractive entry into imaginative sex. Based on the pleasure found in this fantasy she might be encouraged to experiment with many others, gradually building up a repertoire of fantasies, which would produce for both herself and her husband multiple, diverse and incredible dimensions of pleasure.

If the celebrant who ceremonially deflowers her uses an instrument, he must be careful, of course, not to injure her. A finger, used repeatedly for fifteen or twenty minutes, will do the trick, or, indeed, even, say, a weenie. Many women use weenies in masturbating. There is no reason why-that humble gadget should not constitute in this context the instrument of ceremonial defloration. The most important thing is that the woman receive great pleasure, and not be injured or made uncomfortable. If an instrument is used, of course, the male must wait a bit before he gets "his." That is all right. There is plenty left for him. After the girl's virginity has been publicly sacrificed to the stone god, she is removed from the altar. She is now only a "had" girl, a simple captive, and is no longer of any religious interest. It would be unimaginative, and a waste of girl, of course, now to slay her. Instead, she is chained to the temple wall, with other girls who had preceded her on similar occasions, as a temple prostitute. The wall is long and low, and a great many girls, naked, are chained to it by the left ankle. They are there for the use of the faithful. They may be sexually enjoyed for the price of a small offering, a small coin, placed in a brass bowl near them, to the rude god of phallic triumph. This is where the husband gets "his." The girl is already aroused. She is ready for love, and eager for it. She has at least two more orgasms to go. Let us hope he has not forgotten a coin.[1]

[1]*The use of temple prostitutes, incidentally, provides an encouragement for the faithful to attend religious observances and gatherings. It is one way to build up attendance. The offerings, too, of course, tend to add up. There is more than one way to get a new roof on the temple. This beats bond issues and brown-nosing businessmen. In the current rush to bring Madison Avenue into religious matters, one should not completely neglect the old ways.*

16. The Male-Slave-of-the-Imperious-Queen Fantasy.

The male is the helpless slave of the female.

Comment:

In this fantasy a culture or a planet may be supposed in which women are dominant. Perhaps men are smaller than they are on this world, physically inferior in strength and size, so that the actual statistical relation existing on Earth is reversed; if this were the case I have little doubt that the position of men on such a world would be the same as, or similar to, the situation of women on ours; in fact, I would conjecture that men would be far more kept in "bondage" than women on our world; I expect that women are far more practical about such matters than men; a "man's liberation" movement on such a world could not succeed; the women, recognizing the obvious danger in it to their social position, would not permit its success; it would be difficult enough for them to compete viciously with other women for the limited goods of society, without, as an act of incredible moral generosity or practical idiocy, doubling, at a stroke, their competition; they would want men home, to be their comforts and lovers, when they returned, tired and worn, from their daily battles, to be their servants and "wives," to keep their houses and raise their children. Men would be weaker; that is why it would be "natural" to thrust them into such positions; men would doubtless be put in confining garments and would be taught to smile much and be pretty, and not challenge, but serve their masters. And men, smaller and lighter than such women, kept isolated from one another in separate families and houses and apartments, each easily intimidated in his own home by his larger, stronger spouse, kept busy with menial, repetitive chores, would have little opportunity to share society, except on whatever basis the masters accorded them. Too, of course, in such a world, the technology and the weaponry would be in the hands of the dominant sex. Manufacturing techniques, etc. would be the province of the females. In our own world, for example, if we put all the women in New York state on an island, with water and natural resources, they could not produce one automatic pistol. Such a simple device is, actually, a technological triumph, requiring the collaboration of hundreds of skills and processes. Women do not have these skills or know these processes. If women decided to have war with men they would be much in the position of the Indians, who had to rely on representatives of their enemy to provide them with guns and ammunition. This is not the sort of industrial base from which one wins wars. At any rate, it is my conjecture that men, in our world, in their position, are much more generous to women than women would be to men, were the positions reversed. It is difficult to imagine a woman, for example, giving a desirable position to a man over a more intelligent, better qualified woman, simply on the basis of divergent genitals. Yet this sort of thing occurs repeatedly in our own culture. I do not think women would permit it in a woman-controlled culture. It is just too stupid.

In this fantasy, then, it might be supposed that women are larger and stronger than men, with consequent effect on the social position of men. All other determinants, such as intelligence and aggressiveness, being equal, obviously, over a large population, strength and size will determine who it will be who occupies choice positions. These lessons, of course, will be taught the inferior sex almost from the cradle. They will learn who it is who can be first in line if he wishes, whether he chooses to be or not. The fantasy might be laid on another world, or, interestingly, it could be laid on our world, in the future, after, say, certain mutations have taken place, perhaps due to radiation. Perhaps girl babies start growing into larger, stronger organisms than male babies. In five hundred years, this could make quite a difference. On the other hand, one could always suppose that women are as beautiful and desirable as they are now, but that, somehow, they come to a dominant position. Perhaps they learn some sort of mind-control techniques, or some genius woman inventor equips and supplies them with a type of weapon which can cause men great pain if they do not obey. Perhaps men wear "pain collars" which can cause them excruciating agony if they are not pleasing. Such collars may be actuated by the controlling female, or, selectively, or collectively, from a control center operated by female personnel. Each collar responds to a different signal, but there is a common signal to which all respond. Perhaps for one hour, once a year, the common signal is broadcast, to keep men in their place. Further, if the collar is tampered with, the pain commences. Keys to these collars, or methods for removing them, are kept in secret, well-guarded places by superbly trained, well-armed women. Or, if one likes, one may suppose that the male is merely a slave of, say, a Queen or Ruling Female, who has guards and an army at her disposal.

Her interest in the male slave, perhaps observed from her palanquin, is not Platonic. It is sexual. He is as much a sex object to her as any woman could be to any man. He is ordered to her chambers to please her.

This is a good fantasy for women. Although they are not as much oppressed in our society as many of them enjoy believing, there is little doubt that they have more than their fair share of frustrations. The main frustration is doubtless a very basic biological one. The woman is, statistically, smaller and weaker than the man. The child who finds himself at the mercy of bullies is in a position not unlike that of the female most of the time. Just being "loomed over" can induce a feeling of psychological helplessness. The child may grow up and clobber the bully, but the female is going to remain smaller, and, in effect, at his mercy. This is made easier by the fact that the female, interestingly, usually finds "bullies" sexually stimulating; they bring out a feeling of delicious vulnerability in her; and, to some extent, she enjoys being teased and "bullied." She knows that, eventually, in or outside of marriage, she is going to be "had" by the bully, and that, hopefully to their mutual delight, she is, inevitably, going to serve his sexual pleasure. Almost all women want to be had by a man. Those who do not tend, statistically, to be less frequently impregnated, and, accordingly, over many generations, tend to be weeded out of a population. With women becoming economically independent this tendency will be geometrically accelerated. Two hundred years from now man-haters may be extinct. Up to our day, or the last generation, they had to accept impregnation as the price of survival. One great social advantage of the women's liberation movement is likely to be that it will lead, indirectly, back to love, family and the home. There is no reason why love and a home should be societally forced on any woman. Those who continue to feel a powerful impulse toward men and the love of children will continue, hopefully, to be free to follow these impulses. Those who do not should not be forced, societally, I suppose, to marry or have children. On the other hand, the women's-libber-type mind is a valuable strain in a population, and perhaps such women, and Lesbians, for example, should be forced to bear at least one child, that these genes not be lost. At any rate, most women, regardless of their ideology, have excellent reasons, at least from time to time, for resenting men and their dominance. Men do, in effect, run society and women, rightfully or wrongfully, desirably or undesirably, tend to occupy, statistically, less prestigeous positions. The woman, just in standing before a man, is immediately classed with all other women as a certain kind of object, to be accorded certain kinds of treatment. She is seen as a "kind" of thing, pretty, weak, vulnerable, at the mercy of men.1 She is classified as prize, as sexual quarry. One cannot blame a woman for not, upon occasion, resenting this immediate classification of her as a "form" of life with a certain sexual destiny. There are times when a woman wants to be seen by a man as his object, and his prize, but there are other times when she resents, and justifiably, her nature as the always-weaker, the always-hunted. There are times when she wishes *she* had power, that she might look on men as they look on her, that she might own and command them, as they do her, that it might be she, *she*, who is dominant!

This fantasy, then, allows a woman to ventilate these deep,

and justified resentments. It allows her to be on top, to be dominant, to be the master. This can be thrilling to her. I recall reading a fantasy written by a woman. In it men, not women, were kept in harems, and they were controlled by robots, and female officers, who could destroy them at the slightest sign of disobedience. The women were strong, clear-eyed, powerful. The men were divided, bickering, petty, "feminine." One may well imagine how the women used such men.[1] Such fantasies are not uncommon to women. In a sense they are vengeance fantasies. It is very liberating for a woman to be permitted to enact them. If you love your wife presumably you will want her to have this cathartic, hostility-ventilating experience. She has many scores to settle with "men," and also, of course, with you personally. Much as you love one another, you will surely, from time to time, get on one another's nerves. The sweet, open discharge of hostility in the context of fantasy, concluding with mutual exquisite pleasure for both, is a fantastic experience. It is good for getting "it" out of the system of both. (A fantasy particularly good for liberating male hostility, incidentally, is the bitch fantasy. The bitch fantasy is also good for satisfying masochistic needs in women. Some women, of course, are more masochistic than others. No fantasy, of course, should be played unless it is pleasing to both partners.)

[1] *"The Superior Sex," by Miriam Allen deFord. This story was originally published in* Fantasy and Science Fiction, *in April 1968. It is reprinted in* Xenogenesis: Tales of Space and Time, *a collection of stories, all by Miss deFord (Ballantine Books, Inc., New York, New York, 1969.)*

In this fantasy, the "Male-Slave-of-the-Imperious-Queen" fantasy, it is the male who occupies the position of slave and must, in all things, obey the will of his mistress. Whatever she wishes, he must do. If she wishes, he must kneel before her and put his head and lips to her feet. If she wishes, he must, commanded, crawl into her bed. Perhaps she would, first, desire him to wash her body, or her hair; perhaps he must comb her hair; perhaps he must bring her certain garments or adorn her, according to her directions; perhaps he is to read her Oriental love poetry; perhaps he is to prepare food for her and feed her; or fetch wine for her and, kneeling, serve it to her. Perhaps she will command him to wear certain garments; perhaps she will even order him to adorn himself with certain jewelry. Women, for example, are forced to be pleasing to men. Let a man feel what it is like to be forced to be pleasing to a woman. Let him learn to smile and to be submissive and ingratiating. It may give him a real insight into what it is to be a woman. It should make him more human.

A great advantage of this fantasy, incidentally, which should not be overlooked, is that the man responds to the woman's directions. She should, then, instruct him as to how to make love to her. She tells him where to touch her and how. This can be extremely valuable to the male in informing him as to what excites her. It can also be liberating to the wife because, in the context of the fantasy, she must command him. In standard sex she might be reticent to say anything to him. In the fantasy, she gives him detailed and explicit directions. It allows her, in the fantasy, to communicate her wants. Later, of course, in other love makings, he should remember what pleased her. If she enjoys having her breasts stroked and kissed, she should tell him to do this, and make sure he does it exactly as she wants. Similarly, if she wants her clitoris licked and kissed, in this fantasy, she orders it done. There is no embarrassment or hesitation. She is the queen, or ruling female. She orders her slave to do exactly what she wants. He must, of course, with perfection, comply. Feed-back, often missing in prosaic love making, is built into this fantasy. If the slave does not do it right, he must keep at it, until it is exactly as she wants. Furthermore, she, as queen or ruler, will insist on her complete pleasure. For example, she may not permit the male, under her command, to penetrate her until she is, an hour or so later, on her final orgasm. When penetration does take place presumably she will kneel across his body, writhing, taking *him*. Let him lie on *his* back this time. Let *him* look up at the dominant partner, who uses him for *her* pleasure.

If nothing else, when this fantasy is done, the husband should have a wealth of information about the sexual nature of his wife, and some of this information is likely to be new and valuable. In effect, he has been given a detailed lesson in how to sexually stimulate the woman he loves. This knowledge will make him tremendously happy. It is not likely to make his wife unhappy either.

17. The Two-Animal Fantasy.

A male and female animal encounter one another, and mate.

Comment:

Two animals, without speech, who have never encountered one another, and have never had sexual relations, meet. The animals are human animals, but still animal. They know nothing of sex, but, strangely, they feel attracted to one another. They smell one another, they study one another; they circle one another; they growl, warning one another off; they whine, inviting the other's closer approach. They rub timidly against one another, and find it pleasurable. They touch one another, and kiss and lick one another. Soon, driven by their instincts, they mate. They are then companions, inseparable.

This can be a beautiful fantasy, and is useful for teaching human beings the loving body. It is important in this fantasy to really feel oneself as an animal, relating to another animal. It helps human beings, often too cerebral, too complex, too abstract, too ready to conceptualize, meet one another on a level almost of pure attraction and instinct. The animal in man is beautiful, and this fantasy helps to celebrate it. This fantasy, incidentally, is not a betrayal of imaginative sex but an illustration of it. Intelligence and imagination, is a dramatic act, conjoin to remind us that the glories of sexual contact among the mammals are ours by the right of our nature. We, too, are members of this wondrous form of life. We can have much more than they, but we must make certain we never have less.

18. The Rape-in-the-Caves Fantasy.

A cave girl is caught and dragged to the cave of her captor. She is thrust within. There is no escape for her. In the back of the cave, in the dim light, on the furs, she is on her hands and knees, or she crouches against the back wall, in terror, a trapped female. The captor squats in the entrance of the cave, regarding her. Then, after a time, he approaches her. He tears her garment from her. On the furs, in the light of the small fire, amidst the wild shadows, as she struggles, he rapes her. When he is finished with her, she does not desire to leave him. She puts her head against his body. She wishes to be permitted to remain, to be his mate.

Comment:

This is a standard fantasy, which, in fact, is so common and familiar that it is, and has been for many years, delightfully satirized. We are all familiar with the cartoon of the cave man bopping his beauty over the head and dragging her to his cave. Incidentally, if this fantasy is enacted, the beauty is not to be bopped over the head. Broken skulls and severe headaches are not sexually stimulating to a woman. On the other hand, a bit of hair yanking or physical brutality, dragging her about a bit, can be. Many women find a bit of pain, psychic or physical, sexually stimulating. Their favorite fantasy is not the rape fantasy for nothing. The fact that this troglodyte fantasy is so familiar, and so much satirized, is not really a mark against it. For one thing, the satires are not the real fantasy, and bear little resemblance to it; further, the familiarity of the fantasy bespeaks its general power; if it were not as powerful and widespread as it is, it would not be as familiar to us.

In this fantasy, for it to be maximally effective, it is important for both partners to psychically introject themselves into the entire situation. They must think and feel the situation as it would be. There is no civilization. There is rule only by lust and force. Moralities, scruples, restraints, do not exist. There are no marriage ceremonies. Mating is by capture. No social artifices, no glosses, no contracts, no meaningless rituals, conceal the victim's plight, that she will be, by the decision of her captor, sexually subjugated. The primitive realities of the basic biological relation of man to woman, that he wants her, and will have her sexually, are here unclouded by social gimmicry. This is a raw fantasy, a bold fantasy, for those who can dare to enact it. Perhaps the female is bound hand and foot with rawhide thongs and carried to the cave? (Rawhide boot-straps make superb binding thongs for women.) She has no protection. She is at the mercy of the man who has captured her. She is helpless. He can do what he wants with her. We may even suppose that there is very little developed language. It is important, very important, to understand the *rawness* and *primitiveness* of the world in which these individuals find themselves, *very important*. The caves are the jungle, and the female has been caught. She has literally been, understand this, *caught*. There has been speculation, incidentally, that the wedding ring is symbolically reminiscent of the bonds in which the captive female is placed. That seems pretty farfetched. On the other hand, which of us has not carried his wife over the threshold of his first home? That act seems symbolically reminiscent, surely, of capture and carrying the female into one's stronghold, whether it be cave or castle, or Apartment 1A. I suppose that a women's libber would not permit herself to be carried over the threshold, but would insist on walking through at precisely the same time as her contractual partner. That alone should inform him of the time he is in for. When a man wants a lover and wife, it is too bad if he is stuck with another one of the boys, one determined to be a real buddy and pal to him.

Incidentally, whether this "cave" fantasy bears any resemblance to anthropological reality is irrelevant to the fantasy. No anthropologists were present taking notes during the early paleolithic era, so we do not much know. It would seem likely that the brain, morality and civilization all developed simultaneously. It seems further likely that, given primate societies, there was always order and structure in human groupings, leadership by an elite of strong, dominant males, and, thence, downward through a social hierarchy ending up with smaller, weak males, sons of females not mated to dominant males, on the periphery of the group for the leopards. There is always going to be an establishment, in which aggressive, intelligent, often unscrupulous individuals, within whatever political structure is available, are going to lie and knife and fight their way to the top. Trees may come in many different

shapes but the toughest monkeys will always be in the high
branches. On the other hand, even if there was always "law"
in this sense in human groupings, this "law," quite presumably,
did not extend outside the groupings. Outsiders, even of one's
own species, have usually been regarded as fair game for about
anything. To think of mankind as one grouping, to think in
terms of a universal morality, is an achievement of a highly
developed morality. Most of us, even today, except for a few
delightful years in our naive adolescence, find it difficult to feel
it in our blood. The stranger, too many times, has meant danger.
Evolution has contrived us in such a way as to be suspicious
of strangers. If this suspicion should be reduced in the prime
mating years, evolution, too, may have had a hand in that. Those
groups which were suspicious of strangers, we note, tended to
survive. Whether there is any longer an evolutional point in
holding outsiders in suspicion is arguable. Our main hope now
for survival is clearly our rationality. If we make it through the
next thousand years it will doubtless be because of our brains
and not our reflexes.

In short, whether the human situation conjectured in this
fantasy ever actually obtained or not is irrelevant to the fantasy.
It is a powerful fantasy, regardless of what the case might actually
have been, regardless of what anthropology may someday decide
the case actually was. It does seem likely, however, that the
fantasy would correspond to a past reality, provided the captured
female was not a member of the in-group, not a member of the
family or clan or tribal grouping. Such women, as they are with
primitive tribes today, would be regarded as suitable objects of
predation. Further, of course, history is replete with evidence as
to the frequent capture, rape and enslavement of human females,
particularly those of villages, cities, races and nations other than
your own. The capture, rape and enslavement of women was one
of the great historical pastimes of man.[1]

[1]*An interesting variant on this fantasy involves a highly
educated, brilliant,* modern *woman, perhaps an ardent feminist,
or a sexually starved scientist, or both, who is doing work, either
on her own, or with despised male colleagues, on time transduction*

experiments. Needless to say, by an accident, or contrivance on the part of her male colleagues, she is flung back in time to a paleolithic era. She thus finds herself, a modern woman, in such a time. She is, of course, hunted, caught and mated. She is introduced into the savage life of the tribe, forced to do the servile, repetitive work allotted to the cave females. She must, with other women, and children, and dogs, remain at the camp, while the men hunt, and do war. When her cave-man master returns, he uses her sexually, with gusto. Perhaps the camp is raided, and she, with others, are carried off to be the slaves of other cave men. Doubtless she is beaten and bound, and forced to be pleasing. Perhaps then she is rescued. Is she alone with cave men, or do her male colleagues lead double lives, coming and going in time, for their recreation and stimulation, but keeping her in the past as their mistress? There are many variations. Perhaps she bears a wild child, primitively, it taken from between her piteous legs by grim, intent older women. Perhaps she is gagged that her cries, in the night, not disturb the men. Perhaps later she returns to her own time, and sees a young man, younger than herself, to whom she is as far as she knows unrelated. Yet his face bears the marks clearly both of her own, and her cave lover. She realizes that she, sexually deprived and lonely, in her own time, has mothered a still youthful, splendid line. She stands in history, not apart from it. She returns to the machine, to return to her lover of the caves. She chooses not to be without him. The fresh, pristine world of her rape and capture, at the beginning of the human world, is where she chooses to place her reality. She returns to her lover, as his own lover, his own woman, his wife, his slave, his mate, a mother of our race.

19. The Kidnap Fantasy.

The wife is kidnapped for sexual purposes.

Comment:
      The I-Am-Kidnapped-and-Raped Fantasy is a common one for women.
      Obviously, in enactment, it may be performed and elaborated in a number of ways.

A useful introduction, which may serve to get both partners into the mood of the fantasy, is for the husband, in a busy, downtown area, for an hour or so, to follow his wife, keeping an eye on her, sizing her up as a desirable victim for a sexual kidnapping. If she has an hour or so's shopping to do, that would be an ideal time for the trailing. He will probably find it pleasant, observing her, stalking her. Too, she will find it delicious, moving about, as though unaware, yet knowing that he is following her, observing her.

If the family has two cars, he might even follow her, for a time, in the car. Does she observe, puzzled, in the rear-view mirror, that another car seems to follow hers? She thinks nothing of it. She dismisses it from her mind.

The capture might be made at night, in her bedroom. She may be either fully clothed or not, as the partners wish. She is bound and gagged, and taken to the car. She kneels on the floor, crouched over, in front of the front seat, on the driver's right. He presumably has a weapon. A blanket is thrown over her to conceal her body. Then, around town and through traffic, stopping for lights, etc., her husband drives her about. After thirty minutes or so he takes her to "his place." "His place," of course, is once again their bedroom.

In this fantasy she may wish to be blindfolded, or have a sack tied over her head. It is removed, if at all, only when she finds herself in the "strange bed." If she wishes her rape to take place while she is blindfolded, or has a sack fastened over her head and tied about her neck, the husband should oblige. After all, providing she has not seen him before that time, she will not be able to recognize him later. After the fantasy is completed, the partners may then pretend that he has placed her, hooded, nude, bound hand and foot, in some public place, where she will be found in the morning. In such a case she would never even have seen her assailant. She would be indeed a muchly had wench. Actually, of course, when the fantasy is completed, they kiss and go to sleep. He must be up in time to catch the 8:15, and she must scoot the kids in the direction of the local academic custodial institution.

In this fantasy, if acted out otherwise than simply in the imagination, the wife must not be placed in the trunk of the car. That does not provide her with sufficient air. Further, if a sack is tied over the head it must be of some material through which air easily filters. Under no circumstances should an airtight bag, for example, a plastic bag, be used.

20. The "Lady" Fantasy.

A "Lady," to her horror and much against her will, is being fucked. Then, to her horror and much against her will, she finds herself being physically seduced. She begins to be aroused, and powerfully, sexually. Then, shattering the icy and brittle artifices of being ladylike. she becomes a responding, stimulated, sexually vital female animal. She begins to pitch and buck, and moan and writhe. She is then transformed into an exciting and magnificent bitch, responsive, helpless and wild, responding with delicious pleasure, enthusiasm and joy to her thorough and masterful fucking. Afterwards, she does not wish to go back to being a lady, though she can play that role, and superbly. What she wants is to get back in bed and have more, and more! She did not know what a man could do to her body. She did not know what ecstasy could be involved in the yielding of a bitch to a male. She wants to do it again, and again. She has been made "sexually alive."

Comment:

This is a very simple fantasy, and again, one not unfamiliar to women. Women, particularly in the past, were raised to be ladies. On the other hand, in perspiring, urinating, being made restless by the proximity of men, etc., they were aware of their humanity and femaleness. There is, in most women, the conflict between what they feel they *ought* to be and what, upon occasion, they would like to be, or feel like being. In every woman, there is a bit of sweet and secret bitch. This fantasy helps to tap that concealed resource. It is a lucky fellow who, though perhaps scandalized, finds himself married to a sexy bitch. This fantasy, by its dramatic technique, is designed to unlock the sexy bitch

that lurks beneath the most refined exterior of the most elegant
lady. Even if your wife is a member of the League of Women
Voters or the P.T.A., you may rest assured that somewhere,
beneath that efficient, concerned exterior, there lurks a sexy
bitch. Get her clothes off and look for it. See if you can make her
hop and yell. She doesn't have to spill the beans to the P.T.A. or
the League.

The following is a small exercise for the woman who finds
it psychologically difficult to break through her antisexual
conditioning and be responsive to a male. It is a simple exercise.
It consists in standing, while alone, nude before a mirror. You
then repeat to yourself the following, over and over.

I want to be fucked.
I enjoy being fucked.
I need to be fucked.
I will be fucked!
I have a beautiful body and I want it fucked.
I want it fucked beautifully and at length by a strong,
attractive male.

If this is done for fifteen minutes or so an evening, for a week,
you will discover that, at the end of that time, you do, indeed,
wish to be fucked. You will probably find your sexual curiosity
heightened, and your responsiveness intensifying. Being honest
with oneself is the first step in breaking down undesirable
habits of sexual inertia and fear. Admit to yourself that you *do*, if
you do, want to be honest and true to your femaleness. Let this
commitment sift down to the subconscious. Admit to yourself
honestly that you do desire sexual experience, that you do, if
you do, really, really, want it. That, it seems, is about half the
battle. You cease to reinforce undesirable conditioning; you seek
to substitute new mental patterns. It is quite a breakthrough for
many women, even in our age, to openly admit to themselves
that they do want intimate and satisfying sexual experience. It
is common to "say" that they want it, but it is, I conjecture, given
implicit conditionings to which they have been subjected, less
common to really feel in their blood that they want it, and are

not ashamed to want it. How many women, for example, would not be ashamed to tell a man openly they wanted him to fuck them? But no woman should be ashamed to do this. Surely there are more subtle ways to convey to a man one's desire for sexual experience, but then one it talking tactics. A woman should not be ashamed to tell a man she wants him to fuck her. Many wives are reticent even to use the intimate, marvelous, juicy expression 'fuck'. They should not be. It is great English. It is one of the most expressive and happiest words in the language. For a wife who is backward, shy, negatively conditioned in these matters, I recommend that she, on some evening, crawl on her husband's lap, kiss him, and say to him, "I want you to fuck me tonight." She may be lucky to get as far as the bed.

Later on in the week, in the above exercise, the woman may wish to observe, more closely, more exactly, how beautiful she is. She might turn before the mirror, noting her breasts and back, and flanks and legs and ass. She is really nice. "Could a man really want to sexually have me?" "You bet your sweet ass, Girl. He wants to have you, and how!" She may also, if she wishes, pose as a naked beauty. She may then, if she wishes, move lasciviously before the mirror. How exciting that would be to do before a male! That would really knock hubby out of his armchair, wouldn't it? And there, do I detect a bump or a grind? And that rotary hip motion, to music! You never knew you could do that, did you? You had better be careful though. He might chain you up as a slave girl.

Doubtless, in some cases, there are tragic psychological blockages which exist against sexual relations and emotional sexual freedom. In such cases, it may well be that some form of medical attention or therapy is required. The above exercises are, in my opinion, valuable in loosening up a female for sex, and valuable in making her more eager and responsive. On the other hand, of course, if there is some unusual or serious blockage involved, they are not intended as a substitute for the services of a qualified psychiatrist or psychologist. I suspect that imaginative sex, as a matter of fact, has great therapeutic value, but what therapeutic value it has, if any, is up to the determination of the scientific and medical community. The matter is an empirical one, and could only be resolved by the results of experiments and tests. All we would claim is that it can produce great sex.

The "Lady" fantasy can, like others, be elaborated variously. The Lady may wish to begin the fantasy clothed in a rather Victorian manner. She could purchase a long dress for this fantasy, which could be removed from her by her Victorian rapist.[1] Other props might be a bit of Victorian bric-a-brac or a Victorian-type lamp. Most importantly for this fantasy, of course, the woman must, in the beginning, "think Lady" and then, bit by bit, find her-self, as though against her will, being forced to "feel Bitch." In the end, of course, she becomes an uninhibited female animal, raw and responsive and delicious; she is shameless, helpless, enthusiastic, joyous; full aroused, to his slightest touch, she thrills; she belongs to him; she is his bitch and loves her fucking at his hands; she wants more, more! "I love it!" she cries. "I love it!" "What do you want?" he asks. "Your cock," she cries. "I love it!" Now she is a bitch, his. She is like a dream come true. In her fucking, she has become a total bitch, and, to him, she is helpless and glorious.

[1]*A delightful variant on this is not to remove the dress, but lift it. First her ankles are exposed; then her secret calves; then the back of her delightful knees; than the beauty of her thighs is exposed; and then the glories of her beautiful, vulnerable Victorian cunt. Naturally, bloomers are out. The long dress, if full enough, can then be lifted up and tied over her head, pinning her arms and head within. The dress should fasten in the back. Alternatively, it should be belted, and the buckle should be pulled around to the back, where she cannot reach it, to free herself. If she wears panties they are then slipped free, and she is helplessly exposed to you. After a time, as she becomes aroused, she begs for her lips to be free, to kiss you; if it pleases you, you free them, and accept her kisses; her arms are still confined. She wants to hold you and touch you, of course. "Chain me to the bed, if you wish," she begs, "but let me free to hold you!" If it pleases you, you then chain-and-padlock her to the bed, by the throat or an ankle, and let her make love to you, desperately. You take no chances with her, of course. Later, in your*

yacht, if you wish, you may transport her to one of your islands in
the Aegean, where she will be given suitable garments and taught
her new role, that of a slave girl.

Another elaboration on this is more contemporary. The woman
begins the fantasy dressed in an evening gown, black perhaps,
with pearls, and white gloves. She is very much the "Lady." She
does not wish to lay for the man. She is prepared, however, to
do so. Perhaps he knows some secret of hers, something in her
past. Perhaps, if she permits him to make love to her, he might
cancel certain of her gambling debts. Who knows? At any rate,
she becomes his bitch, helplessly his. Even when he refuses to
cancel her debts, and she realizes how completely and perfectly
she has been "had," she still wants him, again and again. She,
an elegant, rich, educated society woman, begs to become his
mistress. He permits this.

And so on! Let the partners devise and elaborate, and love, as
they please.

21. The I-Am-Fucked-before-a-Female-I-Disliked Fantasy.

A woman is stripped and placed in the bed of a strange man. She
is under the casual and scornful observation of another woman,
one whom she dislikes intensely. The man begins to make love
to her. He is a fantastic lover. She cannot long resist him. She
is in agony. She knows she is the object of the other woman's
amusement and contempt. But she cannot help herself. She begins
to yield. Perhaps the other woman smokes a cigarette, amused,
and observes her attempts to control and restrain herself. She is
in misery. She can then resist him no longer. She responds to the
lover, profoundly, helplessly. At length, she yields herself to him
with the uncontrollable, total, shameless abandon of the fully
aroused female animal. She has been "had," fully and perfectly
before the woman she despises. She has been forced to show
herself before her as a fully conquered bitch.

Comment:
In this fantasy, of course, there is actually no third person

present. The "other woman" exists only in the imagination of the lovers, and particularly in that of the female. This fantasy, which is a feminine fantasy, can be very delicious and very powerful.

It is interesting to speculate on the reasons for the power of this fantasy.

The major reason for its power is, I suspect, that it meets the "shame" syndrome head-on. It dodges nothing. Women, on the whole, either implicitly or explicitly, have been conditioned to be ashamed of sex. They hide it. They want to make sure the door is locked, etc. They are even conditioned, tragically, to be proud of sexual aloofness and, for most practical purposes, sexual frigidity. They fear being "had." They fear yielding to a male. Particularly there is a certain insidious prestige ranking among women who compete with their respective frigidity quotients. One's image as a woman with other women is sometimes dependent in part on this sort of thing. For example, a wench who, an hour before, has been quaking with pleasure in Jim's arms, squealing and kicking, if asked about Jim later by another woman, may remark, "Oh yes, Jim. He is very nice." If the other woman, too, should have love made to her by Jim, the first woman is thus protected. In spite of what Jim might be able to accomplish with the body of woman two, to woman one he was merely "very nice." That puts woman one one-up on woman two. Woman two, of course, may find her responses inhibited with Jim because of the remark of woman one. He is not going to turn *her* into a quaking pleasure object. Not her! And if, in spite of her resolve, he does, she, too, may be expected to conceal her transport. "Yes," she agrees later, cooly, with woman one, "Jim is all right." They smile sweetly at one another, and hate one another. Each is afraid that the other will know what her responses were. Each, interestingly, is determined to appear to be the least "had," the most on top of the situation, the least involved, the most frigid. Imagine then the horror, the shame, of a woman forced to reveal herself before another woman, a cool, contemptuous rival, who clinically and scornfully observes her every move, as a helplessly conquered bitch! This might be regarded by them as a "maximum shame" situation. But after one has been helplessly revealed as a sexy bitch, licking and kissing, pitching and sucking, helpless in a man's hands, what is there to lose? One could never again play the phony frigidity game. One has then hit the bottom. And the bottom is very nice. The bottom is glorious. When a woman can say to herself, "I love a good fuck, and the more I'm had the more I love it," she is well on her way to driving herself and her partner crazy with love and pleasure. Imagining, of course, that her conquest has been observed, means that she has nothing more to hide. What others know, she may now admit to herself. She has been "found out." She may now, free and happy, be the bitch she has always wanted to be. If *that* woman knows, that other woman, what difference does it make who else knows? She is now free, sexually liberated, to be the responsive female animal she wants to be.

Perhaps, after she has yielded to the strange man, the "other woman" rises, scornfully, and says, "Collar her as a bitch." The had woman, unresisting, is then collared. Then the other woman leaves. The collared girl then looks to her lover. "Yes," she tells him, "I am a bitch. I know that. I even wear a bitch's collar." Then she kisses him. "But I love you," she tells him. "I love you."

22. The Publicly-Enslaved-Female-of-Noble-Blood Fantasy.

Perhaps there has been a hard-fought war. Perhaps the side which has lost was governed by a proud and beautiful queen, who is now a prisoner of the conquerors. Or perhaps it is the daughter or daughters of the conquered rulers who are captive. In regal garments, chained to the chariot of her conqueror, an emperor or general, walking behind it, the female or females of noble blood are paraded through the streets, exhibited booty of his triumph. At the climax of his triumph they are, in a great square, before thousands, publicly enslaved. They are stripped, branded, collared, and publicly fucked. They are then led away in chains, slave girls.

Comment:

Many women, on one level or another, wish to be proud of their bodies and their sexual responsiveness. They also wish, on some level, to be sexually had, fully and completely. It is hard to imagine a woman more had than one who is publicly fucked, one forced to show publicly, before thousands, her responsiveness, one who is exhibited and owned. The "Enslaved Queen" fantasy combines many desirable elements of female sexual fantasy. High station, pageantry, capture, bonds, exhibition, the reduction from the highest of the high to the lowest of the low, public sex, abject enslavement. The female was once the highest person in her state, uncountably rich, whose word was law. Then she fell captive. Still she was treated with graciousness and honor, great respect. But, in the square, on the high platform, this ends. There she is enslaved. She is now only an article of property, collared and branded, to be bought or sold. She is no longer to be respected. She may now be abused and treated harshly. She must now obey masters. She who was once the queen is now only the female slave of her conquerors. Let us suppose that it will be the general who will keep her as his slave. Doubtless he will well teach her the meaning of her brand and collar.

Here, as in other fantasies, there are many variants. For example, the woman may wish to fantasize herself only one of hundreds of women, bound helplessly on racks, in long rows, who, at a signal, say, a trumpet or clash of cymbals, are simultaneously penetrated and raped. She might also, of course, prefer to think of herself as staked out, in a helpless position, perhaps arched over shields, head down, legs split, to satisfy the lust of an army. If a vibrator is used, each thrill of sensation can be imagined by her as her rape by a new soldier.

23. The I-Need-a-Job-Desperately Fantasy.

The woman, who needs a position, lays for the man who can give it to her. Afterwards, he either gives it to her or not, depending on whether or not he is satisfied with her. Perhaps she must try again; perhaps she must try to please him more, next time.

Comment:
This fantasy may be a bit too realistic. In it, however, the woman finds herself in a predicament. She is forced, against

her will, to try to buy what she needs with her flesh. The male, callous, in a commanding position, imposes his demands. She doesn't have to lay. It is only that if she doesn't, she doesn't get the job. If she does lay, she might get the job. Then again, she might not. Many women, apparently, implicitly, find themselves in such positions. It is not unknown for female advancement and promotion to depend on her sexual prowess. Whereas a situation of this sort, in real life, is an ugly and unpleasant one, in fantasy, it can sometimes provide pleasure for a woman. It has something of the "whore" element going for it, except that the woman performs under "duress." She must, nonetheless, perform. It is a form of "forced sex" and forced sex is a frequently encountered element in sexual fantasy. A tinge of shame and helplessness, if a part of the game, can be sexually delicious. In real life, of course, they would just add to the misery of an already miserable situation. I once worked in the motion picture industry. We might also call this the "casting-director fantasy."

24. The I-Want-an-"A"-Professor Fantasy.

A luscious coed, to get an A in a given course, lays for the professor.

Comment:

This is a form of prostitution, and a rather unpleasant form of it. For one thing, the girl does not really need such a grade. She is trading her body not only for something she does not need but for what, in effect, is trivia. Secondly, the relationship lacks the honesty of open prostitution, which is a commercial transaction and understood as such. The coed will, doubtless, attempt to brown-nose the professor, flatter him, and make him feel smart and wise. Even in bed with him she will continue these obvious, transparent maneuvers. She thinks, I suppose, that he is a jerk.

Now your wife, who presumably has never done this sort of thing, may know girls who have. They may have received grades better than hers in the same courses. Your wife would like to see such spurious wenches get their comeuppance. She can do this in fantasy, by imagining herself such a girl. She makes an appointment to see the professor. She discusses her work with him in the course. She makes it clear to him how desperately she needs a grade. Perhaps she must maintain a certain average to be eligible for a certain prestigious sorority, etc. He tells her to work hard, of course, to study, etc. She crosses and uncrosses her legs, and leans forward, etc. She invites, without speaking, him to place his hand on her body. She looks at him piteously. She is all innocence. She needs an "A" so desperately. Is there no way she can obtain this grade? "I am willing to do anything, anything!" she tells him. His hand touches her body. "Oh, Sir!" He removes hand. She leans forward again. "Yes," she whispers, "anything." Now she is crying. To comfort her, he places his arms about her shoulders. She looks up, helpless, tears in her eyes. Her lips are parted. "You excite me," she tells him. His hand strokes her waist, on the side. "Does this excite you?" he asks. "Yes," she whispers, "yes!"

And so they agree to go to bed. Let us hope he does not take her on his desk or on the couch in his office.

At this point it becomes more delicious to the wife. She is now the coed in his bed. She prostitutes herself and flatters him. She pretends to herself that "she is putting one over on him."

But, slowly, it becomes evident to her that, given the Professor's harsh commands and instructions to her, that she has a great deal more than she bargained for. She is not going to be permitted to lie down and bounce up. He, carefully and methodically, puts her through an incredible set of paces. Never had she expected anything like this. She is forced, in exacting and delicious detail to perform, and perform superbly. When she is finished she has been completely and humiliatingly had.

She is then told to put on her clothes and leave.

"What about my grade?"

She is then informed that she should work hard, and study, and so on

The wife then feigns the rage, indignation and humiliation that such a girl would feel.

At this point the "professor" may again, if he wishes, take her once more in his arms and caress her into a fiercely resented ecstasy.

Is this not what such girls really deserve? Surely that more than "A's."

This is a kind of vengeance fantasy by the wife on women who use their sex to advance themselves. Most women despise such women. This gives your wife an opportunity, in imagination, to revenge herself on such unfairly competing wenches.

As a note one might add that, in real life, sex between students and professors is quite rare, particularly where the professor is not a young bachelor. Besides, it is often unnecessary. Good grades can normally be managed by beautiful brown-nosing girls, provided they are not completely stupid, without getting near a bedroom door. Their smiles and their beauty, and flattery, always pleasurable to a male, are often more than adequate to buy them what they want. Brown-nosing in a male student proceeds on a quite different basis. He must pretend interest in the professor's work, wish to discuss it, criticize it in certain ways, etc. A little of this, of course, is also useful in the case of the female. One good argument, incidentally, for more female faculty members is to get more objective over-all grade averages for lovely female students. Sometime, I think, it takes a woman to see through a woman. On the other hand, it is my general opinion that most instructors in high school and college, with a bit of experience, have little difficulty in telling which students are serious and which are not. The serious student, incidentally, should not be afraid of being mistaken for a "brown-noser," and, accordingly, be tempted to neglect educational resources, consultation, etc., to which he is entitled. The lovely girl, however, even when recognized as a "brown-noser" is still likely to get good grades. It gives me pleasure, for example, to give good grades to beautiful women. It is hard to grade them objectively.

25. The Helpless-Maid Fantasy.

A maid, who wishes to retain her employment, discovers it would be well for her to sleep with the master.

Comment:

This fantasy is much like the I-Need-a-Job-Desperately

fantasy. Many unfortunate, miserable girls, in past generations, have found themselves in this sort of predicament. Jobs were very scarce, and a good position in a rich household was very desirable. There were plenty of girls willing to take your place.

In many fantasies, it is helpful to engage in activities that help one to get in the mood for the fantasy, and, indeed, might even be considered as an introductory portion of the fantasy. The woman, if she is a housewife, might get herself into the proper frame of mind for the fantasy while doing her housework. A wife is, after all, among many other things, her husband's maid. If she is not a housewife, but has a maid, she can dismiss the real maid early and perform some of her tasks herself, to get into the mood. She may also wear a maid's uniform. She can meet the husband at the door, take his hat, address him as "Sir," and so on. All day long, we may suppose, she has, in fear, anticipated that he will indicate his desire to her that she serve him sexually. What will she do? She doesn't know. She is in agony. He is, of course, handsome and strong, and sexually attractive to her. After supper, she will see what happens. But, after supper, he asks her nothing. He merely begins to remove her clothing. "Sir!" she exclaims. But, overwhelmed, stunned, helpless before his boldness, obedient, she is lifted naked and carried to the bed.

26. The I-Am-Raped-by-an-Alien Fantasy.

A beautiful young Earth female is surprised in her own bed by a handsome, powerful alien. She is stripped and bound. She cannot cry out. He has touched the side of her throat, gently, and, to her horror, she finds she cannot speak above a whisper. She is thus free to communicate with him, to plead with him, etc., but she is unable to summon help. He is obviously interested in arousing her sexually. She determines to resist him. He smiles. He begins to apply to her body a small, sophisticated electronic device. She attempts to resist. He is patient. No Earth woman can long resist the device. At last she begins to yield. Then, after a time, in agony, against her will, she is fully responsive. She writhes in sexual heat, a helpless sexually ignited female. Then, her resistance shattered, she begs the alien to fuck her. He must satisfy the incredible need he has aroused! He cannot leave her like this. "Please fuck me!" begs the Earth woman. "I beg you to fuck me!"

While the woman, bound, helpless, aroused, waits in piteous suspense, the alien considers her plea.

Then, with a laugh, masterfully, he fucks her, satisfying fully the need he has aroused.

Afterwards the alien, mercifully, remains beside her, holding her, caressing her gently down from the peaks to which he has carried her.

She has now fallen in love with him, her alien, uncompromising captor.

She begs to be his wife, his mistress, his slave, his love animal, anything, but to be his.

He rises and departs, leaving her behind, still stripped and bound, only a fucked Earth female.

She does not know if her alien lover, whose sexual conquest she is, will ever return to her.

Comment:

This is a very lovely, very feminine fantasy. Many women would be overjoyed to find a loving male to help them to enact it. It is too good to be left entirely to the masturbations of lonely, beautiful women. The electronic device, of course, is a simple vibrator. Many women, intelligently, use such devices to stimulate themselves sexually. It is no secret that a D-sized battery has more stamina than a heavyweight prize fighter. More importantly, there just aren't that many loving, imaginative men to go around. There is no reason in the world why vibrators and men cannot work on the same team, so to speak. Vibrators and men are not mutually incompatible. Undying hatred need not exist between them. Although the suggestion seems a bit far out now, it is not at all unlikely that, fifty years from now, love making will be enhanced by a number of such devices. For example, today, love making is, sometimes, enhanced by such things as candlelight, wine, earrings, silken garments, perfumes, etc. We are used to such enhancements and think little of them. The vibrator, in a generation or two, may be as common and familiar as lipstick.

There is nothing wrong with scientific progress as long as people don't get left out. The invention of silken underwear did not make woman obsolete.

In this fantasy, if the woman is tied, she may be tied variously. Many women are sexually stimulated by having their legs split and having their ankles tied apart to the bedposts. It makes them feel deliciously vulnerable and helpless. Their hands might then be tied, similarly, apart, so that she is spread-eagled on the bed, or they might be simply bound behind her back; another variation which is stimulating and sexy is to bind her wrists together over her head; this way her wrists move against one another, rein-forcing, one upon the other, the sense of capture; further, in this tie, the hands are held far from the body that they are helpless to protect; in such a tie she may feel that her beauty is more displayed, more exhibited, more vulnerable; how could she be, symbolically, more open to her captor's caresses; further, in this tie, be sure that the girl's palms face upward, rather than down toward the bed. The palm of a girl's hand is a very delicate, sexy area. For example, it will make a girl nervous to trace, with a fingernail, a design in her palm. The palm, subconsciously, I suspect, represents to her the sweet vulnerability of her cunt. She will even use the palm, subconsciously, from time to time, to signal sexual desire, holding it open, subtly, as though inadvertently, toward a sexually desired male. Preening behavior, of course, in the presence of a male is also an invitation to sexual advance. In tieing her hands so that both palms are facing up, you maximize her sense of helpless and delicious sexual vulnerability. It also permits you, too, of course, to touch her palms, extremely lightly, which is likely to produce a thrilled response which will, like a chain reaction, be exhibited fantastically throughout her entire body, from the expression on her face to her toes. It is up to you what designs you trace with your fingernail in her palm. She should, of course, understand the meaning of the design. That is a part of planning. Perhaps an "S" for "Slave," perhaps the initial of her first name, followed by an "F," for "Fuck," etc. The trick, of course, is the combination of *feeling with meaning*. In this particular fantasy, now under discussion, one might not wish to trace meaningful designs on the palm, or on the body, at all. It is a possibility, of course. Perhaps at the conclusion of his enjoyment of the Earth woman the alien traces on her body a strange sign. It symbolizes, we shall suppose, that she is his sexual conquest. If this is it, and she is given to understand this, or sense it, it might be acknowledged by her. "Yes, you have conquered me, Master. I am yours. I am your conquest, Master." Or, perhaps, the alien places a small mark on her body, supposedly indelible, which marks her as a woman who has been had by him. Perhaps later, she notes, from time to time, similar marks on the bodies of other Earth women, perhaps a small yellow or red dot. They laugh and try to explain the marks away. They do not know that she, too, on a concealed portion of her body wears such a mark, and knows its meaning. Even her husband, a boring and clodlike fellow we shall suppose, does not know the meaning of the mark on the wife's body. And, too, he does not much care. He does not much care, we shall suppose, about her. He only wants his supper and his shirts ironed.

How does the fantasy end, or continue? We may perhaps speculate that the alien does return for her, and he takes her away with him, powerfully desiring her, as a bound, leashed love animal to his own planet. She has left the unironed shirts behind.

What then?

Whether the fantasy continues with new adventures or not is up to the lovers. Everything is to be as they wish it. Fantasy is yours to elaborate and enjoy. It may, of course, be left implicit that the alien and his love animal, soon domesticated to her new duties, though sometimes rebellious, an abducted Earth woman, will have a fantastic love life and many exciting adventures.

Of course they will!

27. The I-Am-Raped-by-a-Machine Fantasy.

The female is raped by a machine.

Comment:

The machine here can be a robot or it can be something, say, through which, nude and helpless, she is processed. For best results, perhaps this machine should figure in the context of a larger fantasy. Perhaps it is used to punish a disobedient female, and its attentions, hydraulic and mechanical, are unpleasant and designed to drive her back, eagerly and submissively, into the arms of a live male. Or perhaps it is the product of a scientific misogynist, who enjoys, through observation windows, noting the distress and helpless responsiveness of a despised sex. (A turnabout fantasy would be that of the politically powerful Lesbian misanthrope who contrives such a machine to humiliate and rape males.) Another possibility, more interesting, is that it is an advanced culture's device for removing frigidity in captive females. When the machine finishes with the woman she is not only sexually vital, sexually alive, but an incredibly powerful sexual desire, in the throes of which she often finds herself helpless, has been instilled in her. When she comes out of the machine she is eager to go to the slave block. She wants a master, quickly. Perhaps the machine more arouses her than satisfies her. Perhaps it teaches her more what she is missing than gives it to her. Perhaps, in effect, it readies her, and superbly, for male sexual domination. It brings her to the point where her needs now cry out for satisfaction, and at the hands of a handsome, powerful male. Perhaps, when the woman comes out of the machine, she is certified, or stamped, in some way, depending on the adequacy of her responses and the registration of these by the machine. Is "Grade A," for example, stamped on her lovely ass? When she comes from the machine is she simply released from the belt and taken to a slave pen or, perhaps under nonhumanoid aliens, is the whole process more automated, and she emerges stamped and packaged for shipment? Perhaps the aliens, who may resemble sponges or octopuses, capture and "process" Earth females in this fashion for mercantile distribution throughout the galaxy, where such females might be desired, e.g., in remote Earth colonies or among more humanoid aliens, who might desire them as slaves or sex animals. Indeed, perhaps there are some sorts of less humanoid creatures who buy such products. And perhaps some of these less humanoid creatures even use such fair merchandise, scandalously perhaps, for sexual purposes.

Who knows?

28. The I-Am-Raped-by-a-Monster Fantasy.

The female is raped by a monster.

Comment:

Men, perhaps unfortunately, are not the only things females are sexually curious about.

In this fantasy, the nature of the monster is, of course, up to the female. If she is to be raped by it, she should certainly have something to say about its configuration.

Perhaps it is mammalian in nature but obviously alien. Perhaps it is very large and covered with silken fur, and has several prehensile appendages. It is doubtless extremely strong. Its mouth is perhaps large and ringed with teeth. Perhaps it might bite through an entire shoulder of hers, if it chose. The eyes are perhaps large and dark, nocturnal. We may, incidentally, suppose it to be of great intelligence. Indeed, perhaps we may suppose it to be of greater intelligence than human beings. Perhaps it captures her and takes her, gently, in its mouth, and carries her, on four feet, in loping strides, to its den. There it drops her on grasses and soft mosses and, perhaps with its teeth, strips her. When it holds her, in its several furred, prehensile appendages, she is completely helpless. She cannot move. There is no escape for her. It bends more closely to her. She turns her head to one side. She smells its fur, its odors. She sees the large eyes. She feels its powerful, silken, furred grasp. She hears it breathing. She screams, as it penetrates her.

Perhaps the monster, in its jungle, keeps her as a nude pet. When search parties approach, the monster restrains her, not permitting her to cry out. He keeps her to himself. When there are no more search parties, she understands that she must serve the monster. She must gather fruit and nuts for it, and, with her fingers, and teeth and tongue, groom its fur. She is its human slave. In the jungle, too, we may suppose there is much danger. The monster must, frequently, protect her. Hating it and terrified of it, yet she fears to roam far from its side. It is her only protection. It frequently uses her, of course, for its sexual satisfaction.

In time we may suppose, fantastically, and to her horror, she finds herself pregnant with a powerful, squirming animal. She is not permitted to kill herself. If necessary, she is physically restrained. She may be even forced fed by the monster. It forces food down her throat and does not permit her, later, to regurgitate it.

When she goes into labor she is hooded. She does not see what it is to which she has given birth. Afterwards, with great gentleness, almost affection, the monster returns her to civilization.

She, of course, refuses to divulge what, in all details, has happened to her. She has only been "lost" in the jungle.

Many years later perhaps she, and an older woman, a respected companion, are flying over the jungle when their craft has engine trouble. There is a crash landing. Both women survive. But, shortly afterwards, they are stalked by a pride of predatory animals. It seems they must be destroyed. But, from the forest, a monster, rather as the one she had been raped by, years ago, emerges and slays or drives off the animals.

Both women are stunned.

The monster comes toward them and, timidly, touches her with one of its prehensile appendages, or perhaps, with its great, dark tongue, touches her arm. It then turns and disappears into the jungle.

She realizes that it was her offspring. The older woman then tells her of these monsters, alien creatures, who inhabit the jungle. She, too, in her youth, was stolen by them and used, and forced to bear such an animal. They are a highly intelligent species of life, from a distant world, whose rightful females have died, and whose zygotes will produce only male offspring. They are, however, crossfertile with human females. They are, despite their offensive appearance to human females, gentle and kind and loving beasts. On the plane of civilization and morality they would rank higher perhaps than human beings. It is only to preserve their kind that they seek out human females. Without the human female their noble and gentle species would, in a generation, become extinct. They have a complex oral tradition and literature, but have not chosen the ways of technology and weapons. The final commitment of their outstanding intelligences has been to repudiate cruelty, competitiveness and artificiality. They live gently in the jungles, bothering no one and only come forth, when necessary, to procure a mate, that their kind may not die. They form great affections for the females they take, but, invariably, though it causes them great pain, return them to safety when the offspring has been born.

The girl's monster offspring had wanted to touch her, to make itself known to its mother, but then it had turned, and withdrawn to the jungle. It knew that it could never have a mother; it knew that it could only be hateful to and despised of the woman who had given it birth. It had acknowledged her as its mother, and thanked her for the gift of life. Then knowing it could only be feared and hated, it had withdrawn.

Men arrive and rescue the women. The women refuse to explain the slain animals about the fallen craft.

It remains the secret of such women that the beasts exist. The younger woman weeps as she is carried away in the rescue craft. From the jungle the offspring watches the plane depart.

29. The I-Am-Going-to-Have-an-Affair-with-This-Strange-Woman Fantasy.

The husband and wife have an affair.

Comment:

The fantasy element here is, really, only that the lovers are unknown to one another. Beyond that, it is, as a matter of fact, not a fantasy at all. It is simply having an affair with one's wife. She can be, of course, a terrific woman to have an affair with. If she is going to have an affair, it might as well be with you. Why should you be left out? Similarly, if your husband is going to have an affair, why shouldn't it be with you? You can probably give him a better affair than some inexperienced, green wench who, most likely, hasn't even been married yet. Such women, even if they aren't virgins, generally don't know one end of a man from the other. That takes a good deal of experience. Their concept of an affair is usually to lay down and have their meals paid for. Their main advantage over you is that they are probably better at tennis. One of your advantages over them is that you may not play tennis at all.

The affair must be carefully planned.

Ideally it takes place in a new locale, and, preferably, a rather exotic one. The Bahamas will do nicely. The husband and wife arrive separately. If they are rich enough, they can have separate accommodations. If not, then he will "pick her up" and she will share his accommodations. He may "pick her up" in the bar, along the sidewalk, anywhere.

He does not know her. But he is sexually interested in her.

She is, to him, a new woman. Perhaps she has dyed her hair. She is now a blond, or a redhead, or a brunet. She is now something different. He first sees her this way when he first lays eyes on her in the new locale. Moreover, she has purchased new clothes and new jewelry for this affair. He has never seen her dressed and adorned as he does now. Moreover she is probably "his type." If she wasn't, he probably wouldn't have married her in the first place.

They conduct themselves precisely as if they did not know one another. She plays coy. He tries tricks. They fence together verbally. He must be careful how he propositions her. She must be careful how she responds. Neither, of course, wears their wedding rings. The waiters, fellow guests, etc., do not know they are really married. The husband may have to make sure some other males do not "cut in" on the woman he is after, etc. Only the husband and wife know their real relationship. If necessary, one can always let the house detective in on it. Together the husband and wife talk, and walk, and go dancing, and join one another to do sight-seeing, and, in the evening, after supper, make love.

Moreover, this affair should be an important one. In fact, it might even lead to marriage. Both partners should talk to one another about themselves. When you are really interested in another person you wish to know a great many things about them, sometimes even small and intimate things. Do you know your wife's favorite food, for example? Hopefully, you and the woman you meet will find out a great deal about one another.

These should be true details, not made up. This is a time of relearning and reappreciating one another, of reminding yourself of terribly important things you may have forgotten, of finding out, sweetly and deeply, to whom it is, as a unique person, you are married.

In your relationship, of course, you refer to one another by your own first names. "Mom" and "Dad," for example, will not do. Further, though you talk about many things, obviously you do not discuss your marriage. You are, after all, having an affair. Further, you agree not to mention Aunt Mildred and, too, though it will doubtless be harder, you do not discuss the children. You can always call up Aunt Mildred privately, both of you, and check on the kids. But, when you are together, you discuss life, and your desires, and one another.

At the conclusion of the affair, you may propose marriage to her, and, hopefully, she will accept. Then, with your lover, now as your wife, you return home.

Perhaps, for the second time in your life, and the second time with the same person, you have fallen in love.

30. The Bitch Fantasy.

A proud bitch is captured. To her outrage, her captor treats her precisely as the bitch she is.

Comment:

The female's clothing is removed. Bitches do not wear clothing. She is collared. Then she is leashed. She is not permitted to use her hands, only her mouth, tongue and cunt. If the captor permits, she may walk upright. Otherwise she goes on all fours. Under no circumstances, however, is she to use her hands. Similarly, she is not allowed to speak. Bitches cannot speak. She may attempt to signify her needs by whines and whimpers. Human communication, however, is forbidden her. In her training she is taught to respond to tugs on the leach, gestures, voice commands, whistles and the snapping of fingers. She eats and drinks from dishes placed on the floor, using, of course, only her mouth. She may also be fed by hand, or thrown scraps of food. Approval may be indicated by such things as smiles, scratchings behind the ears and expressions, such as "Good girl!" Disapproval may be indicated by such things as frowns and sharp words. She might also be struck with a rolled newspaper or nicked with the free end of the leash. Presumably she learns her tricks swiftly and well. In no time she can beg and roll over, and such. It is supposed that in this the female understands that if she is not completely cooperative and compliant, she is to be beaten or slain. It may be supposed that if she lives, she lives as her master's bitch. When she is fucked, of course, she is fucked in the bitch position, she on all fours, he behind. At night, when he is finished with her, she is chained by the neck to the foot of his bed.

This is a rather rough fantasy, perhaps the roughest of those we discuss.

Obviously it can serve to ventilate male hostility, and, in that sense, serve as a male vengeance fantasy. Few men, for example, have not met, at sometime or another in their life, an irritable, proud, contemptuous wench whom they would not relish stripping and putting through her paces as a bitch. Wouldn't it be delicious taking her clothes off and treating her exactly like what she is, a real bitch. You don't feed her, for example, until she begs, by whimpers, to feed from your hand. Some women deliberately humiliate men. So why should a man not, if only in fantasy, take his vengeance, and with a vengeance?

Interestingly, this fantasy can also have an appeal to women.

This appeal, I suspect, is primarily motivated by two considerations.

First, just as most men are aware that they have often acted like bastards, and don't feel too pleased about it, so, too, most women, not all, know that they have often acted like bitches, and they aren't too proud about it either. This fantasy, then, because it can be felt as undergoing a deserved humiliation, can relieve guilt feelings. Just as a good spanking can, upon occasion, relieve tension in a child and make him happy so too this fantasy, in an adult woman, can let her feel the score for her nastiness has been evened up, and perhaps more. Sometimes there is a deeper psychology than psychology. It is surely better than burning her hand on the toaster. The question, of course, is a bit more complicated than this, or the fantasy would not have ts appeal. For example, the humiliation, as it is experienced, at the hands of a beloved male, is not simple humiliation. In fact, it is not really much like humiliation at all. The humiliation, such as it is, is felt in a sexually stimulating matrix. It concludes, of course, with her sexual pleasure. Once again, we note, however, that this sort of thing is not intended as a substitute for psychotherapy or appropriate medical attention, where these are indicated. For example, if a woman preferred this sort of fantasy, and frequently, she would probably be suffering from guilt well beyond that normally accumulated in human life. In such a case, she should probably seek medical attention. To enact a fantasy such as this, once in a while, when it was pleasurable to do so, however, would seem to me an emotionally healthy outlet for run-of-the-mill guilt feelings. It is probably far superior to smashing the fender of the car so that hubby will yell and scream at you.

A second reason, perhaps, for the appeal of this fantasy to women has less to do with the relief of guilt than it has with the release of sexual inhibitions. Many women, I understand, find it difficult, in their own persons, so to speak, to have good sexual relations. The problem seems to be analogous to the individual who, in real life, is quite shy and reticent, but, given a role, as in a play, can throw himself into it with élan and gusto, and do an astonishing bang-up job that startles everyone. Many genuinely gifted actors, as opposed to Hollywood stars, are rather introverted, quiet individuals. Often they cannot easily be recognized from role to role, they are so gifted. Such talent, of course, would spell doom to a Hollywood star, whose success, commonly, depends on playing himself over and over under different names. One of the general attractions and strengths of imaginative sex, incidentally, is that it provides individuals with roles. People who don't know what to do in their own person, or are afraid to do anything in their own person, can often perform superbly in the context of playing a role. Indeed, some people live life as a set of roles. That, however, seems to be carrying matters too far. Somewhere there is the person, and he must never get lost. At any rate, if a woman does have difficulties with sex, imaginative sex can be great for her. She may begin by acting, but, after some days or weeks, she will presumably shift into feeling. A woman who acts like she enjoys sex is probably well on the way to enjoying it. In the context of the fantasies, of course, the acting is understood as acting, and there is no call for guilt about trying to fool hubby. In most cases, of course, sooner or later, the acting combines with genuine feeling. For example, suppose the woman is acting the role of a slave girl in orgasm. Presumably, if all goes well, she is, with all her imagination and feeling, *from the inside out*, acting the role of a slave girl in orgasm; indeed, if she has sufficient empathy and skill, she will literally feel herself to *be* the slave girl in orgasm; indeed, to speak of the matter as it is *felt*, she literally *is*, and *knows she is*, a slave girl in orgasm; and in all this, of course, the orgasm is quite genuine; it is a *real* orgasm. Similarly, as you have her, you are not having your wife, you are having a slave girl, a wench that you own, but your orgasm, too, is real. Remember, Wench, you are *owned*. You may hold *nothing* back. Yield to him as a slave girl must to her master, totally, irreservedly. Fully. Empty and shatter yourself at his feet. He is all. You are nothing. You are only a sexually conquered slave. Yield in all your helpless, degraded sensuous ecstasy. It is an incredible sexual experience. You will want it often. This matter bears some elaboration. We shall return to it at the conclusion of the discussion of the next fantasy.

Now, for some women, the bitch fantasy, with its exotic premise of the beautiful, rebellious captive treated like an animal and forced to behave as such can be a stimulating role challenge. It is far removed from their ordinary self. Further, for many women, who have been conditioned to believe that sex is ugly and dirty this is a fantasy which, perhaps initially to their minds, is honestly and suitably "degrading." Sex is not for ladies, but bitches, animals. Now they are *forced*, literally forced, to behave as such an animal. They are deliberately humiliated, deliberately "degraded," and then, in the context of this humiliation and degradation they are forced to have sex, and as an animal. This is a fantasy which, in its way, can trick the frigid woman. It does not argue with her that sex is not ugly or dirty. It does not use reason on her but behavior. It appears to accept her premise as to the lack of dignity of sex and, if anything, even amplifies it. This puts her off her guard. Dirty and ugly as it is, she is going to engage in it, and in a way that she may find reassuringly humiliating and degrading. She is not argued with. She is simply given her orders. For example, let us suppose that she is ordered to kneel and lick his genitals. This is something that, as a lady, she could never bring herself to do. As a captive bitch, she has no choice. After she does it, of course, and gets used to the earthy smells and tastes, she has it behind her. The important thing is that she has made her break-through. After this, in many diverse love makings, she will think nothing of using her mouth and tongue to delight her husband. Similarly, after she has been had as a bitch, how could she object to being had as a woman? She has gone as "low" as she can. The only direction left to her then is up. Also, she discovers, to her surprise, that "low" is not really low. It is not so bad, after all. Indeed, it is rather fun. Sex is not so bad after all. She has had it, so to speak, at its putative worst, and it turned out, in the last analysis, to be fun. If humiliation and shame, or a touch of these, can bring a woman to orgasm this is a point in favor of humiliation and shame. After they have brought her to orgasm, hopefully she will also have discovered that there was, really, nothing to have been humiliated and ashamed about. The Bitch fantasy may seem the sexual nadir for a woman. But, for a woman who can only be coaxed into sex by means of the basement door, it is recommended. Anything to gain entrance to the building. After that she can come in the front door, the side door or leap in windows, or land on the roof upside down by helicopter.

Obviously it would be wrong for a man to put a woman he *dislikes* through the bitch fantasy, for then he would actually be, in fact, humiliating and degrading her. That would be cruel, and morally unworthy. Paradoxically, then, the only woman he may treat as a bitch is one he cares for. The distinction, of course, is a simple one. He is not actually treating her as a bitch, but *playing* that he is doing so. Similarly, she is not actually being treated as a bitch, but *playing* that she is being so treated. The Bitch fantasy is a game, a fantasy. Even when both lovers seem most cruel to one another, it is drama, not fact. And their drama, whatever its pleasures or values as a psychological venting mechanism, takes place in a context of love. When this is understood, it becomes clear how a loving husband, for example, could play his role in such a fantasy. Indeed, he would permit himself to act in such a fantasy only with one he loved. If there is some woman he actually dislikes, he may, if he wishes, put her through a bitch fantasy in his imagination; that will help to relieve his hostility; but it would be wrong, of course, if he actually dislikes her, to actually humiliate or degrade her. Compare the case in which he might fantasize the rape of a hated female. His fantasy may relieve his feelings, and thus be a desirable fantasy; but it would be wrong, in fact, to rape her, whether he hates her or not.[1]

[1]*The moral questions here are more complicated than these formulations would suggest, but the formulations, as general assertions, may be permitted to stand. For example, it might be possible to conceive of some case, some unusual case, in which it might be morally acceptable to rape a female. But, even in such a case, it does not seem that there would be a moral obligation to do so. One such case might be when a husband, for his wife's own good, forces sex upon her and rapes her. She might be sexually freed by such a rape, and be the better for it. It might even be the start of a good sex life for them. On the other hand, such cases are presumably rare. Moreover, even if, in unusual cases, it is morally permissible to rape, the rape, whether morally permissible or not, would still be a* legal *crime. Since law, and respect for it, constitutes about the only fragile shield between us and the jungle, there is a general presumption that it is not morally permissible to break laws, even when the law is, in effect, morally neutral. Indeed, even if the law prescribes something contrary to morality, the question must be weighed whether or not the violation of the law is not more morally improper than the acceptance of the moral impropriety advised by the law. For example, it may in certain cases be more moral to obey an unjust law than to violate it. Let us suppose, in a trivial case, that a law exists that students may not be allowed access to the general stacks of a large university library. Let us further suppose that this law has no adequate justification and that it, in effect, is unjust because it allows faculty members such free access, thus*

being discriminatory, and is immoral, in the sense that it makes the work of students more difficult and troublesome; it causes them inconvenience and psychic "pain." It causes unnecessary pain. On the other hand, it may be more moral for the student to obey such a law, or regulation, than to violate it, producing an anarchic power-makes-right situation, necessitating recourse to authority in enforcing the law, etc. The usual thing to do with bad laws is not to break them but get them changed. If it seems impossible to change the laws then a common democratic rule of thumb, coming out of centuries of military and political conflict, is that majority rules. This may not be a great rule, but the alternative, that a minority rules, doesn't seem obviously superior. There just aren't any great rules in this sphere. Optimum moral action is as subtle and difficult as life itself; circumstances may well alter cases. Even a rule like, "Everyone should follow his own conscience and be prepared to take the consequences" isn't plausible, if understood as a universal prescription. The individual who feels he has a moral obligation to kill left-handed Lithuanians is not to be advised to follow his conscience, even if he is prepared to be locked up after the second or third Lithuanian. Morality is not simple. Beware the man who, in a complex situation, clearly sees the right. He is probably either very young or very simple, or perhaps both. Further, it is one thing to see a wrong, and another to figure out how to make it right without producing a great deal more wrong. It is one thing to be able to tell the car is running improperly and another to be able to fix it. Driving it off a cliff will probably not effect the necessary adjustment.

It now being understood that the Bitch Fantasy *is* a fantasy, it is clear how lovers can engage in it. It is a game they play. There is no intention to hurt anyone. On the other hand, in the context of the drama, clearly the fantasy can be, in effect, a vengeance fantasy for the male. Perhaps this is worth a bit of elaboration. First, the captive woman can stand proxy for other women, or for hundreds of them. Men spend a good deal of their time being sexually frustrated. For every thousand women a man sees whom he would like to go to bed with he is lucky if he gets one. The woods are literally filled with beauties he will never get to touch, and kiss and take in his arms. He might like to have a harem filled with all the beauties who have, from time to time, attracted him, but he will not get it. What man has not passed a lovely girl on the street and wished he might simply say to those of his retinue, "That one, prepare her for love and send her to me tonight," and know that it would be done? This sort of frustration is bad enough, but then add to it the frustration beyond this that women may have caused him, women clerks, women teachers, women drivers, etc. Thus, the Bitch fantasy, in effect, permits him, in a controlled, harmless situation, to take a symbolic revenge on all those delicious, troublesome, frustrating creatures. Women have caused him a great deal of pain. This fantasy helps him even the score a bit. Secondly, the very woman he lives with, whom he loves, is when all is said and done, one of that bitchy stripe, too; she will, in simply living with him, have gotten on his nerves; she will have been abrupt and unpleasant with him many times; she will have criticized him and nagged him; she will have, implicitly or explicitly, demeaned and insulted him; it is natural that when two people live together, particularly people as different as a man and a woman, that friction and hostility will be generated. Marriage is not simple; there are yells and screams; it is not all kisses and smiles. Sometimes, even among genuinely loving partners, each will feel real hostility for the other. This fantasy then, in a humorous manner, permits the ventilation and discharge of gripes. It provides an institutionalized avenue for the relief of accumulated grievance. It is an escape valve. It is not clearly inferior to shouting, breaking dishes and slamming doors. (A fantasy with similar escape-valve possibilities for the female, of course, is the Male-Slave-of-an-Imperious-Queen Fantasy, discussed earlier. A version of the "Bitch" fantasy, of course, can be used in which the male is the individual forced to assume an animal role. In such a case, one supposes, for greater dramatic plausibility, the animal would not be a "bitch," a female dog, but something else. This, of course, is up to the lovers. If the woman has a real pile of irritation to unload she might wish the male, precisely as she was forced to do, to enact the role of a captive *female* animal, and *she* will be the *male* keeper. That might teach him what it is to be a woman under the domination of men. Moreover, it might excite her to play the role of a man dominating a degraded female. What would it be to be a man, seeing such a beautiful creature helpless at your feet? What would it be to be a man, knowing that you are stronger, and can dominate, and sexually exploit, at your pleasure, such a delicious, vulnerable thing as a female? Once she understands something of the male's power feelings, commonly concealed, and the ecstasy of his masculine domination, she may find her own female role far more meaningful and exciting that it would otherwise have been. She will now understand more of how she appears to the male, and how the males sees her. This should make being a female, understanding herself as game and quarry, as being weaker and at his mercy, as being intensely desired, as being forced to be submissive and obedient to his lust, a far more thrilling act. The normal female will prefer, generally, the role of the captured woman, at the mercy of the dominant male. This is truer to the nature of her most frequent sexual fantasies. On the other hand, if she understands something of this relationship from the standpoint of the male, her own portrayal of the captive is likely to be far richer and more satisfying, both to herself and the male. The normal woman will normally prefer to be dominated; but, too, it is normal for her, sometimes, to wish to dominate. Similarly the male, normally, will prefer to dominate, but, too, it is quite normal for him, sometimes, to wish to be dominated. It is an unusual woman who wishes always to dominate and an unusual one who would never wish to dominate; similarly it would be an unusual male who always wishes to be dominated, and an unusual one who would never wish to be dominated. Statistically, the male should dominate and the female submit; but, occasionally, these roles should be reversed. Universal generalizations aren't much better in sex than in history or science. The needs and desires of the partners should determine relationships, not abstract rules. Reality takes priority over recipes.)

Other values of this fantasy, apart from its utility as a male (or female) vengeance fantasy, is that it can, in some cases, as we have noted, relieve guilt feelings and lower sexual inhibitions. Presumably the relief of guilt feelings could occur in the case whether the dominated subject was male or female; and the lowering of sexual inhibitions, too, could occur with either partner playing either role.

One thing not to be lost sight of here is that this fantasy, like all others, is to be engaged in lightheartedly. It, nor the others, is not meant to be taken seriously. It is meant to be enjoyable, to be delicious fun. Pompous fantasy is ridiculous; inventive and loving fantasy can be marvelous.

The bitch fantasy, incidentally, may be put in the context of a larger fantasy. For example, a sophisticated, educated, highly intelligent, beautiful female enemy is captured. To degrade and humiliate her, she is forced to be a bitch. Perhaps she is a top espionage agent for a foreign power and you, her captor, also an espionage agent, but of a different power, after months of frustration and search, have taken her. She is now yours to do with as you please. You will make the proud bitch pay well for the trouble she has caused you.

What about a poodle collar?

I expect a beautiful female spy, stripped and put in a poodle collar, with a leash, would look ravishing. What would you think? You must be careful, of course, not to ejaculate at the mere sight of her. You must not take her until she has become fully aroused and, by whines and whimpers, begs you to have her. A poodle collar, of course, might be right for some women, and not for others. You can always experiment. In what sort of collar does your beautiful female spy look best?

31. The I-Am-His-Slave-Girl Fantasy.

The female is the male's slave.

Comment:

In its thousands of variations this is perhaps the most provocative sexual fantasy that a man and a woman can share.

It has something of capture and rape going for it. For example, how do you suppose the woman becomes his slave? But, the relationship is institutionalized and backed up by an entire culture. She has nowhere to go, nowhere to run. The authorities will not free her; they will return her to her master. Moreover, hundreds of women, hundreds of thousands perhaps, enjoy this degrading status. She is only one, of an entire class of human beings. She has no hope of freedom; she must learn to serve, and serve well. She may be bought and sold. She is only property.

This fantasy, of course, answers to the male's desire to own and dominate a woman; too, of course, it answers to the woman's desire, instinctive in her, to be owned and dominated by a man. We have discussed biology and evolution in such matters. The problem, of course, is that these desires mingle with many others. For example, the male also desires to respect and love the woman; and the woman also desires, paradoxically, to be independent and free. The strength of these relative desires doubtless varies considerably from individual to individual. For example, interior anatomy differs considerably among human beings. For example, different individuals, of the same sex, may have different size and shape organs, different numbers of valves coming into the heart, etc. If these features were visible, doubtless sexual selection would have eliminated certain human types and, anatomically, we would be much more standardized than we are. Similarly, if there is this much gross anatomical difference among human beings, it seems qutie probable that there is also considerable psychological divergence. We probably differ much, one from the other, in emotional capacities and neurological dispositions. It seems quite possible that one woman might have a desperate desire to surrender sexually to a male and another might not even catch on to what the other was talking about. The more masculine woman, who is more aggressive, etc., of course, should not be permitted to impose her own value judgments, indexed to her hormones, perhaps, on those of more glandularly normal females. Because the more aggressive woman is more outspoken is no guarantee that she is going to talk sense. A gentle female, who desires a man's touch, is just as worth listening to. Most women, it seems, like men. Let us hope they are not talked out of it by women who, perhaps genetically, cannot understand what it is to desire sexual experience. At any rate, let each woman be true to her own self. Let each not pretend to be the other. Let the woman who hates men or, more likely, who cannot sense their attractiveness, not be placed under pressure by society to pretend to be sexually attracted to them. For example, it seems piteous hypocrisy when certain women, obviously seething with hatred and resentment for men, pretend that they are really sexually normal. The sexually normal person just doesn't hate whole sexes. He may hate people but it will never have occurred to him to hate an entire sex. This is not to say that a woman cannot, from time to time, be genuinely annoyed with "men" and that a man cannot, from time to time, be genuinely annoyed with "women." There is surely justification for both attitudes; men can be real bothers, and so, too, can women. This sort of resentment, however, is a different thing from holding a standing hatred for an entire modality of human being. Similarly, let the woman who cares for men, and is attracted to them, not be ashamed of her desires, and not feel that she is somehow betraying her sex by finding the opposite sex of sexual interest; she is not somehow uninformed, despicable, unworthy, out-of-date, stupid or iniquitous for wishing to be held, and kissed and loved. Those who say, or imply, she is are, most likely, glandularly deficient.

Now there is little doubt that love and freedom are desiderata of civilized life. On the other hand, there is, too, little doubt that men, from time to time, for one reason or another, do desire to own and dominate women and that women, statistically, from time to time, relish a bit of being owned and dominated. A likely compromise then is to shoot for love and freedom in reality and, in fantasy, give our less civilized side its delightful due.

I deleted the following paragraph from a novel. I do not recall precisely why. Perhaps it did not fit, or something. At any rate, it is of interest:

"It might have been a firelit picnic, on a beach on Earth, in which the boys and the girls had played the game of Master and Slave, a bit of cord on the wrist, or ankle, or throat, of the girl to mark her as Slave. But that is a dangerous game. Nothing so excites a man as to have a woman admit herself his slave, his to do with as he wishes. Similarly, nothing so excites a woman as to feel herself his slave, to feel herself his, and to know that she must do what he tells her."

Those who understand this paragraph, in their feelings, as

opposed to merely intellectually, will understand the force of the fantasy currently under discussion.

Because use the fantasy is dynamite, it is recommended, of course, that it only be played between husband and wife. It leads too naturally to intercourse to be risked in a situation where intercourse is either not possible or not desirable. Similarly, since this is a fantastic fantasy, it should not be permitted to precipitate marriages, which, on other grounds, might not be suitable. These pleasures had best be reserved for adding delight to marriages which are based on valid, independent considerations, such as independently motivated love, common values, common interests, and such.

In this fantasy, as in all others, there should be no enactment that is not mutually stimulating and pleasurable to both partners. For example, if either the husband or wife do not feel this fantasy, in their blood, so to speak, there is no need for them to practice it. They might try it, to see if they can make it work for them, but, if they do, and it doesn't, that is all right. Imaginative sex is not for everybody; it is, frankly, only for imaginative people; further, not every portion of imaginative sex is for everyone who enjoys imaginative sex; some fantasies might just not grab one, others might; one can like food without liking blueberry pie.

The variations on this fantasy are limited only by one's ingenuity. Settings can be historical, contemporary, exotic or futuristic. Once again, of course, character analysis and attention to realistic detail can improve a fantasy. Props may also be of value. Most important, always, of course, is the imagination.

A small, private Roman banquet can be fun to prepare and serve, in which delicious, exotic foods, with splendid wines, may be served from a low table, or on the floor, while guests recline on cushions. And that luscious, captivating slave girl, with loose hair and golden earrings, in her brief tunic of red silk, fastened on the left shoulder by a golden clasp, looks somewhat like your wife. But she is not. She is your slave. When, during the banquet, you want her, you may remove her garment, or order her to do so, and then, after perhaps having commanded her to dance for you, you take her by the ankle and pull her down to the cushions beside you, or, if you wish, you order her to the cushions beside

you, and you then take her in your arms. She will doubtless
yield well to her master.

Exotic or futuristic settings can also be delightful. Perhaps
you have stolen her, an Earth woman, and have taken her to
your own planet, in our own times, to be your slave. Or, perhaps,
in some distant world of the future, human slavery will exist,
as it does in certain places today, and used to exist, almost
universally. The expression 'slavery' might not be used, but the
relationship might obtain. Perhaps such slaves would be bred
for passion and pleasure. One might suppose a brilliant girl,
resentful and rebellious, who has been so bred. She is a beautiful,
proud girl, a fighter, but, when the hand of a man touches her,
she finds her responses becoming uncontrollable. In agony, and
then joy, she yields to him, as a slave girl to her master. She
then, with her whole heart, her brilliance, her sweet softness,
conquered, loves her master. She acknowledges herself his. She
cannot help herself. She has been bred to belong to a man; and
he is the man to whom she belongs. Or perhaps such slaves are
selected as the result of tests during childhood. Perhaps they do
not have incredible aptitudes, perhaps essential to fitting into an
intricately organized world of the future. Perhaps their I.Q.'s are
less than 140, by current standards, and society cannot profitably
employ such imperfect units for responsible work. Rather than
let such units multiply themselves by uncontrolled breeding,
producing inevitable frustration and social stress, doubtless,
if a revolution were averted. quotas would be established for
their numbers. Unborn revolutionaries, those with I.Q.'s less
than 140, do not build bombs. Since voluntary controls on such
matters are useless, they being adopted only by the moral and
responsible members of society, who thus diminish their own
numbers, some form of involuntary control appears necessary.
The deliberate sterilization of free women with I.Q.'s less than
140 after, say, their second child, would be likely to provoke
political recriminations. Unlimited childbirth candidates, even
if ludicrous to any rational mind, would be certain of political
victory. Their slogans, of course, would be for "voluntary
reduction in family size," in the name of "freedom" and so on,
or, in short, a return to the policy of no reduction in family size

at all, except in those families of greater moral responsibility, of whose children one could use more, not less. The people most likely to practice rigorous population control are precisely those who might be well advised to exceed their quotas somewhat, at least if the object of the program is to produce more intelligent, more gifted, more moral human beings. One solution of this sort of problem, of course, is to control women with I.Q.'s of less than, say, 140. The woman, of course, is the desired object of population control. Without her there is no child, and it takes her the better part of a year to produce one. Sterilizing ninety-nine men out of one hundred is not as effective, since the one hundredth man, theoretically, given modern techniques of artificial insemination, could in a period of a month or so, impregnate a million women. There is no more effective way to control a woman than to reduce her to slavery. If the programs of the women's liberation movement become adopted, over the next centuries, and the family is abolished, and state control of human beings is instituted, this enslavement of the female population, say, those under 140 I.Q., will be easy. The men with I.Q.'s less than 140, properly conditioned, will not defend these women, particularly when they may be assigned them for their quarters in virtue of their merits in the eyes of the state. It is assumed that women, free women, with I.Q.'s over 140 will be seldom, statistically, impregnated by sub-140 males. This solution, the enslavement of women with I.Q.'s under 140, frightening though it might be, could, in given historical contexts, be quite practical. It would provide a statistically effective means of controlling the numbers of a certain strata of the population. If the family is abolished, something of this sort seems likely within the next thousand years. The word "slavery," of course, would never be used. Indeed, the women involved might technically be the property (controlled units) of the state, not of private individuals, and might be conditioned to regard themselves as a certain form of specially privileged and protected citizen, necessary and loyal daughters of the great, loving mother, etc.

Now, in fantasy, one could imagine a woman, a highly intelligent, sensitive woman, who, because, say, of the spite or vengeance of a clerk or functionary, who tampers with records, is improperly categorized as a sub-140 specimen. She had accepted the system until now, to her horror, she becomes its victim. There is no appeal from the results of the tests, twice given, twice altered. Her case is closed. She is then, say, trained in detail, with inferior women, as a service daughter. She is trained to wear her uniform attractively, to cook, to clean, to make love, and so on. She, in her training, comes to realize what society has done to many of its women, and now, similarly, to her. She sees through the hypocrisies of her world. Let us then suppose that, after her training, in a display area, a given male bids a high rent price for her. She is, of course, beautiful, and for *bona fide* bidders, is exhibited naked. On the other hand, she may be simply assigned to him. Let us suppose, in either case, he is a high-order male, over 140 I.Q. She is, of course, we shall suppose, his equal, or nearly his equal. He, of course, cannot accept that. He has the results of her tests on her forms. Further, the tests were repeated, and their results conformed. To him, she is merely one of the "lower orders." He has little concern for her feelings none for her as a person, for, technically, she is not a person, but a controlled state unit, a service daughter. He knows "what she is" and will use her for precisely what she is. Moreover, he is irritated by her resistance and apparent intelligence. He will not tolerate such insubordination and pretense. He keeps her under cruel and close discipline. She is forced to serve him helplessly as a slave. He treats her offhandedly, casually, commandingly. She resents this furiously but, too, to her horror, something in her womanness finds herself thrilled to be commanded by him. The situation, we may suppose, is complicated by the fact that, to her misery, she finds him irresistibly powerful and attractive. Let us assume that, in his arms, she truly finds herself, in all the helplessness of her vulnerable womanhood, a slave, and that she, to her misery, cannot help responding to him, precisely as he expects her to. In his arms, against her will, she becomes only a spasmodic, moaning service daughter. Further, to her horror, she finds that she has fallen in love with him. Does she manage to communicate her true nature to him? Can she soften him? Is she taken from him, and assigned to other masters? Does the clerk or functionary, by managing her records, continue to manipulate her? Does he want her for himself? Does she gradually begin to believe she is only a service daughter, fit only to be a slave girl? Does the clerk or functionary, to whom she may now be assigned, sadistically explain to her what he has done to her, and then command her to serve him? Must she do so? What are her responses? Does he truly "have" her? We shall suppose so. Does her original "Master" or "controller" still seek her? Does he steal her and take her to a place other than the civilization which formed them both? If so, how does he treat her? Are they both now fugitives? Does the society, and the clerk or functionary, pursue them? What happens? Do they, and, in particular, she, fall into the hands of others? Is he forced to become a sex slave to "high-order" females? Do they find one another again? What happens?

Another variant on this general form of fantasy utilizes a contemporary milieu. One need not go as far as the Middle East. One may take contemporary life, as and where one lives it. One may imagine camps or resorts, say, where kidnapped girls, behind high, electrified fences, in lush surroundings, are kept as slaves to serve the members of the clubs or the proprietor's customers. Similarly, one might suppose that there is a sedate, respectable couple, putatively a man and his wife, a very attractive couple. They have, of course, a secret. She is not truly married to him. He has some fantastic hold over her. As soon as the door to their apartment closes, she is his slave girl, completely. He dominates her and will accept her only as such. For some reason, she must obey him in all things, submissively and perfectly. If she shows the least sign of resistance, or if he is not pleased with her, he reminds her of the hold he has over her. She becomes again then his perfect slave. Indeed, if he is annoyed with her he treats her harshly and even beats her. There can be no objection. She is his slave girl.

These fantasies can be elaborated in thousands of exciting ways. Attention to detail can be important, and mutual planning of detail will produce fuller patterns of pleasure.

Women are marvelous at the production of seductive costumes. One would almost suspect that they had the seduction of men built into their bones. Indeed, they may. Doubtless, in the course

of history and evolution, the most seductive women, whether
obviously or subtly, would tend, statistically, to be the most
sought and the most frequently impregnated.

With respect to detail, consider even so simple a matter as
stripping the woman you intend to enslave. How should it be
done? For one thing she should be, commonly, fully dressed.
She should be so marvelously attired that she would turn the
head of every man she passes on the street, even to lipstick and
cosmetics. Then, article by article, slowly, it is a joy to reveal her
to yourself. Divesting a lovely woman of her clothing can be a
festival of pleasure to a man. How far do you strip her down?
She is naked, of course. But, do you leave her her earrings? Do
you wipe even the lipstick of civilization from her mouth, baring
her totally to you? Do you leave her a necklace, bracelets, a
slender black choker? How do you remove the clothing? Do you
do it elegantly, but a bit roughly, or how? When you unhook her
brassiere do you simply let it fall, or do you jerk it away, startling
her? If she wears old clothing, of intent, it may be torn from
her, of course. Perhaps she is stripped with great courtesy, with
gentleness and elegance, and then, by contrast, rudely ordered
to the bed or floor as a captive whore. Perhaps the girl is treated
with marvelous gentlemanliness and respect until the anklet or
collar is fastened on her, and then, by contrast, she is harshly
and brutally commanded, as the mere slave girl she now is.
Shifts of treatment accorded to the woman can often be sexually
stimulating to her, shaking her up and making her relate, in the
context of the love fantasy, suddenly, differently to you.

Many small acts can be symbolic and can be sexually charged.
For example, let us suppose the woman, naked, frightened, now
in her collar, crouches in the corner, and you throw her a brief
garment. "Put it on." "What is it?" "The garment of a female
slave."

Even putting on such a garment, or costume, can be sexually
stimulating to her. It can bring about a change in her fantasy
personality. She stands there before you, as though furious, her
fists clenched, in the garment you have commanded her to wear,
that of a slave girl. Later, of course, she may be ordered to remove
it, or you, if you wish, may take it from her. While she wears

the garment, of course, she must serve you in some way. Perhaps she prepares food and brings it to you, or gives you wine, or performs some small task you set her, like carrying an object from one room to another, and then returning.

Another act that can stimulate a woman is the unbinding of her hair. We shall suppose that other than the woman herself, only a master is permitted such an act. She looks at him. "You have unbound my hair," she whispers. "Yes," he says.

If you think your girl would look well with a tiny ring in her nose, you can find an earring for girls who do not have their ears pierced, and, gently, that you not hurt her, clamp this to the sides of her septum. She must be permitted, of course, to see how she looks with such a scandalous pagan adornment. A full-length mirror in the bedroom is desirable. Women love to see how exciting and desirable they appear. If they see how marvelously they "look the part," they will enjoy, even more, playing the part. Women are born actresses and lovers.

It sometimes adds to the pleasure of such fantasies to be able to signal your desire earlier in the day. Anticipation tends to whet the sexual appetite, as it can that for food or drink. Let us suppose that the wife wishes to be his slave girl that evening if and only if she wears a certain set of earrings. This is an understood signal between husband and wife. Perhaps he has a certain ring he wears. The earrings may be understood as "those of a slave girl," the ring as "that of a Master," etc. Thus, even in the presence of a family, or relatives, or business acquaintances, etc., secretly, the husband and wife communicate to one another their desires and intentions. It is another secret which they, as lovers, share. The others do not suspect.

Other devices, though perhaps less effective, because they do not work psychologically over a long period of time to prepare the other partner, can be as follows. When she turns down the covers she finds, to her surprise, a bit of slave silk beneath the covers. She is to prepare herself for her master. Or he, perhaps, finds some such signaling device beneath his pillow, perhaps a padlock, a bit of chain, a strap, an earring, etc.

Or perhaps the wife, when her need is much on her, simply

kneels before the man she elects as her master. She puts her head and lips to his feet. "Make me a slave," she begs.

Perhaps he then simply chains her by the ankle at the foot of the bed and, on the floor, over the period of an hour or so, makes love to her. Perhaps, on the other hand, they inaugurate a lengthy and exquisite fantasy, complete with characters, with capture and rape, and enslavement, and so on.

Remember that in all these fantasies, verbal exchanges, conversation, is extremely important. Talk is sexually stimulating, extremely so. The surest path to orgasm lies through the brain, which controls these matters. Do not neglect that you can think. Body sex is for psychiatrists. Body and brain sex is for lovers.

Different women, and men, find different things sexually stimulating. Investigate one another's preferences and desires. For example, does she like, while lying bound in bed, to be fed crusts of bread, or given drink from a canteen or bottle thrust between her teeth? Does she like to be forced to eat chocolates, perhaps pretended aphrodisiacs (see Fantasy 2), while she is chained and you are caressing her clitoris? Does she like to pretend she is forced to eat from a pan on the floor, her hands bound behind her back? Does she like, lying on her stomach, a pillow stuffed between her legs, to pretend she is being beaten?[1] Does it thrill her to respond, as a slave, to signals, such as hand clappings, snapping fingers, gestures and, even, let us suppose, whistles? Does it thrill her to drink wine from a cup which you hold for her, she perhaps bound or chained? Does it thrill her to be ordered to dance naked before you, etc.? Human beings differ very much, one from the other. Almost every human being will have a number of ideas which will seem exciting or delightful to him. Something that seems delightful to A, of course, may not seem so to B, and vice-versa. But, surely in the pool of sexual imagination, a large one where two sexually alive human beings are concerned, the husband and wife should have great fun in planning a mutually satisfying, marvelous fantasy, or, more likely, fantasies. Honesty and openness is desirable in sex, as well as in human relations generally. Fear and shame inhibit human happiness. First, few ideas that can produce pleasure are stupid. Second, if an idea is stupid, it is well that it be examined, and, rationally, be determined to be such. Unusual ideas are not necessarily stupid. Third, there is not all that much wrong with stupid ideas. They are not so terrible. Lipstick is a rather stupid idea, but it is a very nice, very sexy idea. Familiarity and acceptance reduce stupidity. Consider women's and men's fashions. Today's stupid idea is tomorrow's norm. Was it really stupid or not?

[1]*This brings her clitoris into contact with a stimulating surface. Further, as she is "beaten" she psychologically imagines the pain and "feels" herself into her role. When you then rudely unfasten her and turn her on her back to you, she looks up at you, her master, whipped to obedience, psychologically readied, physiologically warmed. She puts her arms eagerly, fearfully, about your neck. She lifts her lips to yours. She will serve you well.*

Let us have some concluding remarks on the I-Am-His-Slave-Girl Fantasy.

Remember, Wench, in the context of the fantasy, he *is* your master. Treat him as such, literally. Remember that you are nothing; you may be bought or sold, or disposed of; you have been captured or purchased; if it pleases him, he may have you whipped or slain; fear him, he owns you; struggle to please him, knowing what may be your fate if you do not; hope that he will be kind to you; be frightened that you might not please him; and you, Husband, look upon her; she is not your wife; she is only a slave; be harsh; command her; treat her as such. In the context of the fantasy, realities are transformed. You may not even have seen this woman before the evening. Gone is the marriage and the past. The only reality now is the new reality. Look at her. She is not bad, your new female slave. What will you do with her?

Did you buy her at the market? Was it your bid that took her naked off the block? Or did your servants bring her home, hoping that she might please you? Is this the first time you have seen her, as she brings food to you? Did a business associate give her to you? Did you get a good price on her? Was she a bargain? Or did you pay more than you wished, and you now feel hostile

toward her? Doubtless you are determined to get more than your
money's worth. Or did you capture her yourself, on one of your
campaigns, binding and leashing her in the streets of a burning
city? Was she perhaps the daughter of a senator, the daughter
of one of your enemies, chained with her other women in their
burning palace, before being led to the locked slave carts, or
being tied by the neck to your stirrup? Now, again, look at her,
again closely, very closely, as she serves you. No. She is not bad,
your new female slave. Command her; she is yours to do with as
you please.

Perhaps she kneels before you, head down, and lifts a
wineglass to you. You do not take it immediately. You examine
her. She is beautiful, in the brief, diaphanous silk of a slave.
You are not displeased. You regard the lineaments of her beauty,
beneath the silk. It is yours, when you wish it. You take the
wine, dismissing the girl to one side. She kneels aside, her eyes
not yet permitted to meet yours. You strip and rape her with
your eyes, to her collar, as you enjoy the wine. You order her
to drink some, too, which she obediently does, her eyes not yet
permitted to meet yours. When she is ready, the wine hot in her
body, you tell her, "Please me." Her eyes suddenly meet yours,
for the instant defiant. Then, beneath your gaze, her eyes fall,
her lip trembles. She is terrified. She, a female, has looked into
the eyes of a dominant male. "Yes, Master," she whispers.

See that her subjugation is complete, helpless and exacting.
A slave girl must yield all to her master; she is not permitted
inhibitions or reservations. Command her; enjoy her; own her—
every beautiful, forced-to-yield, fuckable inch of her. When
she weeps "Master! I yield me! You own me! I am yours, yours,
Master!" you may permit yourself, if you wish, to be pleased
at your conquest. Perhaps you are surprised. Perhaps you had
not expected it so soon. It was, of course, sooner or later, given
your ownership of the woman, your power over her, inevitable.
She did not know that. But you knew it. With such words,
inadvertently escaped from her as she twists in the throes of
her orgasm, she puts her own stamp on her slavery, not that it
was in the least needed, either legally or humanly. It is merely
that she, as she breathes and leaps, must even herself cry out

her bondage and your mastery, rejoicing in the depths of her femaleness in her complete subjugation, her complete, deeply desired domination by an uncompromisingly triumphant male. Each woman is incomplete and partial until made whole by her surrender to a male. A slave girl cannot, regardless of her pride, withhold this surrender. It may be simply taken from her by her master. Some women learn love only in chains. They do not wish a choice; for their pride will force them to refuse; they hunger, rather, to be ravished. In the sexual sense, the slave girl is forced to be the most complete of human females; she is most at the mercy of men, her masters. Afterwards, if it pleases you, you may give the yielded, piteous slave some brief moments of tenderness. You may then, if bored or irritated with her, rise and order her body from your sight. Perhaps you command her to the kitchens, or to her kennel, where a guard will see that she is chained for the night. If you are generous, however, and fond of the slave, neither bored nor irritated, you might, as an unusual privilege, permit her to remain the night in your compartments. She might be chained at the foot of your vast couch, that of the master. Or, if you wish, you may permit her to curl up, lovingly, obediently, at your side, beneath the covers. If she should be defensive about her surrender, should dare to challenge its validity, now that the ecstatic miseries, the throes, of her orgasm have subsided, she may again, summarily, be reduced once more to bondage. This time it will take even less time. This time, when you are finished, she knows well her slavery, as she puts her head to your side, her hair about your body. Look upon her. Do you feel kindness toward her? She looks up into your eyes, her eyes shining with love, your slave. "Go to sleep," you tell her. "Yes, Master," she whispers. You look upon her again. You will grow fond of this one. She is not displeasing. But beware. You are the master. She belongs to you. Do not grow weak. In the morning you will have her beaten, to confuse her and keep her in her place. She will then, fearing you, not understanding you, struggle even more to please you. But you will not have her whipped often, for you rather care for her. Could it be that you might grow fond of a slave, a mere slave? How foolish that would be. You resolve, in all things, not to forget that she is a slave. She is only a slave. You look again upon her, tenderly. She presses her lips gently to your side, and kisses you softly, like a flower. If necessary she may be, upon occasion, put under the lash. The whip, you recall, is an excellent device for reminding a woman of her station.

And you, sweet wench, remember that in the hour of this fantasy, you are a slave, literally. For an hour *you are a slave girl*. You are one; be one. The mixture of the mental and physical is an incredible psychological alchemy. Yield as what you are; yield as you must; yield, helpless, vanquished slave! Let the irons and leads, the baser metals, of common, heavy, prosaic, unimaginative love makings be in this hour boldly transmuted into the coinage of untrammeled exoticism, into adventure's gold, into fantasy's gold, into romance's gold, as you lie, perhaps chained, upon the anvil of his lust, being formed and beaten, yielding, by the hammer of his pleasure into an ecstatic, yielded prize, more rich than rings and bracelets, and plate, the most coveted of treasure, the most sensual and delicious of properties; the conquered female, her master's yielded slave.

Try this experience, woman.

What woman is complete who has not been at least once so conquered?

32. The I-Am-a-Love-Prize-in-a-Barbaric-Lottery Fantasy.

The female is selected to be the love prize in a lottery. She belongs to the male who wins her.

Comment:

This is again a fantasy which, with elaboration, can be exquisite. The girl is selected randomly, we shall suppose, from a population of beauties, deprived of her freedom, marked and collared as a love prize, to prevent her escape in the society, and then given detailed and thorough training in the arts of giving sensuous delight to a male. Perhaps there are "prison schools" for such women, and perhaps, in a given lottery, several are used as prizes. Doubtless the lottery should be state controlled, in order that its conditions be carefully regulated. The girls, for example, must meet high standards for health.

This fantasy allows ample scope for the woman's feelings to be fully explored, perhaps when she is selected, while she is being trained, when she waits, tantalizingly clad and handcuffed, to be won, when she is delivered to the winner, when he brings her to his home, etc.

Perhaps she is won by someone she had found sexually repulsive, or unworthy of her notice, before. Perhaps she is won by a complete stranger.

If the lottery is not state controlled, perhaps the girls are entered as prizes in an "underground lottery," controlled by the underworld, in which tickets are high priced and are made available only to rich, screened buyers. Perhaps a girl visiting a foreign country, perhaps a student, is seized, either for a state or private lottery.

A type of variant here would be the woman who is seized and used as some sort of prize. Perhaps she is captured by primitive tribesmen, stripped and tied to a stake, and given to the victor in some form of contest of skill. Perhaps she is released and allowed to flee into the jungle and then, after an hour or so, she is pursued. Her captor gets to keep her, say, as a sex and hut slave. The tribe's territory, of course, is isolated, and her chances of rescue are slim. Perhaps a civilized man does find and buy her but, to her horror, rather than release her and return her to safety he keeps her in the bush as his own slave. Does he permit her clothing? Does he put a bone in her nose? What is her relation to him? Does she yield, at last, to him, as a raw, helpless, conquered, primitive woman to her master, not otherwise than as other primitive women of the village? Another variant here is the woman who is captured, say, by an important international criminal, to be given, say, on an island, to one of his lieutenants, or perhaps one of his sons. She is a "gift," a reward, to the lieutenant or son.

33. The I-Have-Been-Sold-to-Pay-My-Family's-Debts Fantasy.

The girl is sold to satisfy her family's creditors.

Comment:

Perhaps the girl is publicly auctioned. On the other hand, she might, if one wishes, pass directly into the hands of a hated creditor. Perhaps he had earlier offered to cancel the outstanding debts, if she had accepted his proposal of marriage. Now, court proceedings later, she is consigned to him. She is stripped. Her police handcuffs are removed. His are placed on her wrists. She is now his.

Perhaps, as a master, she finds him irresistible. Perhaps she now cannot help but yield herself completely to him, emotionally and helplessly his property.

34. The I-Have-Played-a-Dangerous-Game-of-Chance-Which-the-Loser-is-the-Prize Fantasy.

A rich, reckless playgirl, perhaps at a casino of the future, engages in a game of chance in which she, herself, stands as stake. She has not thought of losing. She is "out for kicks." To her horror, she loses. To her even greater horror, she is not permitted to buy her way free. She had counted on that in the unlikely event of losing. Her legal representatives can offer a thousand times the going price of a beautiful female for her, but her winner is not interested. He wants *her*. We may further suppose that there has been much rivalry between the winner and the loser, and that they have hated and despised one another. Now, to an agony of horror, she realizes she belongs to him. What will he do with her? What will be her fate?

Comment:

This fantasy can be a joy for a woman to act, for, once again, there is an enormous gamut of involved emotions and responses. It can very well begin with her in earrings and evening gown, with a roulette wheel or cards, and an entire imagined background of onlookers, gamblers, waiters, croupiers, etc.

Perhaps, when she loses she faces him, eyes flashing, demanding to know what price he wants.

He draws forth a pair of handcuffs from his tuxedo, and tosses them to an attendant. "Put her in these," he tells him.

Will he brand her?

What will he do with his beautiful slave? How will he dress her? Where will he take her?

35. The Outwitted-Female-Executive Fantasy.

The scene is a setting of future worlds and commerce. Faster-than-light space travel is, in some fashion, feasible. It is a time of great interplanetary trading empires. One such empire is controlled by a young, beautiful, brilliant, ruthless female executive. She inspires terror in her own organization and rules it with an iron hand. All humane values are sacrificed to simple profit; all decisions are indexed to this sole parameter. Using her brilliance and her lack of business scruples, in one fashion or another, legally or illegally, she drives one competitor after another to the wall, ruining them, tending to dominate and consolidate under her own command vast organizations of producers and manufacturers, commercial unions and trading fleets. There remain only some four or five alternative, smaller organizations which remain competitively viable in the face of her vast holdings. She is now attempting, of course, to corner these and drive them from the field. It appears she will be successful, and they, to escape without complete ruin, total bankruptcy, must sell out to her, rather on her own terms, which are, deliberately, economically implausible and degrading. The business meeting in which the appropriate papers are to be signed, giving her their holdings, is scheduled for a small, little-known planet. It is conveniently located, however, for such a meeting.

The meeting begins and she, much in control of matters, dominates the discussion. She makes it clear to them that they have little choice but to sign the papers. It is that or, soon, to be bankrupted. To objections as to the degrading implausibility of the terms of her response is scorn, amusement, simple power. "Business is business." She is at the pinnacle of her triumphs. When these arrangements are concluded, she will be, undisputedly, the principle governess of the commerce of the galaxy.

"Sign the papers," she commands.

"I think we have heard enough," says one of the gentlemen at the table.

They then remove her clothing.

Unknown to herself, the planet is one on which women are slaves.

Intentionally, in her briefings, she had not been informed of this. She, powerful as she is, was yet at the mercy of her organization. She looks at her male subordinates, her attorneys and her guards, and realizes that they knew of this. They are partners to the conspiracy. She was much hated. The mantle of her authorities will now be divided among them, her department heads, her executive directors. Indeed, her empire, to the relief of the galaxy, will be split into a hundred companies and organizations, restoring a competitive pluralism to interplanetary commerce.

She stands there naked, her arms held, now only a stripped woman among men.

She has only one chance.

The laws of the small planet, since she is not native to its shores, permit her to attempt to retain her freedom. If she can elude capture until midnight of the day on which her right to freedom is being tested, she will be released and returned to her own world. If she cannot elude capture until midnight of that day, she is simply enslaved. She is taken to a back gate of the great estate at which the meeting was to take place and, to her consternation, released into the brush. She knows she has until midnight of that day to prove, by the laws of the planet, whether she is fit to be free or a slave. She is young, and in perfect physical condition. She flees into the brush, a beauty, brilliant, her freedom at stake. After an hour the four or five men, young and strong, we shall suppose, her business rivals, whom she had so abused, in hunting garments, carrying ropes, leap into the brush after her. One of them, well before midnight, the strongest and most handsome, we shall suppose, captures her. Perhaps he binds her hand and foot and carries her back to the estate, like a caught deer. Perhaps he ties her hands behind her back and puts a rope on her neck and leads her back, as though a lovely animal on a tether. That night, well before midnight, she is branded and collared. She is then fingerprinted, and her prints are broadcast throughout the galaxy as those of a slave. Each planet respects the laws of others. Therefore, no matter where she goes in the galaxy, or is taken, she can be only a female slave. The new slave then, just before midnight, begins to serve the men at their feast of celebration. She brings them food and drink, which she serves to them, and dances naked for them, and, on the cushions and rugs, lays for them. The men much use her, and well. She belongs specifically, of course, to her captor. He has only, as an act of courtesy, made her available to his guests. We may suppose further that, in the arms of her captor, at least, she finds herself, to her horror and astonishment, a conquered, loving slave girl. We shall suppose, too, that this is what, subconsciously, she had always desired, to belong sweetly and fully, helplessly, to a strong, dominating, sexually magnificent male; her aggressiveness and her ruthlessness and cruelty, and her hatred of men, had been subconscious compensations for the sexual starvations and frustrations she had intellectually, as a matter of fear and pride, imposed on her body; sensing what men might do to her, and the vulnerability and yielding weakness that their touch might induce in her, she had feared and hated them; she had attempted to humiliate and degrade them; fearing sex, she had sought its common substitute, power. But matters are now no longer in her hands. She lies now, a rightless, powerless slave girl in the arms of her master, only a wench among hundreds of thousands of others also in bondage. Does she now miss her empire, with its vulgar, cruel gratifications of power? It does not matter whether she does or not. They are no longer hers to enjoy. Everything is now in new, sudden perspective for her. Such gratifications are as out of the question for her now as they would be for a frog or a rabbit. Her principal task now is to relate well to her master. If he is not pleased with her, he may even slay her. But she does not seem to miss her empire. She looks up at her master. There is a new light in her eyes. She hopes only that he will be kind to her. The gratifications of power seem trivial and remote in the face of the newly discovered, joyously accepted, emotions that now flood and dominate her. She loves him. He shakes her lovely head with his large hand and she, shamelessly, a loving slave, presses her lips to his thigh.

Comment:

A delightful fantasy, involving complex role playing, capture and enslavement, and sexual conquest.

Further, of course, there is no reason why the fantasy need stop here. Other adventures may be devised and enjoyed. The possibilities are manifold.

36. The Common-Chain Fantasy.

A man and a woman are fastened together.

Comment:

Body closeness tends to build sexual desire. If one wishes to encourage mating between a given couple, even if they do not, initially, much care for one another, one might simply handcuff them together, say, for some eight hours a day, even under the watchful eye of chaperones. They are separated during the eight hours only to be permitted to go to the bathroom. When they are finished, they are again cuffed to one another. If both are right handed, as is normally the case, the right hand of the girl is handcuffed to the left hand of the man. This restraint on her right hand makes her feel more vulnerable; and, of course, it leaves his right hand, the love hand, dangerously free. After a few hours of this the woman is almost bound to have at least a proposition from the fellow; and, if it is prolonged, for more than a week, it is not unlikely that she will be pondering a proposal of marriage. Being fastened to a woman is a very sexy experience. If a husband and wife have not made much love lately, and seem to be "growing apart," this is one way to remind him of her essential and desirable femaleness. For best results, of course, the couple must be fastened together for some hours before they permit themselves to make love, presumably still fastened together. The wait builds sexual tension and desire.

Handcuffs, of course, need not be used. Cord or rope tieing the two wrists together is also effective, and, too, permits more freedom. If the hands are separated by some two feet, it will be easier for them to work on supper together, etc. A light chain, fastened with padlocks, is also good. The chain may be of the length desired. Presumably it should not be more than some two feet in length. Chain is very sexy, probably because of the connotations of bondage and forced sex, and its hold is obdurate; one does not free oneself from a chain; thus, subconsciously, one feels oneself more a helpless prisoner; this can be sexually stimulating, particularly to the weaker partner, the female, who finds herself in a sexual situation without escape; she is at the mercy of the man to whom she is fastened. If chain is used, of course, one must be careful not to spend half one's time picking up broken glasses, swept off kitchen counters. Sweeping up shattered goblets is *not* sexually stimulating.

In bed, perhaps, for greater freedom, if one wishes, only the two ankles need be fastened together. If both partners are right handed, presumably it would be his left ankle to her right.

This arrangement, of course, can be placed in the context of a larger fantasy. Perhaps the man and the woman have been captured by aliens, and are simply fastened together as specimens. Perhaps their mating is intended. Perhaps she is a captured criminal, or spy, and he is an apprehending officer, who has unusual plans for her, or another spy, who will take her to some secret place where she can be suitably interrogated, emptied of information, and then kept as a sex slave, etc.

Who knows?

At any rate, it is a very sexy thing to be fastened to a woman.

It is not simply that there is a sweet, enforced closeness, but her movements are such that, via the link between you, you are very conscious of them; and, of course, vice-versa. The link causes you to sense her much more deeply. We tend, incidentally, to have certain body-separation distances which are observed in our culture. Normally these are violated only in emotionally heightened situations, as in combat or love. If the couple is so fastened that each is, always, on the borders of, or within, the other's space, this generates, psychologically and mechanically, a very intimate and overwhelming awareness of one another.

It is hard for a man and a woman to become intimately and overwhelmingly aware of one another, and be physically close, without becoming acutely conscious of the potentiality of, and desirability of, the other as a sexual partner. Linking the partners can thus lead them persuasively to the pleasures of sexual congress.

The Common-Chain Fantasy is a love trick, well worth playing, eyes open, on one another.

It is fun.

What man would not be likely to make love to a woman, in time, to whom he is chained or tied?

How long could he resist her beauty and his impulses? And, if she is his wife, why should he continue to resist? She is his.

Let them love one another.

37. The Blindfolded-Lovers Fantasy.

A man and a woman, blindfolded, make love.

Comment:

In making love, commonly, one wants as large a variety of stimuli available as possible, tactual, visual, olfactory, etc. In this game, however, one concentrates on nonvisual stimuli. The point of the game, of course, is to learn to sharpen the senses for the reception of nonvisual stimuli, the sound of breathing, the moving of bodies, the texture of surfaces, odors and tastes. If one makes love in this fashion once or twice, or a few times, one's awarenesses become broadened and deepened. A woman's body, for example, with its delicate, sensuous geodesics, its subtle sweetnesses to the touch, the tongue, its sounds, as it moves and breathes, vital with life and passion, its wet, hot odors of sexual heat, is a most marvelous object, quite apart from its visual beauties, and its glorious emotions and intelligence. Such a body is well worth celebrating and being aware of, and alive to. It can be thrilling, for example, to know the feel and sound of her body in orgasm, even not seeing it, to hear her breathing, to hear her cries and moans, to feel her ass and her hot, wet cunt quaking, your hands on her beauties, to sense the writhing of her legs and feet, the helplessness of her marvelous sexual surrender. This kind of experience makes you much more aware of the vulnerable, passionate glories of your female's physical reality. She is marvelous. This game helps you to understand more of her. Then, imagine the thrill of seeing her, too, the expressions on her face, the movements of her beauty! This game constitutes, in effect, an intimate course in woman appreciation. From the woman's point of view, too, of course, unable to see the man, she can become, too, undistracted by visual stimuli, much more aware of additional dimensions of sensuality.

If one wishes, of course, this sort of thing may be placed in a larger context of a fantasy. Perhaps, for example, you are slaves being mated, and the owners do not permit you the dignity of seeing the mate; perhaps they do not wish complications which might arise from your seeing one another, such as, perhaps, later recognizing one another, or, perhaps, falling in love. Perhaps the slave masters do not permit the slaves to speak to one another. The relation, to the degradation of the slaves, is reduced to that of a stud male and a breeder female. Another variant on this type of fantasy is to have only one of the partners blindfolded. This makes the blindfolded partner feel much more at the mercy of the nonblindfolded partner. This can enhance the pleasures of helplessness on the part of the blindfolded partner and enhance the pleasures of dominance on the part of the nonblindfolded partner. When a woman is "had" blindfolded, she can be in no doubt as to having been "had." Hoods, of course, rather than blindfolds, may be used. Care must be taken, of course, that there is no difficulty or impairment in breathing. A hood, tied under her chin, covering her entire head, can make a woman feel very helpless, particularly if she is naked.

38. The Unwilling-Mind-Moving Fantasy.

A woman's body, perhaps electronically, against her will, is forced to engage in intimate carnal relations.

Comment:
Imagine that you did not wish to go to the store, but, suddenly,

to your horror, your body got up, put on its hat and coat, left
the house and went to the store. You are fighting this with your
will, but the body, as though in some hypnotic phenomenon,
performed behaviorally precisely as if you wished it to do what
it was doing. Anyone watching would never guess that you did
not want your body to act as it was doing. Perhaps it even smiles
and says "Hello" to people, and acts as though nothing unusual
were going on. You, however, wild with horror, cannot control
its actions. Only you realize that it is performing these actions,
as though autonomously. You seem, your will, your mind, to be a
prisoner within yourself. Your body is now acting "on its own."

Now, suppose you are a beautiful woman. You encounter
a man to whom you are attracted, but of whom you are also
frightened. He points a device at you. It emits a tiny signal.
Suddenly your body begins to behave toward him as that of a
hopelessly enamoured female. You accompany him, helplessly, to
his room. You remove your clothing. You dance for him. When he
gestures, you swiftly leap to the bed and lie upon it, provocatively,
awaiting his caresses, holding your arms for him, your lips as
though to kiss him. He enters the bed and you, fighting from
within but unable to help yourself, make incredible love to him.
You are a terrific lay for him. You even say things to him that
scandalize and shock you. You have a fantastic orgasm.

At the end he gets up and prepares to leave. As he goes out
the door, he takes out the small electronic object, and turns off
its signal, releasing your body to your own control again. You
are horrified, naked in bed. You know you cannot charge rape
for many saw you come, lovingly and willingly, to the room.
You have been fully and completely "had." As he leaves, he lifts
the electronic object and tells you that he will see you again,
sometime.

A variant of this fantasy, which is also powerful, permits the
woman to express herself dissidently in speech, while her body,
against her will, lovingly performs. "I hate you," she weeps,
while performing with perfection an act of fellatio.

This fantasy can be an excellent one for a woman who
finds sex difficult. Her will can be as much against sex as she
pleases. It is her *body* which must act, she willing or not, as that

of a passionate woman. This fantasy permits her the luxury of theoretical repudiation of sex coupled with its most detailed and intimate behavioral consummation. She may feel any way she wants, but she must *act* as though she were a hopelessly enamored, skillful, passionate lover.

It is, of course, supposed that, eventually, a coherence develops between her acting and her feeling.

Acting like a hopelessly enamoured, skillful, passionate lover, she might suddenly discover, to her horror, that she is one. Perhaps, at the end, she can resist no longer and, with her full will, her rigidity crumbled, yields herself to him, *completely*. He looks into her eyes. She is no longer frigid. She is now his, completely. "Yes," she tells him, "I belong to you now. You have at last conquered me. You own me. I yield myself to you fully, not only in body but now, too, in mind. I love you. I love you!"

The electronic device, then, of course, is no longer needed.

She is now, truly, his hopelessly enamoured, passionate lover. We may suspect, as well, that her skills, and her scandalously uninhibited intimacy, originally electronically induced, will not desert her. They will remain an important part of the love-making of the sweet, conquered wench. That fellow, we may suppose, is one lucky electronics genius. He has got himself a great lay.

After having been made his, she became his.

39. The Safari Fantasy.

An arrogant, rich woman, a huntress, wishes to hunt and kill animals for sport. But, in the bush, she is stripped and put in a cage, for shipment to a slave market.

Comment:

This is a fantasy that is likely to appeal to animal lovers. It is also a fantasy of the "turnabout" type. The cage aspect and the shipment aspect here can be sexually stimulating. Which of us has not wanted to put an irritable beautiful woman, stripped, in a cage? Which beautiful woman, in her fantasies, has not at least once imagined herself so confined, at the mercy of a man? The

cage, I think, ideally, is a small one, which closely confines her,
so that she must sit, or crouch or kneel. It is barred all around,
or, say, at only one end? Is there enough room to rape her in the
cage? Or, must she be dragged from the cage for her rape, only
to be then thrust back in, after being had? Does the cage have,
roughly, the proportions of a bed, say, one of those old brass
beds, with bars at the foot and head? If so, she may as well be
raped in the cage. Perhaps the cage is about bed-sized, but its
ceiling is only about two feet high, so that she can only recline
within it? One interesting idea is two cages, a small holding cage
and a love cage. She may be poked with sticks from one to the
other. You are waiting to rape her in the love cage, of course,
and then she is returned, when you are finished with her, to the
holding cage. She is fed and watered as an animal, of course. Is
there straw in the cage? Must she clean it herself, or do you hose
it down from the outside? Do you speak her language? How is
the cage shipped? Is it placed on a truck, with other cages? Is it
placed on a native dhow, in the hold?[1] Is it perhaps shipped, with
other cages, by air? If so, it would be tied in place with ropes,
so that it would not slip in flight. Is she given, while passing
through civilized areas, perhaps in a van, a gag injection, which
precludes her crying out above a whisper? Or, perhaps, similarly,
she is forced into drinking a liquid which, temporarily, paralyzes
the vocal cords? In the time of shipment she has a good deal of
time to anticipate and consider her fate, to become miserable and
wild, to let the horror of her approaching slavery grow in her. In
her being transported, she becomes ever more desperate in her
attempts to win her freedom, by threats, by bribery, by plotting
escapes. But, we shall suppose, that she is, in these attempts,
unsuccessful. She arrives safely at the market, as they all do,
only another caged beauty to be processed and sold.

[1] Or is it placed on the deck, tied down, a square of canvas
thrown over its top, to shield the captive from the sun? Should
another ship approach, the cage, of course, would be placed
below decks. Perhaps then, too, the girl's hands would be bound
together, behind her back, behind two bars of the cage, and her
ankles would be crossed and tied to two of the bars opposite.

Another rope or strap, by her neck, ties her head back against the bars. Another, by the belly, looped twice, tightly, pulls her back against the bars, fastening her yet more securely in place. Are there rats in the hold? Is there water? It is dark, it stinks. She begs piteously not to be confined there. But she is a woman destined for the slave block. The men do not pay her attention. "Please," she weeps. A heavy wadding is thrust into her mouth. Rolled silk, passed twice about her face, slipped deeply between her teeth, knotted tightly behind the back of her neck, holds the wadding in place. Her eyes are wild over the gag. She squirms, helplessly. They eye her appreciatively, then depart, taking the lamp with them. She is left in the darkness. For hundreds of years women have been brought to market in such ships. A rodent darts across her naked body. She throws her head back. She is already learning what it is to be a slave, to be at the mercy of men. If the boat is boarded by officials, say, inspectors, her cage is simply covered. A small bribe is sufficient for the inspectors, who are prepared, for a gratuity, to sign whatever papers are necessary to clear the ship for port. The inspectors, of intent, given their gratuity, barely glance into the hold. She can hear them, but cannot attract their attention. She has been gagged and bound by slavers, men who are masters at the art of securing women. She is cargo, as much as a bale of tobacco or a barrel of oil. She is goods, lovely goods, a shapely female slave on her way to market.

Perhaps a millionaire playboy, whom she knows and despises, buys her, and has her sent for him to his desert palace.

There, in luxurious surroundings, far isolated from civilization, she is trained as a slave girl to serve his pleasure.

She has slain her last animal. She must now devote herself to the arts of love. She must try desperately now to be pleasing to her master.

If she does not please him she does not know what her fate will be. He owns her.

40. The Mating-Bag Fantasy.

Two Earthlings, a beautiful woman and a strong handsome man, slaves of aliens, are placed naked in a mating bag.

Comment:

Perhaps you were wondering what to do with that sleeping bag when not camping, or even when camping?

Some sleeping bags are so designed that two may be zipped together. This produces a larger bag. It is one way to get your wench in the sack.

It is fun to make love, sometimes, under confining conditions. It is a different sensuous experience.

A fantasy might or might not accompany love under such conditions. If it did, the "mating-bag fantasy" seems an obvious possibility.

We may suppose that the couple, on the alien's planet, manage an escape. He takes the female with him. After all, she is his mate.

They may have adventures, of course, attempting to survive, being pursued through the exotic flora of the alien's planet, etc. Perhaps they are again recaptured. Perhaps the alien women enjoy raping Earth men; perhaps the alien men enjoy raping Earth women, etc. The couple, we may suppose, again escape, etc.

In the mating bag, originally, they attempted not to mate; they attempted to resist one another; but they had been specially selected by the aliens' science to be mated; they were selected, like many others, out of a population of millions, because they were perfect mates, because they would be totally and irresistibly attracted to one another. If it were not for the aliens, who, of course, are interested only in breeding animals, they would never have found one another. In an orgy of shame, the man and woman, helpless under the circumstances to resist the floodtides of their instincts, have no choice but to mate. They later, however, as we recall, manage to escape.

In this fantasy, perhaps the slaves have no names. Perhaps they have only numbers. "I am female animal 672." "I am male animal 4462." In this fantasy it must be remembered that you are new, strange, fresh lovers. You have never seen one another before. Remember, too, that it is the first time you have ever touched one another. It is clearly love, and irresistible love, at first sight. It could not be otherwise. You are perfect mates. Aliens, for their purposes, not yours, have brought you together to breed. "Do not weep," he tells the woman, sheltering her in his arms. She looks up at him. "I do not understand," she whispers, "I have only seen you this instant, but I cannot help myself—I love you—I love you!"

Another variant of this type of fantasy involves having the lovers chained belly to belly. One way of doing this is to have the wrists of each, separated by an ample length of chain, chained about the body of the other. Each wears a belt, with a ring in the back, through which the other's chain passes. This keeps the lovers in proximity, facing one another, and gives them enough room to hold and touch one another.[1] In this variant, of course, their escape becomes practical only when the chains are removed. Perhaps he manages to break out of his cage later, and find her cage, and free her, too. The aliens, one supposes, keep the males and females separate except for purposes of breeding. After the female is impregnated they would separate her, we may suppose, from the stud male. They flee together, a fugitive pair of mated slaves, into the exotic flora of the alien's strange planet.

[1]*Suppose, for example, that herds of males and females were captured on the planet Earth and must now, stripped, be transported to the aliens' planets. Suppose, further, particular breedings are not required by the aliens. We might then suppose large, common holds, steel-walled, straw-strewn, dimly lit, on the cargo ships, in which the captives would be so chained, in pairs. Each hold contains numerous pairs, perhaps more than two hundred. The ships of the aliens are gigantic; they are cargo ships, for slaves; the holds, numbered, are deep, and spanned by catwalks. The ships do not enter the Earth's atmosphere, or that of their own planet, but remain in orbit, loaded and unloaded by lighters. They were even, we may suppose, built in orbit. The slaves, packed into these lighters, are brought to the cargo ships; by nets, they are lowered into the holds; the sheer steel walls of the holds are some forty feet in height; there are no floor-level doors to the holds; the nets, emptied, are removed; the human beings look upward at the catwalks, occasionally manned by guards; from the catwalks the concave water depression in the floor*

is filled when empty; similarly, food, tasteless, nutritious, in cubes,
is thrown to the slaves; they, chained, compete for it as best they
can; they must roll, using primarily their mouths; the stronger, the
swifter obtain more; sometimes the male feeds his female, mouth
to mouth, that she get enough; but the food, all things considered,
though not abundant, is ample; the aliens do not wish their slaves
to starve; occasionally, of course, randomly, a day is skipped in the
feeding, that the slaves may more effectively learn their dependence
on their masters; once, for twelve hours, the water depression was
left dry. The hours are long in the hold. There is little diversion.
This arrangement guarantees that each female will arrive on the
planet of her slavery pregnant. Perhaps the aliens keep Earthlings
in mated pairs, slave pairs, to serve them; the males may be easier
to control with a lovely female given to them as their mate (is this
not the way males are controlled on our own planet?); for example,
if he is recalcitrant, she might be taken from him, and given to
another slave; or she might be exchanged for a less desirable mate,
or he might be deprived of a female entirely. There are numerous
possibilities.

41. The Husband-as-Wife Fantasy.

The husband, for a few hours, does the wife's work, and is
treated by the wife with the casualness most men vouch-safe to
their spouses.

Comment:
    This fantasy takes a few hours, preferably a day, to enact. In
the morning the wife goes "off to work." She may, of course,
spend the day shopping, or visiting, or whatever, but she is out
of the house. Before she has left, she gives the "wife" a set of
instructions, as to what to do. If she doesn't he may not know
what to do.
    He gets her breakfast before she leaves for work, and is left
alone in the house after she leaves. She may give him, if she
wishes, a kiss as she leaves. He cleans up the dishes. During the
day he does housework. He will dust and vacuum, and perhaps
clean the stove and the bathrooms. He will do the laundry. If

they have two cars, he may do the shopping. It is not a bad idea for the wife to have him mop and wax the kitchen floor, too, as that is a nasty job it will be desirable to palm off on him. If she is not worried about him destroying garments, she might also have him do the ironing. She should give him more work than she normally has, if only to make him understand, clearly, the nature of keeping the house. It is not hard work, but it is repetitious, servile work. He should, moreover, during the day, attempt to think of the work as though it was his work, and he was to be doing it all the time. Toward late afternoon, of course, he must make supper. Further, it should be a "good" meal, requiring real imagination and effort. After all, the spouse has been busy at work all day and deserves a treat when she comes home. She has been doing the important things, and winning the bread for the two of them. When she comes home, she relaxes, perhaps reading the newspaper, while he finishes setting the table, cooking the vegetables, etc. They then eat. Afterwards he, while she reads or watches TV, finishes the dishes. She speaks very little to him. At the end of the day, he, in bed, on his back, is pressed down beneath his lover-raper. After he ejaculates, he is abandoned and she cleans up and prepares to go to sleep. She kisses him, says good-night, and turns off the light. They may then, if they wish, turn the light back on and make real love.

This fantasy can give wives a break, in permitting them a day free from the housework. For example, even when they "have a day off," they usually have to get breakfast in the morning and, often, supper in the evening. This gives them a "real" day off. It also gives her a chance to get some work out of hubby. Her day off is not, thus, followed by two days' work squashed into one the next day. More significantly, however, this fantasy gives the husband an insight into what it often is to be a woman. Hopefully, it should make him a much more tender, understanding, appreciative husband. All human realities are flawed, both those of men and women. A fantasy of this sort, however, can help the husband be much more sensitive to what is often involved in being a woman, indeed, in being his wife. In this fantasy, in the hours of its enactment, she is to treat him as the average husband treats the average wife. She is not to be cruel to him; she is just not to pay him much attention; she is just to take him, largely, for granted. And, for his part, let him learn what it is like to be expected to smile, and be pleasant, and helpful, and solicitous and ingratiating. Let him learn what it is to be expected to behave toward a male as a woman is expected to behave towards a male. The studied and careful, felt enactment of these two roles should convince both wife and husband that their marriage, whatever it might be, must not be permitted to be the average marriage which they have, in the instructive enactment of this fantasy, portrayed. Two loving human beings must not permit this uncaring, tragic routine to entrap them. They must control their marriage, not it control them.

42. The I-Am-Raped-in-Public Fantasy.

The woman, in a nightmarish situation, is pursued among crowds, which do not appear to notice her. She cannot attract attention. Even policemen do not seem to hear her, or notice her. If someone does notice her, they are not interested in listening to her or helping her. They turn away. They continue on their own business. Always the man pursues her, nearing her, following her, coming even more close. He follows her on subways, through streets, in buildings. She flees, ever more helpless, more terrified. At last, in a public place, where many people pass to and fro, he apprehends her. She is caught. She screams, she struggles, but no one seems to hear her. No one pays her attention. Perhaps this occurs in a large railroad station in a heavily populated metropolitan area, perhaps in Pennsylvania Station in New York City, near the Information Booth. She is stripped, thrown across luggage, and raped.

Comment:

Obviously the "rape" occurs in the privacy of one's own bedroom. On the other hand, the pursuit can be public. The husband can, through buildings, etc., follow his wife, before he eventually apprehends her at home. This can give the wife the female thrill of being game, and the husband the male thrill of being the hunter. She is, fleeing, walking swiftly, etc., in the crowds, unable to elude him.

In the fantasy, in its rape portion, if the lovers prefer, they may imagine not that individuals, unnoticing, pass them; but that a sizable crowd gathers, interested, perhaps amused, to watch her helpless struggles. Her forcible seduction, at the conclusion of which she yields helplessly to her rapist, a naked, conquered female, is completely public.

The analysis of this fantasy is of interest. Let us consider it in its "observing-crowd" variation. It is a rather complex one. It has an obviously cynical aspect to it, namely, the element that each of us, in important things, like facing danger, is much alone, and that human beings tend to be selfish and unconcerned for their fellows; each of us probably suspects that he can count very little on the aid of other human beings, perhaps when most he needs it; human beings on the whole are self-centered, timid, prudential organisms; if they were not, organized crime and violence would be impossible; antelope, acting together, could destroy lions, but they will not, or cannot, do so. Cynicism, of course, has its pleasures. If it did not, there would not be cynics. On the other hand, in this particular fantasy, the cynicism, as in all the best cynicism, is not actually warranted, or not fully warranted, as the cynic well knows. The situation is fantastic, and, in actuality, the woman would, in a civilized situation, be amply protected. The fantasy thus has something of the pleasure of a bad dream which, at the time of dreaming, is *known* to be a dream. It is a bit like acting a part in a play. Wouldn't it be horrible if it were happening, but you know, very well, *it is not really happening*. This sort of comprehension can produce pleasure. There is the thrill of excitement, but, too, the knowledge that there is *no real danger*. Perhaps, even, a sense of relief, that there is no actual danger, contributes its part to the pleasure. One gets the cynic's pleasure, thus, of saying, in effect, that all human beings are nasty, while knowing full well that this is not really true, not exhaustively or completely. If it were, there would be no one to tell it to. The cynic is in the strange position of telling everyone that everyone is nasty and having everyone agree with him and offending no one. There is enough truth to it to make it worth saying, and it is enough false, obviously, that no one will take it altogether seriously or be offended. But, besides the cynicism aspects of the fantasy, the entire situation, because of its unusual nature, has the stimulation of wildness, implausibility and novelty. It also has built into it a unique, almost dreamlike mode of female helplessness, being completely at the mercy of an attacker while theoretically in the midst of competent, immediately present defenders. There is a literary value of paradox and irony here. How helpless can one be? Feigned helplessness can be sexually stimulating to a female; actual helplessness, of course, would just be miserable. There is also in this fantasy, of course, aside from obvious elements like pursuit, capture and rape, the fantasy of public sex. The woman is publicly exposed as being beautiful, desirable and sexually vital. Her orgasm is induced publicly, before a crowd. She can no longer keep her sexual responsiveness a hidden secret. All the world now knows that she is an intensely vital, wildly sexually responsive female. Her extreme desirability has been publicly exhibited. This appeals to the narcissist in her, and there deserves to be narcissism in all beautiful, vital females. They are marvelous, and should be recognized as such. When her rapist leaves her, does she see, emerging from the crowd, to her horror, other men, to have her? Is she raped repeatedly throughout the night? Perhaps it is only early in the morning that she is permitted, lamely, to dress herself, pulling her torn clothes about her, and return to her apartment.

43. The Invisible-Rapist Fantasy.

An individual exploits his property of voluntary invisibility to take what women he pleases.

Comment:

Perhaps this fantasy is most powerful as a feminine masturbation fantasy. The woman struggles as though held, she is perhaps as though thrown to the bed or floor. She writhes, terrified, in the grip of an unseen assailant who then, with adept caresses and then penetration, brings her to orgasm in his arms.

Perhaps a knife blade is held across her throat, quieting her for his touch. In this fantasy, she may imagine that his actual appearance, which is concealed by invisibility from her, is whatever she pleases. On the other hand, she knows nothing of his appearance. He might be the most handsome or the most ugly man in the world. She knows only she cannot help responding to him, cannot help yielding herself to her strong, invisible lover. She may set this fantasy, of course, in a larger context. Perhaps the invisible lover follows her about sometime, during the day. She does not know when he is with her and when he is not. Perhaps, sometime, at her work, he whispers in her ear, startling and terrifying her, telling her that he will have her that evening. Perhaps sometime when she is alone, or not alone, she feels his hand at her waist, or on her breast, or leg, or throat. Perhaps sometime he kisses her at the back of the neck. She can tell no one. They would think her insane. She is helpless, victimized. She hurries home, to rush within her apartment and lock the door. But he is waiting for her. Is he within the room or not? She does not know. She never knows. She prepares her bachelor-girl supper. She begins to be confident that she is alone. She feels safe. She becomes lighthearted. She begins to sing. Then, suddenly, by unseen hands, she is gagged from behind. She is stripped, her hands are bound. She is then carried to the bed and thrown upon it. She is his for another night. He may have her much when he wishes. For example, she must fear, even in taking a shower or bath, for he might surprise her there, perhaps even taking her in the water.[1] When she retires and steps naked to her closet to reach for her nightgown, perhaps he emerges from the closet, unseen, taking her frontally in his arms and smothering her cries with his kisses. He then warns her to silence and carries her, helpless, obedient, terrified, to her own bed, where at his leisure he rapes her. After, say a month of this, perhaps the woman becomes enamoured of her strange lover. She has never seen him, but he has conquered her sexually. She begins to prepare herself for him, with gowns, cosmetics and perfumes. At last, one night, in his arms, she cries helplessly, "I love you. I love you!" He then becomes visible to her. It is, perhaps, a man whom she had hitherto ignored. She had never truly "seen him" until now. He had been, in her past life, so to speak, "invisible" to her. Now, in his arms, she finds him both marvelous and desirable. She has discovered him, and loves him. To his proposal of marriage, her eager response is "Yes, yes!" A variation here, perhaps with more appeal to the woman, is that the man turns out to be one who had, as far as she knew, ignored *her.* She had been not "seen" by him; she had been "invisible" to him. Perhaps he is an extremely desirable, first-rate male who had never, to her consternation, given a tumble. Perhaps she had envied other girls, more sleek and striking than she, more bedizened, who had dated him; perhaps she had resented them and considered herself too plain and poor for such a male. How could he ever care for such a one as she? But now she learns that he was struck with her, and fallen much in love with her long ago, but that he had taken her modesty and pride for disinterest and aloofness; he was too shy, being terribly attracted to her, even to make an advance; he had thought that she did not want anything to do with him; he had thought that she regarded herself as too good for him. In fury, then, that of the putatively spurned male, he had, with his formula or device for invisibility, decided to take a vengeance on her, seen as a cold, haughty bitch. He had decided simply, in vengeance, to make her his rape slave. He now discovers, however, to his delight and joy, that his beautiful, helpless rape slave loves him. To his proposal of marriage she, joyous, tears in her eyes, holding him, kissing him, responds "Yes, yes!" In a short time we may suppose that his beautiful rape slave becomes his loving wife. Their mutual acquaintances are surprised. The office is startled. The other girls are indignant and jealous, furious. "What does he see in her?" Only the two lovers know the whole story, the strange story. The lovers are marvelously happy together. They share their secret. Sometimes, at the eager request of the wife, for the delight of it, as before, he makes love to her under the delightful mantle of invisibility. Surely, at least, on the night before their anniversary he should do so.

[1]*No electrical appliance, incidentally, should be used in or near water. It is extremely dangerous to do so.*

44. The Slave-Girl-Exchange Fantasy.

A space ship, crewed by four men and one woman, due to instrument failure, deviates considerably from course and, eventually, months later, crashes on a small, uncharted planet, one of thousands in the galaxy. The four men are all highly educated, extremely intelligent civilized gentlemen. They all have doctorates, too, ranging from computer science to astrophysics. The woman, too, is a worthy member of this crew. She, too, is extremely intelligent and holds, say, a doctorate in mathematics or physics. Let us call her Doreen Elliot. In spite of her education and intelligence, she is something of a pain in the ass to them, for she is arrogant, sharp-tongued and given to put-downs. She uses her education and intelligence as weapons in wars the men do not fully understand and would just as soon not fight. The chip of frustration, of course, is on her shoulder. She would be much happier if the four of them would pay more male-female attention to her, for example, giving her a good raping and slap on the ass and then sending her back to her important duties. They try not to see her, of course, as a beautiful, nasty, sexually deprived female, but, as she verbally insists she be seen, rather too often, merely as a fully equal, respected, competent crew member, one of them, even another neuter component in the operational loop of the ship's system. That she happens to be a female complicates the operation of the ship, but perhaps not so much as her constant insistence that the fact is unimportant. The men would be willing to try to forget it, if only she would shut up about it. She does not shut up, of course, because, subconsciously, she wants it to be constantly on their minds. The matter is further complicated by the fact that the men, when all is said and done, are rather found of Dr. Elliot, their beautiful, bitchy colleague. Even with her nastiness, they would rather have her around than not. We may also suppose that, in accord with her program of professed, determined neutership, she wears a severe hair style and a concealing uniform, consisting of coveralls.

A week or so after the crash landing on the uncharted planet, the party is contacted by aliens, native to this new world. They are humanoid. There are five of them, four males, barbarians, and a female, an exquisite, excitingly clad creature, collared and branded, who serves them as a slave girl. The Earthlings, who are lost on this new world, are much in need of the help of the aliens. Communication, by gestures and words, is managed. The aliens visit frequently. On these occasions the beautiful alien slave girl serves all food and drink. She is beautiful and submissive, and concerned to be pleasing. The Earth men are stunned with the unexpected pleasure of being treated by a woman as though they might be important. The alien beauty is in awe of them, and only because they are men and free. She herself is only a lowly female slave. Suddenly, as never before, unusual emotions, primitive emotions, flood them. Their blood is suddenly aware, as it never was on their own world, of their masculinity. They are men! In the eyes of the girl they see that they are dominant over her. They realize, with sudden comprehension of power, never intellectually permitted them in the context of their own conditioning, that they are the dominant sex, and that any-thing else, whatever its political or economic justification, is falsehood and hypocrisy. They look at her, her beauty, the lovely slenderness of her body, her breasts, her legs and ankles, the delicacy of her head and expressions, and know that she, that beauty, with all her luscious desirability, belongs by the right of nature to the larger, coarser animal, the dominator, the man. There is immediate friction, of course, between the lovely slave and Dr. Doreen Elliot, our ill-tempered female-Ph.D. crew member in her coveralls. It is to be expected. They are two very different conceptions of female. The slave, in the presence of Dr. Elliot, feels her servitude much more cruelly. Further, Dr. Elliot, resenting the slave's obvious attractions to the male crew members, among whom to that time she has been the only female, treats her with great harshness. The slave, of course, vulnerable in her scanty garments and ornaments, must accept whatever abuse a free person, in this case Dr. Elliot, cares to heap upon her. The poor girl suffers much at the hands of our arrogant female Ph.D. On the other hand, the leader of the barbarians does not fail to recognize that Dr. Elliot, herself, in her coveralls, with her severe hair style, is also a female, and, too, a young and desirable one. He is puzzled to see the insolence and abruptness with which she treats her male colleagues. Does she not know she is a woman?

The barbarian leader suggests that an exchange take place, that he trade the lovely slave girl for Dr. Elliot. Naturally the men refuse to do this. That night, in the shell of the wrecked ship, in their makeshift camp within it, Dr. Elliot heaps scorn on the barbarians, and is much amused at their preposterous suggestion. It is as though they had asked them to trade her, a high-order, highly educated, extremely intelligent human being, one of their own crew members, a person, for a camel or some such animal. How preposterous! How delightful! The story will bear mirthful retelling when they return to Earth. The poor, simple-minded barbarians! She is, of course, also, very flattered, though it would not do to admit it. The slave girl was very beautiful. That night, alone, naked, Dr. Elliot views herself in the mirror. She is pleased. The reflection that faces her is that of a naked, statuesque, very desirable female. She regards herself as "better," even as a mere naked female, than the lovely slave girl.

In the morning, however, their camp is surrounded by hundreds of barbarians.

Clearly the barbarians wish to have the woman, if necessary by force.

Resistance is useless. The woman is to be theirs, either with or without bloodshed. The men's choice is quite simple. Either they surrender Dr. Elliot willingly or, after they are slain, she is taken by force. "Do not give me up!" she cries, for the first time in her life understanding the dependence of women on the voluntary protection of men. Her Ph.D. forgotten, she finds herself appealing to them as a woman, begging them to defend her. "Take her," says the leader of the Earth men. "She is yours."

Dr. Elliot is forced to kneel. Chains are snapped on her wrists, slave chains. She is led away, crying and screaming, a weeping, captive, terrified female.

The beautiful slave girl remains. She kisses the feet of the men and begs to serve them.

The barbarians return from time to time. It seems that on

their world women are kept as animals and slaves. It is a decision
they had made, long ago, as men. In their history women had
once been free, as on Earth, but, over centuries, they had grown
ever more unpleasant, hostile and competitive. They had made
the lives of men miserable. They had gathered wealth and power
into their hands and, through education and conditioning, were
attempting to turn males into conflict-ridden, guilt-torn inferiors.
Using claims of justice and morality, subtly perverted to their own
ends, they managed, finally, to achieve a misery-laden, unstable
political dominance. The next step was to bring about the total
enslavement of males, beginning with male children. A swift,
brutal revolution, however, took place, and it was the men who,
their patience at an end, overthrew the women, making slaves of
their beautiful would-be oppressors. They reasoned that women
would make slaves of men, if they could, but they cannot; so why
should men not make slaves of women, because they can? All
female children on the world, then, were raised to be beautiful,
and to be pleasing to men, and to be their slaves. And, of course,
they are given lengthy, detailed and exquisite training to this
end. If either the men or the women must be slaves, let it be the
women. So reasoned the natives of this strange world.

    Their barbarism, far from being a rudimentary stage in their
cultural advance then, is actually the result of a deliberate
cultural choice on the civilization's part. It is a deliberately
selected, rationally determined phase of cultural development,
superseding an era of hypothetical equality but, actual subtle
female dominance. It represents the repudiation of the social
experiment of feminism, splendid on paper but, frought with
natural consequences of misery for men. Hostile, selfish,
competitive women, hating men and attempting to degrade and
humiliate them, whatever the theories may be, do not produce
large amounts of human happiness, either for themselves or
others. On paper, feminism seemed both practical and moral,
as mankind, without artificial distinctions, joyously, hand in
hand, man and woman, marched forward to new technological
and cultural achievements. Unfortunately, love became no
more frequent under feminism than it had under democracy,
and women, as animals, proved to be quite as grasping and

self-seeking as men ever were, and so what began as a moral, humane program, with appeal to all rational minds, became in its practical development the attempt to politically manipulate males and obtain special, discriminatory privileges on the basis of female genitalia. To the men of the barbarian culture, however, the distinction between male and female did not seem an artificial distinction, but a quite natural one. The fact that one sex is smaller and weaker than the other did not seem an irrelevant consideration in the determination of which sex is to be dominant. It is not an irrelevant consideration among other animals, so why, among men, who are more intelligent than other animals, should it be irrelevant? It is, of course, natural that the smaller, weaker animals should insist on its irrelevance. The larger, stronger animals, however, must make up their own minds on the matter. Further, the men of this alien culture never subscribed to the "hollow body" theory of human beings, namely that the human being is merely a product of his environment. This is obviously false with other animals, and there seemed no reason to suppose it is true with human beings. The human mind is not a "blank tablet" on which the government or those in control of media, claiming they represent freedom, may inscribe what they wish. Verbal stimuli are insufficient to mutate the human species. The alien civilization then, the Earth men learn, has instituted as a conscious social advance, superseding an era of misery, masculine control of females. Unconditional surrender was the only alternative extended to females in this planet's "war of the sexes." Surrendered, the lovely prisoners were then reduced, if they wished to live, to total bondage. Their heads on the block, the choice of slavery or death was put to them. The beauties begged for chains. When the chains were brought, they were forced to kiss them before they were placed on their bodies. Then, chained, they were taken to be sold or distributed to males. From the point of view of the men, the imbonding of females constituted an advance, a step toward social progress, toward a more harmonious, stable, happier society. The bankruptcy of militant, manipulative feminism repudiated, masculine dominance was societally instituted. In the struggles of the sexes, the men, weary of lies and cant, impatient of propaganda, refused to

be fooled into oppression and subservience. The aliens reason
that either men or women must be dominant, if only in virtue
of group-identification phenomena, and that men and women
cannot both be dominant; accordingly they, the men, having
the power, decided that it would be they, not the women,
who would be dominant. Accordingly, sharp, exact divisions
between the sexes were instituted on the planet. This was made
possible, in part, because of the earlier abolition of the family,
one of the major victories of radical feminism, which saw the
family, in odd paranoia, as an institution designed to suppress
females. Anthropologically, of course, the family is an institution
which functions to protect the female and her young. Pseudo-
men, of course, do not need young. She sees through them. She
understands their societal function. It is to facilitate her further
oppression. As soon as, in effect, the state became the great
mother of the children, the cruel revolution of the aliens became
feasible. The islands of love and understanding, in the interests
of ideology, were systematically destroyed. Two antagonistic
opposing classes remained, each vieing to dominate and control
the limited resources of the community. This ugly situation of
male and female animals snarling at one another and snapping
for the same pieces of meat was socially and psychologically
unstable to achieve long historical persistence. The aliens
resolved the situation simply.

Men are masters; women are slaves.

The ambiguities of our civilization, for better or worse, are
thus avoided, in which conflicts for dominance, with their
attendant miseries, are endemic. Social stability, in sexual
relationships, is thus categorically, definitively achieved. If there
must be an oppressed class in any civilization, why, reasoned
the aliens, should it not be women? They are easily recognized,
desirable, beautiful and weak. Why should it not be they who
are the slaves? Men, tired of conflict, will have it so. The women
will simply be enslaved. The women in this civilization, too,
interestingly, have responded beautifully, amazingly, to their
bondage. It is almost as though they, in the lovely biological
core of them, recognized that they were not the dominant
sex, and wished their biological status as the desired, hunted,

had organism be institutionalized, thus relieving them of the stresses of ambiguity and competitiveness. To the amazement of the Earth men, they come to realize that women, under this apparently tyrannous regime, are, though superficially resentful, statistically, profoundly, gloriously happy. They love men and, as women, wish to be women, the women of such men. They find their pleasure and fulfillment in being women, not in being pseudo-men. There is no hypocrisy and pretense in their loving submission to their masters. They are simply, factually, mastered.

They do not dream of the honor of being a free person, or a wife. It is not within their ken. Further, they know why they are kept as slaves. If they were not slaves, they would try, unable to help themselves, to be masters. But, deep within them, they do not wish this. They most respond to a man who understands their true nature, and will keep them in their place. They have no respect for a man who pretends not to be dominant. He is like a lion who pretends to like vegetables, perhaps not a lion at all, surely, at least, a liar. Who does he think he is fooling? He is a man, and they are only women. They despise him for his weakness, or his hypocrisy. If they can, they will make his life miserable. They are pleased most when they lie stripped beneath his paws, held down as his desired prey, feeling his great, rough tongue on their beauty. They wish to be the doe cornered in his lair, not two cows sitting by the road, one with a penis, one without one. Women do not care for women-men. This does not mean they care for cows that pretend to act like lions. They, too, fool no one. The lion need not roar. He dominates, and loves and feeds. He is sufficient unto himself. The lair is his. He will spare the doe to serve him. She will attempt to serve him well. She might escape if she wishes, but she does not wish to do so. She is proud to be the doe of such a lion.

The Earth men make their first mistake with the lovely slave when they attempt to treat her with excessive kindness. Sensing this in them as weakness she immediately becomes petty and lazy, irritable and petulant. When the leader, putting aside his scruples, his Earth conditioning, cuffs her twice, bringing blood to her mouth, she realizes, suddenly, that these men, as much as the men of her own planet, are males, and must be obeyed. This brief administration of physical discipline works a transformation in the girl, and, thenceforward, deliciously, joyfully, she serves them. They have demonstrated their dominance over her, and their refusal to accept insubordination. She has tested them, and found them strong. Reassured, knowing now they are truly men, truly her masters, she serves them happily and marvelously as a slave girl. She has forced them to teach her the lesson she desperately wished to be taught. She only wished to find out if they were strong or not. She may have cried a bit when struck but, in her heart, later, she was pleased to find that they were strong; no slave girl wants a weak master. It degrades them. All female slaves desire strong, masculine masters. They are slaves, and wish to be treated as such. They are happiest when they know they will be lashed if they are not pleasing.

After some months, the aliens return again. This time they bring with them a new, beautiful slave girl. She wears scanty, diaphanous garments, rude, barbaric ornaments, sensual, slave cosmetics. She is, of course, Dr. Doreen Elliot, who has now been trained as a slave girl. Obediently, submissively, as the other slave girl had done, she serves them all food and drink. The Earth men are astounded. They had never realized she was so beautiful. All of them, immediately, desire to lay her. They are further startled at her submissiveness, her unquestioned, self-effacing servility. She obviously fears her masters much. Through her diaphanous garments they see that her thigh has been branded. About her throat, however, there is no collar.

The barbarian chieftain, before leaving, again proposes an exchange of women. Doreen looks at the men. pleading with them to accept her. They have, of course, in the past months, grown fond of their young alien slave. Doreen's eyes plead with them. She dares not speak, of course. The men look at one another, and understand one another. The trade is agreed upon. Before departing with his former slave, the barbarian chieftain gives the leader of the Earth men an object, wrapped in silk.

The Earth men, and Doreen, now returned to them, go into the wrecked ship, in which they have their makeshift camp. She is almost hysterically grateful at her rescue. She weeps. She is now safe. "If you only knew," she weeps, "what they made me do, what they made me learn!" The men, of course, have a very good idea of the training to which the beautiful Earth woman was subjected.

She stands there and faces them, clad in the diaphanous garments and barbaric ornaments of a slave girl.

"Bring me my coveralls," she commands them.

The men do not move.

She is suddenly startled. "Bring me my coveralls!" she demands.

The men regard one another. It is unlikely that they will ever be rescued.

"We do not need now a Ph.D. in mathematics," one of them says to her.

"What do you need?" she asks, in a whisper.

"A woman," responds the leader of the Earth men.

Doreen looks at them, shaking her head. "No," she whispers. "No!"

"Prepare to be beaten," says the leader of the Earth men.

Doreen's wrists immediately cross themselves and present themselves to him, for binding.

She looks at them with horror. She has been well trained.

"Don't beat me," she begs.

The leader of the Earth men unwraps the object, wrapped in silk, which had been given to him as a parting gift by the chieftain of the barbarians. It is a steel slave collar.

Doreen looks at him with horror.

"Kneel to be collared, Slave," orders the leader of the Earth men.

Numbly, obediently, Doreen, the female slave, kneels to be collared.

The collar snaps about her throat.

"Whose slave are you?" asks the leader of the Earth men.

Doreen looks about at them. "I am your slave," she whispers, "—Masters."

The leader of the Earth men then takes her in his arms and carries her to a room in the ship, where he places her on his bedding.

The others will, in their turn, similarly enjoy the beautiful slave.

By evening Doreen realizes that these men of Earth are in no way inferior to the mighty men of the barbarian planet. They, too, are males, and, as much as the mighty alien men, are her masters. She realizes that to them she is now no more than another slave girl, and will be forced to serve them, perfectly, or be beaten. They will not hesitate to use the lash on her if she does not please them.

She prepares supper that evening, and does it beautifully. She is, of course, their second dessert. She is, too, we may surmise, their late snack.

When late, well after midnight, Doreen is locked in her small quarters, and pulls her blanket about her, on the steel plates of the ship floor, she is not unhappy. She will try, of course, to be worthy of sharing the blankets of the men, perhaps each night being chained at the side of a different one. She no longer wants to sleep alone. She wishes to sleep next to a man, one of her masters.

When Dr. Doreen Elliot goes to sleep, she is not now unhappy.

Somewhere the barbarian chieftain, his former slave girl now again in his arms, smiles.

The leader of the Earth men lies awake. Sometime, he tells himself, the family must be reinstituted. There are women here, and, perhaps in time, other Earth women, with other parties, will arrive. The family is best, he tells himself. But the girl is not yet ready for the family. She is still learning to be a woman. "I will keep her slave," he muses. "After years as a slave she may understand better the dignity and gift of being free, bestowed upon her by men."

And the barbarian chieftain, looking at the lovely slave sleeping in his arms, too, thinks not of domination but of love. Love involves risk. Yet is it not worth what risk it might involve? He looks at the lovely woman in his arms, now only his slave. Perhaps he will free her. He loves her. He wants her to bear him a child.

Comment:

This is a rich, complex fantasy, with various roles. In particular, there are two major female roles, those of Dr. Elliot and the lovely alien slave girl, and two major male roles, those of the leader of the Earth men and the leader of the barbarians. The entire fantasy, further, is set in the context of a conflict of two cultures, both of which have their respective histories. These roles, in sequence, of course, may be played by the wife and husband. Dr. Elliot is first at the mercy of the barbarian chieftain, who doubtless teaches her swiftly and well what it is to be a female slave, perhaps even to the kiss of the whip; she is secondly at the mercy of her own crew men, and particularly at that of the leader. The leader of the Earth men, for his part, along with his fellows, learns to his pleasure what it is to be served as a master by the lovely alien slave girl. He is doubtless sexually aroused, and his vanity is pleased, to be the master of a beautiful, helpless female slave, who must serve him intimately and deliciously in all respects. He further learns, of course, that such a wench is most superb and responsive when, to her pleasure, she is subject to the strictest of masculine discipline, when she is most thoroughly and uncompromisingly mastered. Later, of course, the leader of the Earth men, and his fellows, have a new slave girl, a beautiful, exquisite one, the statuesque, enslaved Dr. Elliot. They will treat her, we may suppose, in vengeance for her former arrogance, as even more a slave than the beautiful alien slave girl, to whom she had been so cruel. And Dr. Elliot, now a conquered beauty, in orgasm in their arms, loves them for it. She acknowledges them now as her masters. She begs them now only for their touch.

Other possibilities in this fantasy, of course, are the enactment of historic roles pertinent to the transition in the barbarian civilization, from female dominance, to revolution, to female enslavement. The woman, for example, might wish to enact the role of a female executive, a female dominator, caught in the revolution. She flees, perhaps, from a male employee, or subordinate, to whom she has been, in the time of her power, peculiarly cruel and unjust. He takes her, of course, strips her, and makes her his slave. We might suppose that the women

captured during the revolution by men are given to the men who
have captured them. She learns, we may suppose, to serve her
new master well. We may further suppose that, at last, unable
to help herself, she yields herself to him, completely and utterly;
she is then no longer the proud female executive; such status is
not permitted her; she is then only a female slave, conquered,
submitted, ecstatic, in the arms of a male, his, her absolute
master.

Dr. Elliot's field, of course, need not be mathematics. If your
wife, for example, knows more about, say, physics or anthropology,
they will do quite nicely.

45. The Woman-White-Collar-Criminal Fantasy.

The scene is the future.

A brilliant, beautiful woman, a successful, white-collar
criminal, betrayed by her associates, is arraigned, tried and
convicted. Her sentence is to be sent to a public, penal brothel.
In her cell, naked, chained by the left ankle, she services anyone
who pays for her use in any way they specify. Her clientele
consists largely of common citizens who wish a lay. On the other
hand, some of her visitors are men whom she had bilked, who
are now, for her small price, permitted to take their vengeance
out of her ass. They are not too kind to her. She must serve them
well. Other visitors are her former associates, who betrayed her,
who now enjoy seeing her in this condition and enjoy fucking
her. To her shame and fury, she cannot help responding sexually
to them. The guards, of course, may have her for free. The money
made from her use goes to the state. It is used for the upkeep
of the brothel and her keep. Profits go partly to repayment of
moneys she had stolen and partly to a building fund for new
state brothels. Her upkeep, accordingly, is not a burden on the
tax payers.

Comment:

The role of the woman here is a demanding one, calling for
a range of responses and reactions. In this fantasy, as in almost
all of these fantasies, the pleasures are multiplied in proportion

to the capacity of the players to literally "become the characters involved," to feel as they feel, and react as they would react. Remember that you are, in these fantasies, *another person*, to whom these things, in their full reality, are in fact occurring. Imagine your responses and miseries, for example, to find yourself a public, state-controlled prisoner prostitute, at the mercy of anyone who can pay a small price for the use of your body. Imagine seeing a man enter your cell, whom you had defrauded of a large amount of money. Imagine your misery when he told you to kneel and suck his dick, or lie down and split your legs. And, too, imagine your misery when those who betrayed you to the police "visited" you and made you serve them, and well. And the guards, too. You would be at their mercy. Perhaps they do not feed you or they treat you harshly unless you are especially "nice" to them. Perhaps you fear and hate some of them but must, as a prisoner prostitute, serve them with perfection. And, too, perhaps most to your shame and horror, time and time again, you find yourself, as you lie in the arms of these various men, trying to resist them, clutching at them and yielding to their touch, responding to them, to their scornful amusement, with mad, helpless orgasms. You have the reputation of one of the best lays in the brothel. You are miserable. You cannot help it that a man's touch, for some reason, crazes you with sexual passion.

Another variant on this type of fantasy is to suppose that you are wrongly convicted, or framed, and yet, though innocent, are condemned to the public brothel. Perhaps the individual who framed you, whom you once spurned as a lover, now visits you regularly and makes you serve him, perfectly. As you respond to him in orgasm you beg him to again propose marriage to you, but he merely calls you a bitch, and leaves you to your chain, behind the bars.

This fantasy, unfortunately, may not be as wild as it seems.

We have state-operated and controlled off-track betting parlors in New York. Probably, twenty years ago, this would have been unthinkable. Times have changed. Currently, penal brothels are unthinkable. But, it is possible that times will continue to change. For example, today, and throughout history, it has been regarded as a right of the state to enforce labor on convicted criminals. Further, as our attitudes change toward sex and fewer people regard it as "wrong" but as an act entirely appropriate to human beings, it seems possible that forced labor for a female might well be in a sphere to which she is eminently suited. After all, the convict does not like splitting rocks, either. So, it seems, public brothels are a possibility of the future. We must become a bit more liberal than we are now, of course. Further, public brothels, medically controlled, etc., might help to contain and prevent the spread of venereal disease. Further, it seems they would be profitable to the state. One would have all the proceeds, and have to pay the girls, in effect, nothing. I do not recommend public penal brothels, regarding them as wrong. I do, however, note that with the rise of technocratic, elitist liberalism, with its concurrent disrespect for the individual and his rights, it is quite possible that they will become a reality in the future. Indeed, if they should be economically renumerative, there is great danger. What is economically desirable usually does not have to wait long for arguments to be manufactured to prove that it is also morally desirable. For example, a utilitarian argument, that such brothels would produce more happiness than unhappiness, statistically, across the population as a whole seems a natural. What is the humiliation of a few thousand lovely women compared to the pleasure of several hundred thousand worthy, tax-paying citizens? Besides, the women are criminals and deserve to be "punished." It is up to society to determine how they pay their debt. Besides, they enjoy it, etc. Sometimes it is difficult not to be irritated with human beings.

46. The Captured-Foreign-Agent Fantasy.

A lovely spy, captured, finds herself processed, to her surprise, through unusual channels. After being thoroughly interrogated, and being forced to reveal all she knows, she is drugged and crated. The crate is opened in a remote, mountain resort, a secret recreation area for agents of the power on which she had spied. There, to her horror, she is given detailed training in how to be pleasing to men. She is also, even more to her horror, taught how to cook and clean. She is used, of course, at the resort for a variety of tasks, ranging from room maid, changing linen and such, and responding to bells, to dancing girl and sex slave. Her skimpy garments, for example, her scandalously short black, white-laced "French maid" costume, do not permit her escape across the bleak, snow-swept mountains. The mountains themselves are the walls of her prison. Also, should she attempt to escape she could, doubtless, be hunted down swiftly with dogs.

Comment:

This is a "girl-in-a-trap"-style fantasy. To be well played, it should be understood as a situation in which the girl deserves whatever she gets, and perhaps more. Imagine the humiliation of a beautiful, intelligent female espionage agent, captured, forced to perform as, say, a maid and sex slave. For example, she might be forced to make the bed, perfectly, and then to remove her clothing and get in it. Afterwards, perhaps, she may be expected to again change the linen, make the bed up properly, and then leave the room, to attend to her other duties. Perhaps the guest in the room commands her to dust or vacuum the room naked, perhaps while hobbled.

Incidentally, in the enactment of this fantasy, of course, no actual drug should be used. Drugs are dangerous. Imagination is more than sufficient.[1] Similarly, presumably no "crating" actually occurs, though a cardboard box, if one is available, might be fun. At any rate, if any "crating" does occur, obviously there must be provision for the safety and oxygen of the occupant. For example, one doesn't flip crates around with a tied-up wench inside. This could be anatomically dangerous, particularly to the neck. Secondly, air holes should be more than ample. A half-suffocated or wholly blacked-out wench is not a wench having a good time. As in all fantasies, care must be taken not to injure or frighten a partner. If this sort of thing is not a type of happy play, it should not be done. There is nothing desirable about pain, fear and misery. All fantasies should be enacted only between people who respect and love one another.

[1] *Similarly, no syringe should be used. Syringes can easily become contaminated, and they are also extremely dangerous with respect to the introduction of air into the system.*

A variant on this type of fantasy is that in which the lovely spy, thinking she is to obtain secret information, accompanies a male agent to this "mysterious hotel" in the mountains, thinking to buy secrets with the pleasures of her body. She obtains no secrets, of course. Rather, any secrets which she might know herself, she is forced to reveal. The pleasures of her body, as she learns, are then completely at the disposal of her enemies. She has been lured into a trap. She has been outwitted and tricked. She has been "had."

One may continue this type of fantasy, of course. Perhaps, somehow, the girl does manage to escape. Perhaps she is pursued. Perhaps, in a foreign capital, months later, she is again apprehended, kidnapped, and returned to her duties. Perhaps she has been again apprehended by the very guest whose room she must now set about tidying.

Perhaps, after months or years, relations between the two international powers become regularized, and civilized, and she, with other prisoners, on both sides, are released. Perhaps there is, however, one "guest" with whom she would like to stay, in his own home, if only as his "maid." When they are, say, married, his friends envy him his beautiful, foreign, exotic wife. Only he and she, together, know the full story of their romance.

47. The Aristocrat-to-Slave Fantasy.

Let's put this fantasy on a distant world, one of the future, following the colonization of distant planets, those of other suns.

Certain of these planets have governments, we shall suppose, which are controlled by hereditary aristocracies. Aristocracies, particularly of a hereditary sort, which limit competitions for power to limited sets of individuals, with similar backgrounds and aims, tend to produce stable governments and well-ordered communities. Moreover, it is natural for individuals who accumulate military or economic power to wish to perpetuate this in their heirs. Thus, the successful bandit or chieftain becomes the first of a line of kings. There is no particular reason, given social engineering techniques, particularly the manipulation of communication media, why hereditary aristocracies might not be practical in a complex world. They need not be associated merely with a barbarous feudalism. It is assumed, of course, that the aristocracy is a benevolent one, which concerns itself, if only out of *noblesse oblige*, to look after the welfare of the lower orders. Certain unusually promising individuals, of course, might be, by marriage or ceremony, introduced into the aristocracy, thus freshening and strengthening the aristocracy and providing a release valve for the pressure that might otherwise be created by unusually gifted individuals of lesser birth. Further, in a complex world, there are many prestigious, lucrative positions which might be occupied by those not of noble blood. It is mainly that positions of *power* are confined to those of the blood. Presumably, of course, there would be competitive noble families. Their competitions, of course, for the most part, would leave the body politic, as a whole, tranquil. There is no basic, ultimate division between these families. For example, one of them does not advocate the abolition of aristocracy and the institution of democracy. The same people might not come out on top. Similarly, whoever did come out on top would presumably try to perpetuate their power in their heirs, and a new aristocracy might be formulated. There would only be new princes and new kings. As a matter of fact we now have something of this sort in our country. Power, in its economic form, is transmitted usually along familial lines and among limited sets of families. A child born into one of these families may be the heir to power which would have been the envy of kings of simpler ages. The "words," of course, of aristocracy, etc., are not used. The lower orders might not like them. We no longer call our kings kings. It is not to their advantage to be recognized as royalty. The aristocracy can be much more effective when diffused and concealed. There is no essential connection between aristocracy and naivety.[1]

---

[1] *Incidentally, philologically the word 'aristocracy' suggests rule by the best. Accordingly, as least semantically, there is something to be said for the notion. Most people, at least unreflectively, would respond to the question, "Do you think the best people ought to rule?"*

affirmatively. Indeed, traditional American democracy, not war-democracy or quota-democracy, might be regarded as an instrument for achieving aristocracy. The theory, of course, is that the electorate will attempt to elect the best individuals possible to govern them. For example, are we not encouraged, in a presidential contest, to vote for the "best man"? The essence of democracy is not rule by the people, which is politically impractical, but responsibility to the people. In a democracy, the electorate can change rulers and thus can exert important pressures and influences on policy decisions. (Classically, of course, democracy could mean rule by the people, in the sense that the citizens of the Greek polis could take direct votes on substantive issues. Compare, too, the New England Town Meeting. In referendums, too, of course, you have classical democracy, in which the people directly decide issues of importance. On the whole, however, modern political democracy is not rule of or by the people but, hopefully, for the people, with effective sanctions integral to the system for removing rulers who do not rule in the best interests of the people. What a fantastic thing modern democracy is! Imagine matters relevant to genuine importance and power being decided not by the knife, poison, the hand grenade and the machine gun, but by voting. What a strange, historically unusual, marvelous development. Perhaps only those with sense of history and the nature of human beings can appreciate how fragile and perhaps, tragically, evanescent a flower of rationality democracy may be. In our own country we find totalitarian governments praised by idiotic young people and a true democracy, our own, depreciated as a fascism. Perhaps, in a thousand years, after the destruction of this political achievement, coming out of generations of wars of intolerance, something like it may arise again. We may live now in the dying time of a Golden Age. People may come to look back on America as, for example, others, rightfully or wrongly, looked back on the Athens of Pericles. America did not come to be easily. Hers was not an easy birth. When she is gone, I do not think we will find her again, not in the next thousand years. The Huns are within the gates.) The word 'best', of course, is vague. Any ruling group will regard itself as the best, or the most fit to rule. Can you imagine a ruling group saying, "We are obviously the worst rulers possible, but we intend to go on ruling." Can you even imagine them thinking it? As a practical matter, of course, individuals wish to rule. They do not really care if they are the "best," in some sense or not. The most honest answer most people could give to the question, "Do you think the best people ought to rule?" would be, "Not unless they rule in my best interest." We want to be ruled in our favor. To achieve this, we would cheerfully elect the worst over the best ruler. To vote for the best man would thus, in most practical circumstances, have all the charm and rarity of a moral act. We are not concerned with the moral quality of our leaders, truly; we are only concerned with what they will do for us. Let us suppose that we had two candidates, one a gifted, moral man with a program that would make the distribution of the goods of society equitable, say, in a given instance, that the income of physicians would be reduced seventy-five percent, and his opponent is a political sharpster, well known for his chicanery, etc., who insists that the income of physicians be left to the "free market" (i.e., "pay or die"). Which candidate do you think would receive the support of the American Medical Association? One might, incidentally, distinguish between "plutocracy" and "aristocracy," but the distinction, except verbally, is not easy to draw. "Plutocracy" would be rule by the rich, and "aristocracy" rule by the best. If we define the "best" in terms of the richest, as rich people do, then the two forms of government become identical. "Best" is, of course, as noted, vague. "Best at what?" "Best in what way?" Morally superior? (Which moral code is best?) Best at governing? Best at getting votes? Best at satisfying voters? As a historical note, of course, the historical aristocracies generally were economcially powerful. There is more than an accidental connection between kings and riches. You could have poor aristocrats, but, as a whole, the aristocracy was always economically powerful. Poor relatives are sometimes not without rich families.

In the context of our fantasy, of course, let us suppose that we have an explicit aristocracy, with ranking and titles.

Let us also suppose that two or more groups of aristocratic families have been struggling for power in the state. That party which has lost the battle is then, by the victors, tried for treason.

A beauty, an Aristocrat, barefoot, in a simple one-piece prison tunic, in prisoner chains, stands before the bar of justice.

She is officially stripped of her title and her rank. She is now no longer of the aristocracy.

Court guards then, permissibly, remove her single garment.

The judge appraises her. "Your body is suitable," he muses.

He offers her the choice of execution or, if she is a natural slave, of slavery.

"What are you?"

"I am a natural slave," she whispers.

"Speak up for the court, Girl," orders the judge.

"I am a natural slave," she says, clearly. A buzz courses through the courtroom. There is shock. Her statement is entered into the transcript of the proceedings.

"It is wrong," sternly reprimands the judge, "for a natural slave to have pretended to have been an aristocrat."

"Yes," she whispers.

"Speak up," orders the judge.

"Yes," she says, clearly.

"Is it not true," he demands, "that such a miserable slave should be punished?"

"Yes," she cries.

"And is it not true that a natural slave should be legally designated as what she is, a slave?"

"Yes," she weeps.

"Do you not beg then," he asks, "to be legally enslaved?"

"Yes," she weeps.

"Yes, what?" he demands, sternly.

"Yes—Master," she whispers.

"Speak so the court can hear you," commands the judge.

"Yes—Master," she says, loudly, clearly.

"Let this slave," decrees the judge, "be officially registered as a female in bondage; let her body wear the brand of servitude; and let her throat be encircled with the collar of the state."

She looks at him, in misery.

"And then," continues the judge, "let her, after being suitably trained in the duties of a female slave, be transmitted, with other service and recreational materials, to polar outpost 7A." The gavel strikes three times.

The miserable woman, formerly an aristocrat, now only a woman criminal, convicted of treason, destined for slavery, is led from the bar of justice.

Her world has crumbled.

At the door from the court, her arm held by the hand of the bailiff, she stops, and looks back, agonized, at the judge. But he does not notice her.

His gavel strikes again. "Next case," he orders.

By the arm, the bailiff's hand upon it, the girl, naked, is led through the door from the court.

The door closes behind her. The attention of the court is now on the next case.

We may suppose, of course, that polar outpost 7A is the most remote of the civilization's facilities in the barren, frigid regions of the planet's wind-swept polar caps.

It should provide a quite suitable environment for the introduction of the girl to her new status, that of a female slave.[1]

Comment:

The balance of the fantasy may well be left to the ingenuity and imaginations of the enacting couple.

---

[1]*Behind the door we may suppose the girl is remanded into the care of matrons, who will conduct her to the chamber of enslavement. Little time is lost in such matters. By nightfall she will wear her brand and collar. In the morning her training will begin.*

The actual imprinting of the mark and locking on of the collar, of course, is done by men. It is they who, for whatever reasons, perform the actual reduction of the girl to slavery. Besides, it is said that only a man knows how to brand a woman. This may be true. The best brands, for example, are those imprinted by efficient, strong men. A study was conducted, interestingly, and it was discovered that women, sentenced to the iron, demanded, almost unanimously, in a sample of thousands, to be marked not by women, but by men. "If I must wear a brand, I want to be branded by a man," was a

*common response. A woman regarded it as an extreme insult to be
branded by another female. A woman who must be branded desires
fervently that it will be done not by a woman but by the hand of a
man. Interpret these results as you will. (Women's Libbers ascribe
the result totally to the conditioning of the unfortunate women. An
interesting case is on record where a relatively prominent member of
the Women's Liberation movement, convicted of the destruction of a
considerable amount of government property, for political reasons,
she not desiring to take it home with her, was sentenced to slavery.
At the last moment, naked, in the very branding rack, locked, seeing
the white heat of the iron approach, she begged that it be placed
into her body by a man. The magistrate granted the request, to her
hysterical relief. It is said that she has made a splendid slave. Her
number is 106-74-3781. Her current slave name is Vonda. (Slave
names change frequently. Different masters often give their girls
new names.) Her failure of nerve, at the last moment, is denied by
many members of the Women's Liberation movement, but others,
convinced by the sound-motion-picture record of the event, ascribe
the result to her succumbing to her conditioning. All members of
the Women's Liberation movement are required, legally, to see the
film.)*

They may wish, in detail, to consider the woman's reduction
to slavery, the imprinting of her body with the mark of her status,
the locking on of the state collar, her training, or, perhaps better,
concentrate on her adventures, feelings and experiences after her
arrival at the polar outpost. These are not, of course, mutually
exclusive alternatives.

This fantasy, like the preceeding one, is a "girl-in-a-trap"-
type fantasy. For example, what escape is there for her, in her
brief, light silk, that of a slave girl, standing before the thick
glass windows of the facility, looking out at the fierce, wind-
swept wastes of the polar cap? And how do the rough soldiers of
the facility take to her, a former aristocrat, now only a slave for
their use? How do they treat her? How does she feel? And does
she, to her misery, find herself responding to them, as only a
slave girl to the touch of masters? What does this do to her self-
image? Is character conflict created within her?

Perhaps in the arms of one man she comes particularly to love her collar. What does this mean?

Perhaps she whispers to him, "To you I am a natural slave girl. Every woman is the natural slave girl of some man, but most women, tragically, never encounter their master. I am more fortunate than most, for I have found him."

If the girl, in her transmittal to the arctic post, is crated, attention must be paid, as in the former fantasy, to make certain that there is no danger to her, either from the movements of the container or the lack of sufficient air. We would want her to arrive, naturally, in good condition. Similarly, too, to the preceding fantasy, if it is supposed the lovely shipment is drugged, let it be pure imagination. No actual drug or syringe is to be used. Drugs are dangerous; and, as also mentioned, syringes can easily become contaminated, and, too, are extremely dangerous with respect to the introduction of air into the system.

As in the preceding fantasy, one can always get the girl out of the trap. Perhaps, somehow, she escapes, perhaps with a man who abducts her, perhaps there is a war, perhaps there is an attack on the polar outpost by aliens, etc. Perhaps all the humans at the post are captured and taken to another planet, etc. Many plots and situations can develop intelligently within a given context of background and characters. In the end, let us suppose that the lovely former aristocrat obtains her freedom and becomes the companion of a man she has come to love. There is then, we shall suppose, a new order of society. The old regime has crumbled. They are both now citizens. Human beings may now, as not before, address themselves to the most precious of intricate and arduous tasks, that of love.

48. The Psychiatrist Fantasy.

This fantasy is laid in a world of the future, either on this one or on another planet.

Society, putatively functioning in terms of a set of humane, clinically enlightened values, is, in some respects, in theory, a Utopia. For example, criminals, etc., are regarded as ill, and consigned for treatment. Punishment is regarded as primitive and barbaric. Treatment, of course, unlike sentences of limited terms, etc., may be prolonged to any extent deemed in the best interests of the patient. Accordingly, the inmate, in his rehabilitation, or cure, or what have you, is at the mercy of the physicians in charge. These physicians, over a period of generations, through their professional organizations and the prestige of their putative science, have attained a great deal of political power. They have, in effect, set the stereotypes which will count, in their society, as normalcy. These are, of course, stereotypes largely of their own construction, which reflect their own values. What is not approved is automatically discounted as "sick," etc. For example, metaphors such as "social disease," for which there are no germs, are now, by psychological slipperiness, taken as actual illnesses, etc. Everyone has an eye on everyone else. Everyone is anxious to be "well," to conform to the current health patterns. There is little historical awareness, in any meaningful sense, as to the cultural relativity of such transitory norms. Historical awareness, so called, serves primarily to propagandize the current norms, represented as the ultimates for which mankind had been clumsily groping, until aided by developments in psychological "medicine," etc. As in almost any culture, the current norms are taken as the ideals, the ultimates. They are particularly guarded jealously by those who make their living according to them, warping, cutting and diminishing people to conform to them. Psychological testing, of course, is much advanced. For example, on the basis of such tests, individuals may be remanded for treatment, even before having committed a crime or performed an antisocial act. Individuals who object to such techniques or to this form of control are treated as "subnormals," as primitive minds, as "conservatives," as "sick," and their arguments are explained away by reference to speculations as to their motivations, rather than analyzed on their own merits. If they become a real nuisance, they are committed to sanitariums, at the discretion of the psychologists, for treatment, for cure. Everything is done in their "best interest." Horrifyingly, most of the psychologists take this thing seriously. They believe their own propaganda, which makes them serene in the prosecution of their own ends. They, believing in their "science," etc., radiate confidence and authority, which tends to intimidate others less in command of studies, experiments, statistics, etc. Experiments, of course, can be rigged, consciously or unconsciously. It is no surprise that the science of an era generally tends to support the dominant value ethos of the period. Soviet science, for example, tended to underwrite Marxism; Nazi science "proved" the superiority of Aryans; Western science "proves" the environmentalistic theses essential to melioristic political liberalism, etc. As women become more politically powerful, new experiments will be designed to "prove" whatever the currently popular theses happen to be. Counterevidence will be explained away; experiments which do not yield the proper answers (they know what they are supposed to be) will be redesigned, etc. Statistical studies will be prepared which will point to the relevant, desired political conclusions. If necessary, funds may be withheld from certain areas of science, and certainly from certain individuals. A scientist who dares to go against the dogma, the orthodoxy, of his time, will find himself in obloquy, not reappointed, his research not supported, etc. There will be enough opportunists to give those in power the sanctions, now from "science," which they find expedient. In such a world, let us suppose an uncritical, reflex liberalism has reached its majority. The world is now, for most practical purposes, a psychiatrist's Utopia. People now have, happily, enough to eat, decent shelter, etc. Beyond these things, of course, society, in the best interests of the individuals involved, is organized on the basis of aptitude tests, screening examinations, etc. Freedom, in any pluralistic sense, is now as impossible as it is currently in China or Russia. People may be, for example, assigned to positions; must have permissions to leave them; they have cards, coded into computers; everything is controlled and organized for "happiness" and "harmony." Dissidents, if necessary, are sent to security hospitals. Pharmacological companies are lucrative, dispensing tranquilizing chem-icals, etc. Recreation, hobbies, "outside interests," "sex," etc., are all organized and programmed by experts. A managerial elite of psychiatrists and psychologists benevolently controls the society. It is still a democracy, of course, only those who can vote must be psychiatrically certified, and prove themselves responsible, etc. Education, etc., is also enlisted in forming the value responses of the population. Most people, shambling about, happy, tranquilized, well adjusted, are content. The machine is in working order.

Not all psychiatrists and psychologists, of course, are fools. Some of them, particularly the more insightful and brilliant, and perhaps the less scrupulous, realize precisely what they are doing. They have a good thing going for them and they do not wish the boat to rock. It is a world which, in effect, they have built for their own power and aggrandizement. Most people do not question such a world. It might be taken as a manifestation of abnormality to do so, as a symptom of some more serious underlying disorder, which might take years to adequately treat.

Let us now suppose we have a beautiful girl, desired by some psychiatrist.

He has her remanded, committed, on the basis of tests, to a remote private hospital. She suspects nothing. She packs her bags, and takes transportation, and eventually, a cab, to the remote hospital. She "reports herself in" to the desk. She is taken upstairs in an elevator. She notes that heavy steel doors close behind her. A burly nurse guides her.

She is taken into an empty, lofty, white-washed room. There is one window. It is tall, and barred.

The nurse takes her bags and leaves her in the room.

In a few moments the nurse returns and tells her to strip herself, completely, putting the clothing, even to hair-pins, on a table in the room.

The girl complies and, in a few minutes, the nurse returns and takes the clothing.

The girl is left, stark naked, in the room. She is exquisitely beautiful.

After a time two nurses, the former one, and another, also large and strong, come into the room. They look at her. The girl is frightened. Suddenly she realizes they are Lesbians. They put her in a strait jacket. She is exposed below the navel. She is thrust through the long institutional halls, barefoot. She passes many rooms, locked. She is thrust into a hospital room, with a single bed, with crisp white sheets. There is a small bureau in the room; a tiny lavatory adjoins it. The Lesbians sit her on the bed. She is still in the strait jacket. Then, to her horror, from the bureau, they take a chain and collar, and fasten her, by the throat, to the head of the bed. They then leave her, turning off the light, locking the door, which is of steel, from the outside.

In an hour or so the psychiatrist comes to the room.

He snaps on the light.

He explains to her that the values of the society are, in large part, a constructed fraud, designed to keep an elite in power. Indeed, from his historical knowledge, he informs her that values have always been manipulated for this purpose, sometimes clumsily, overtly, and sometimes, as in the present world, subtly, covertly, brilliantly. Different establishments, in diverse political structures, have agreed in this tacit societal arrangement. There are always those who control, and those who are controlled. The pluralism and freedom of, say, the midtwentieth century made such control difficult; there were too many checks and balances; too much opportunity for individualism and difference; the triumph, however, of "liberal, humane meliorism" with its environmentalistic, enlightened social ethics, gave the putative experts in these matters, psychologists and psychiatrists, unusual power; the individual was superseded in favor of the state, guided by the opinion of these experts; the rhetoric of individualism was retained, but the fact was eroded; liberalism, a noble if naive philosophy of politics, largely the creature of aristocrats and academicians, unacquainted with the ways of men, in a prebiological century, became perverted to the ends of the new establishment. Liberalism was "taken over" to be the instrument of the new elite, the new controllers. Psychiatrists were not unaware of the power of its rhetoric; they were also, knowing men better than the liberals themselves, aware that in it lay the seeds for the most insidious and effective domination of human beings in the history of the planet. The most essential thesis of maligned, backward conservatism is perhaps that men must guard themselves, one from the other. The central thesis of liberalism is rather that such safeguards are unnecessary, or may be surrendered to a benevolent state. The conservative, fearing his own exploitativeness and cruelty, does not expect the state, made up commonly of competitive, ambitious men, perhaps much like himself, or worse, to be automatically benevolent. Why should it be? Would they not be fools to govern in the interest of others, truly? He knows that men, where possible, govern in their own best interest. This is the point of democracy, a practical politics, that it *is* in the interest of the governors to govern in the interest of the governed. If they do not, they are discarded. In the liberal state, however, the elite, highly trained, selecting its own successors, inhabiting managerial categories, tends to be invulnerable to such repudiation. Moreover, controlling education and media, they can, in effect, guarantee their continued power. Controlling education and media they control, in effect, the minds of men, particularly as long as society functions, as long as there is an adequate distribution of goods, etc. Should there be social breakdown, of course, crime, starvation, pestilence, their power might crumble. In the "Utopia," of course, there is no starvation or pestilence. Crime, too, in virtue of the effective control of the population, is considerably diminished. A thief, for example, may be assigned on medical grounds, even though evidence is insufficient to convict him, to an indefinite tour of duty on a collective farm, perhaps on a distant island. Sterilization of criminals, for their own good, to relieve them of the burdens of parental responsibility, is also common, and over a period of a generation has played an important role in reducing crime. The legal system, unable to cope with crime, found ineffective in controlling it, is replaced with a medical system, which is self-sufficient, and need not be concerned with niceties of evidence and court procedure.

The psychiatrist regards the girl lying before him on the bed.

"Is this part of my treatment?" she begs. "What's wrong with me? Why are you saying these things to me?"

"Do you wish to know why you are here?" he asks.

Chained by the neck to the bed, in the strait jacket, from the waist down nude, she looks at him. "Yes," she says, "Yes!"

"You are here," he tells her, "because I wanted you."

"You're lying!" she cries.

He puts his hand on her, intimately. "No," he tells her.

She tries to draw back, but cannot escape his hand. The collar and chain by which she is confined strikes the bars at the back of the bed.

"You have been brought here as a sex slave," he tells her.

"No!" she whispers. She cannot escape his hand. "Please, stop!" she begs.

"There are many hospitals such as these," he informs her, "Where we keep women for pleasure."

She twists her head to one side.

"You will be trained," he says, "to give exquisite pleasure to men."

"No!" she cries.

"Did you see the nurses?" he asks.

"They are Lesbians," she says.

"Yes," he says. "Do you wish me to give you to them?"

"No! No!" she cries.

She begins to writhe under his hand.

"Will you be good?" he asks.

"Yes, yes," she weeps, "I will be good!"

"You will be trained," he says, "to perform exotic dances, to serve men at their orgies."

"No," she weeps, "no!"

"I see that I must give you to the nurses," he says.

"No!" she cries. "I will be good!"

"Will you do precisely what you are told?" he asks.

"Yes," she weeps.

"Yes, what?" he asks.

"Yes—Doctor," she says.

He then, at his leisure, without removing the chain or the strait jacket, rapes her.

Later, stripped, the jacket and chain removed, responding to the proper bell, and instructions, her door automatically unlocking, she takes her cup and spoon and goes down the long hallway, barefoot, to the feeding room. She passes many doors, some of them barred. Where she is seen from within, by other captive beauties, she is jeered. One beautiful blond girl, nude, holding the bars of her hospital cell, says "Stupid bitch."

Her training begins.

She is taught many things. For example, she is taught to kiss, to grovel, to serve wine, to dance to the snapping of whips. When she is slow to learn, or not sufficiently pleasing, she is given for beating to the Lesbian nurses. She fears them much. They are, generally, her guards and jailers. They hate her and treat her cruelly, because she is feminine and beautiful. It is her greatest fear that she will be given to them sexually. They have pliers and irons.

"Yes, Doctor," is commonly on her lips.

She learns there are many women such as herself. Moreover, they are sometimes exchanged among institutions.

She knows that her freedom is gone. She is a sex slave.

At these hospitals there are also kept packs of savage police dogs and Doberman pinschers.

These are used to hunt girls who might escape.

She holds the bars of her cell, looking out.

Comment:

An interesting fantasy, which we shall hope remains far from any future reality.

We may suppose, of course, that the girl does manage, somehow, perhaps in transit between institutions, to escape. Perhaps a male, who understands her plight, and the nature of the society and the power of the "doctors," be-friends her. Perhaps he, himself, has escaped from "rehabilitation." They try to elude pursuers. They have adventures, in the strange society.

A pillowcase, incidentally, with a hole cut for the head, and a pair of man's belts, makes an effective "strait jacket."

49. The Man-as-Female-Slave-of-the-Woman-as-Male-Master Fantasy.

The man plays the role of a *female* slave, and the woman of the *male* master.

Comment:

There are four logical relations which are worth exploring in this type of fantasy.

Consider the role of the female slave first as the male wishes the role played, and, secondly, as the female feels it is ideally played. For example, the male might wish the female-slave role played as a girl who, cringing and overwhelmed, stunned, knows her master at the first sight of him, and the female, though ultimately wishing to be completely conquered, wishes it to be a real battle for him, wishing to act the role of a proud, independent girl who though entrapped helplessly in the institution of slavery nonetheless tries to retain a shred of dignity until at last it is forced from her and she yields, and totally, submitting to her master. There are no reasons, of course, why there can't be many varieties of female slave, depending on their backgrounds, etc.

Consider the role of the male master first as the male wishes the role played, and, secondly, as the female feels it is ideally played. For example, perhaps the male wishes to play it casually, insulting his wench by taking her for granted, and the female might wish it played much more dominatingly, more cruelly, more ruthlessly, paying her more attention as a helpless object to be dominated. She might wish her master to be the sort of man who takes her by the hair and throws her to his feet, scornfully, at whose feet, in terror, she is forced to kneel, head down. Perhaps only such a man, who is ruthless and powerful, uncompromising, would be strong enough to dominate *her*. There are no reasons, of course, why there can't be many varieties of male master, depending on their backgrounds, etc. Perhaps Jason takes his women casually; perhaps Haakon dominates them ruthlessly. (Similarly, perhaps Linda grovels; perhaps Melanie fights.) Similar remarks, of course, pertain to male slave and female mistress roles.

This fantasy is an excellent learning experience. Whether or not one would wish to add it to one's repertoire of sensuous adventures is up to the players. In this fantasy, the male can communicate to the woman his fantasies regarding *her* in the role of female slave and she, as she directs him in her part, can communicate to him her fantasies regarding the role. Similarly, he can communicate to her his fantasies of the master role, which she must then act, and she, in turn, can communicate to him her concept of the masculine role, which she is then playing.

The four possibilities here then are that she directs him as female and herself as male, directing both roles; that he directs himself as female and she as male, directing both roles; that she directs him as female and he directs her as male; and that he directs himself as female and she directs herself as male.

I think this sort of thing works out best, incidentally, when there is considerable discussion prior to any attempted performance. In short, both lovers speak to one another on their conception of these roles. Then, in fantasy, they can try out their ideas, get practice, etc. In this fanasy, incidentally, which is, for most purposes, one supposes, a learning fantasy, each partner is free to comment on the other's performance, and to assume the other's role to try out new variations. For example, the wife might say, "If I were a female slave, I would make the gesture as follows," and then show him; and, similarly, he might say, "This is what a master would say in those circumstances," and then tell her. Needless to say, the female will be much better in the role of slave than of master, and the male will be better, generally, as master than slave.[1] This fantasy, however, can deepen and enrich one's conception of both roles and can be a delight.

This fantasy, incidentally, can have a bonus for the woman. Most women tend to feel hostility not only once in a while for men, but also, interestingly, toward other women. Women often feel irritated toward their own sex.[2] As far as I know, men may occasionally feel hostility toward "women" but they will not feel it generally toward men. They may have male enemies, but they are not likely to feel contempt for men. Accordingly, this fantasy gives the woman a chance to dominate a "woman." Let her pick out some pretty little "nothing" thing who smiles, is pretty, wiggles and uses men to obtain special favors; then let her treat that pretty little "nothing" thing as she deserves, as the pretty little sex object she is, putting her in chains, enslaving her, whipping her, if she wishes, and then, bluntly and ruthlessly, raping her. This might also be enjoyable for her to do to some female she dislikes, her husband acting that role, she acting the role of a rough, ruthless man who makes her respond to him, and "puts her in her place."

[1] *This has to do with biology and evolution, psychology and the parameters of physical strength and size. Hormones, incidentally,*

are quite possibly of great importance here. Testosterone, for example, is clearly linked to male aggressiveness. Large bodies, stimulated by testosterone, aggressive, strong, lustful, are suitable for the bodies of masters. Smaller bodies, slight, curved and beautiful, made delicious and vulnerable by estrogens, make excellent slave bodies. When one adds to this the biological desire on the part of the female, when in heat, to yield herself to male domination, to submit to him completely, there seems little doubt as to who, in these fantasies, is the appropriate slave. It is she, the beauty, who in her heart desires to yield, to submit, and totally, to her master. Under his touch she cannot withhold her surrender; she must yield; it is her destiny. The master/slave fantasy, accordingly, presents the act of sexual congress in its most basic and searing realities. In a sense it is far from being a fantasy; in a sense it is one, perhaps, of the rare moments in which the truth is spoken. Truth need be no stranger to art; where but in art can truth be clearly spoken; in what other context could we face it? In what other context could we dare speak it so openly? In art, truth may be spoken, while we pretend to look elsewhere; it may be spoken, and we may hear it while we pretend not to listen. But too much has been said. Love women, and free them; but in the hour of their heat do not be too kind to them; when their heat is on them do not be reluctant to enslave them; they will love you for it; in their heat they wish to be held, to be dominated, to be penetrated and mastered; in each woman there is a companion and a slave. Give each, effectively and mercifully, her due. Treat the companion as a companion; treat the slave as a slave.

² This, quite possibly, does have something to do with conditioning. There are objective reasons, of course, why women might feel irritated with women; but then, too, there are objective reasons why men might feel irritated with men, and they don't; conditioning seems a likely hypothesis in such circumstances; one advantage of the Women's Liberation movement (there must be some) is that it might help women to think better of themselves; they certainly should; they are great. There might, of course, be nonenvironmentalistic explanations for this irritation of women with women. Any woman, for example, might in theory constitute a rival for a desirable male; what if the hunter of the tribe should notice the other woman; what if he should be attracted to her; is she trying to attract him, that she may attach herself to his group? The male, on the other hand, does not regard all men as potential rivals; each can hunt his own food; further, he does not expect, usually correctly any given woman to be attracted to any given man. A man might be attracted to almost any woman, but the converse is, biologically, improbable. A man, idiotically, will entrust his beloved to the attentions of his best friend; no woman would be that stupid. Men tend to trust one another; women, perhaps knowing better, do not.

There could also, of course, be a nonenvironmentalistic explanation along the lines that the woman recognizes her sex as weaker, and, in this sense, is irritated not only with it, but, perhaps more cruelly, more irrationally, with herself as well, as a member of that weaker, intimidatable group. The answer here, of course, lies in her objective acceptance of this weakness, and, when sexually aroused, in her surrendering of herself, as a woman, to her master. Resentment of the childishness, pettiness and vanity of many females, of course, would seem warranted; such childishness, pettiness and vanity, of course, might be largely the results of conditioning; there is no particular reason, as far as I can tell, why so many women should be vain, petty and childish. There are too many women who are not this way for these traits to be regarded as "feminine." On the other hand, I think it is true, for better or worse, that pettiness, childishness, and vanity in a woman can be sexually stimulating to a male; they make the female seem inferior and thus tend to augment his own ego conception (he overlooks naturally, rationally, happily, his own pettiness, childishness and vanity; they are all right) and, more importantly, tend to trigger his sexual aggressiveness. (Weakness in a woman is sexually stimulating to the male; indeed, perhaps evolution has bred certain weaknesses into women, they being more often sought as mates. Strong women make fine nurses and excellent mothers, but they are not much fun to go to bed with. The trick here, of course, is that a woman who can be strong out of bed often, in bed, her glands secreting, helplessly, becomes weak.

At this point three cheers for biology are in order. Consider them given. To make strong women weak in bed, of course, is a pleasure. To conquer her, if she is really conquered, if she is turned into a helpless, sucking, loving, whimpering, moist-eyed bitch, is a victory. Strength in women tends to vary inversely with the angle of their backbone to the perpendicular. There is no reason a woman who is strong and independent on her feet cannot in bed, in the arms of a dominant male, in the hours of love, hot and helpless, kissing, yielding, touching, be reduced to total slavery. This is one reason for putting a woman in a dog collar. It makes her clearly an object of exploitation. It makes her role clear, that of slave. Further, it generates aggressive sexual behavior on the part of the male. She is his, to be had. In bed man wishes to be dominant; no woman in a collar can be dominant. Collar the strong woman; teach her she is a female. "Why did you make me yield to you like that, as a helpless slave?" "It pleased me." "I love you.") The answer to what men tend to see in empty-headed little women is partly this: quarry. Furthermore, aggressive sexual behavior in a male tends, often, to produce, it seems biologically, submission behavior in a female. For example, she yields in your arms to your kiss. She may even, for no apparently good reason, feel a thrill of fear. Does she tremble? It is as ancient as the caves.

Consider the following three sex experiments:

1. Take your wife, stripped, standing, in your arms. Make sure that, before you do so, she is not aroused; for example, her lovely cunt is dry. And, as you kiss her, touch her. See how long it takes for her cunt to become sweet and wet. Then, at another time, repeat the experiment. This time, before you kiss her, tie her hands behind her back. (Silken cords or leather boot laces are excellent. A man's necktie is also good.) This time you will discover that she is hot and wet to you almost immediately. This time she knows she is completely in your power, that she is "captive," that you control her, that she is yours. This inspires a bit of fear in her. A woman is always frightened, somewhat, to be bound, even by a trusted lover. Can she really trust him? What will he really do with her now? This bit of fear, mixed with her helplessness (she tries vainly to free her hands), and her sense of the lover's desirability, and that he will have his way with her, produces, normally, exquisite submission behavior. She yields.

2. Make ordinary love one night, and see how long it takes for your wife to attain orgasm. On the next night, vary this only by one simple alteration. Before you begin to make love, she kneels before you and kisses your feet. Her orgasm will be attained in less time.

3. Make ordinary love one night, and see how long it takes your wife to attain orgasm. The next night, vary this only by one alteration. The wife, to herself, thinking, saying nothing, fantasizes that she is a helpless slave girl who will be forced to orgasm by an imperious master. For example, perhaps she is a new girl; perhaps she has feared all day that she would be called to his bed; perhaps he saw her in the women's quarters, naked, and she knew, seeing his eyes, that he would have her sent to him that night; now she moans to herself that she is only a woman, only a female, only his slave; she tries to fight her comprehension that he is the strongest, most attractive man she has ever seen; she tries to restrain herself; then, as she is driven into heat by his touch and kisses, she finds herself, bit by unwilling bit, being forced from climax to climax until at last, a conquered slave girl, she yields to her master, surrendering in ecstatic orgasm to his uncompromising domination. The husband then, since she will not be interested in doing so, can see at what point the orgasm was precipitated, before attending to the bringing her down with tenderness from its heights. It will have been attained in a much shorter time than the one on the preceding night.

The complementary learning fantasy to this, of course, would have the female playing her role as slave and the male his role as master, and first, she directs both roles; secondly he directs both roles; thirdly, she directs herself as slave (plays the role as she wishes) and he directs himself as master (plays the role as he wishes); and, fourthly, he directs her as slave, and she directs him as master. In most fantasies, of course, the partners will know one another so well that little direction, from anyone, will be desirable or necessary; the fantasy will have been planned; further, the roles will be "understood," researched, and allowed to unfold, under the inventive imagination of the partners. Part will be planned; part will be developed in progress. The third situation mentioned above, incidentally, where each plays the role as they individually wish, can be useful; but, in a genuine fantasy, as opposed to what is, in effect, a learning exercise, there must be congruence; the roles must, in detail, and exactly, fit one another; presumably, each makes certain concessions to the other, until a mutually satisfactory development of roles takes place. Remember that variety and experiment are desirable. Sexual fantasy is marvelous fun, and well worth some happy effort to perfect. Anyone who enjoys reading fiction or acting should take to sexual fantasy like a slave girl to chains.

Names, we remind ourselves, are important. For example, the wife, in directing the performance of the female slave, would presumably use her name, and the slave would respond, of course, to it. Female slaves usually address their owners by the title of "Master," indicating the difference of status between them. Surely no girl in bondage would dare use her master's name to address him. Such privilege is reserved for his peers. On the other hand, the master would, commonly, not address the girl as "Slave," though he might upon occasion, for example when she is new to him, or he is being cruel to her, for example, "Be silent, Slave." Normally he would use her name. This, of course, must be a slave name. A name must be found which is suitable, and sexy, to the slave. "Jane," for example, is not a good slave name. "Hura," "Mira," "Rena," "Vonda," seem pretty good. Of more familiar names, "Sandra" seems to me an excellent name for a female slave. Any name, however, which for one reason or another seems good, is good, e.g., "Elizabeth" or "Stephanie." Sometimes an aristocractic name is good, the name contrasting with the lowliness of the slave who bears it. In such a case, it might be supposed that it was the person's original name, before she was enslaved, and her master has leniently permitted her to retain it, or, more likely, has, to insult her, given it to her, but *now as a slave name*. The actual name, of course, of the wife probably should *not*, generally, be used. In these fantasies, she is, commonly, someone else. Accordingly the name should be different. If the husband is acting the female role, of course, and the wife is directing, then she should give him a name. This teaches him, of course, what his wife might regard as a good slave name, or type of slave name. Further, he must accept it. A slave has no say in the name which is given to her. Her own slave names, as she acts the female role, of course, should be mutually stimulating. It should be a name which makes her feel vulnerable and sexy; and a name which makes him feel sexually hot and aggressive. It must be a name under which she feels it delicious to submit herself as his slave; and it must be a name such that it seems exquisitely appropriate in his eyes to be the name of the helpless woman he conquers.

50. The What-Will-He-Do-with-Me? Fantasy.

A beautiful woman, stark naked, is placed in a room with a man she has never seen before. She knows nothing whatsoever about him. But she is completely at his mercy. He then does with her whatever he pleases.

Comment:

The uncertainty here can be stimulating, as well as psychologically imagining the entire situation, on the part of both partners. When she enters the room, she knows only she is at his mercy. She must obey, perfectly.

The turnabout fantasy here, of course, is for role reversal to take place, and for the man, naked, to be introduced into the room of the female, at whose mercy he is, completely. He must obey her, and perfectly. She then does with him whatever she pleases.

Variations here may be contextual. In what one might call the "Millionaire-Playboy" version, the man perhaps waits for her, sitting, in an easy chair. Perhaps he wears a tuxedo. He reads or smokes. When she enters the room, perhaps he glances up, and then returns to his reading, or he continues to smoke, regarding her. Perhaps, until he is ready for her, he tells her to kneel beside his chair, her head down, hair falling forward.[1] When he wishes, he then does with her what he wishes. (Have you ever had your wife remove your clothing with her teeth?) In another variation, what might be called the "Aggressive Lesbian" variation, she waits for him, and he enters the room. She waits perhaps in fatigues, and boots. She then does with him whatever she wishes. Presumably she hates men, and wishes to degrade and humiliate them. This is useful as a female vengeance fantasy. The husband, for example, may play the role of some male whom the wife dislikes, or who had been contemptuous of her. She then makes him pay, and a thousand times over. Other variations, of course, in context and role, may occur to the players. The important common element of the "What-Will-He-Do-With-Me-?" fantasies are that only one partner directs; the other complies. The uncertainty, particularly in the case of the woman, produces a fringe of fear. Fear in a female is not at all incompatible with her sexuality. A bit of fear, and not knowing what is to be done with her, makes her more vulnerable, more submissive. This stimulates aggressiveness in the male and facilitates the attainment of submission-orgasms in the penetrated female.

[1] *Another variation is to have her enter the room blindfolded, her hands tied behind her back. You open the door for her, "Come in, my dear." You then guide her to a place beside your chair. "Kneel here, my dear, and wait." She kneels, back on her heels, blindfolded, hands tied, head down, hair falling forward. She is exquisitely beautiful, and yours. When you remove the blindfold, who does she discover you to be? A stranger? A former lover, perhaps spurned? A ruthless leader and hero of the people, feared and desired by women, who takes those that please him as slaves? A detested enemy, whom she knows will now exact from her helpless, unwilling beauty astounding pleasures for himself, even, insolently, forcing her to share them, forcing her, against her will, to find in his arms the ecstasy of the completely dominated slave girl? She fears him, for, looking into his eyes, she knows that he can and will force her, against her present will, to fall madly in love with him. How much she will be at his mercy then, not merely his rape victim, but his sexually conquered, loving slave. When he's finished with her she knows that she will adore him, and be his slave.*

51. The Male-Livestock Fantasy.

Herds of men are kept by large, alien women, a herd to a woman, who controls them perfectly, perhaps by signals, perhaps by whips, perhaps by alien "doglike" creatures, who drive them back to their stalls at night, where they are locked in. The energy systems of the alien women are such that the function of the men with respect to them is rather as that of milch cows. In the morning and the evening they are "milked." Their semen furnishes the large women with energy. They are "milked" on their backs, with the large women kneeling across their bodies. After their morning use they are driven to the pasture, perhaps by the doglike creatures; after their evening use they are returned to their stalls, again perhaps running before the nipping, snapping jaws of the large, fierce doglike creatures.

To the women they are only animals, and are bought and sold, and bred as such.

They are naked, of course. Animals wear no clothing. A given female may mark her herd in a given fashion. Such distinguishing devices, naturally, would be officially registered.

Comment:

This is a simple fantasy, but it might be elaborated. For example, there could be interesting relations between such a member of a herd and breeder-females of his own species. Human females, by such alien women, are presumably kept for stock purposes, perhaps on special ranches. Perhaps a member of an alien woman's herd escapes with a breeder-female of his own species. Perhaps they have adventures together. Perhaps they are pursued. Perhaps they are captured, and again escape, etc. Perhaps, somehow, the alien women can be driven from the planet. Or, perhaps their own men, hunting for them, find them and carry them off in their star ships, leaving Earth once again to humans, permitting the adventure of mankind to begin once more, from the taming of fire to the reaching for stars.

A love trick that might fit in a fantasy of this sort, or, indeed, in any woman-dominant fantasy (what about male harems?) would be the smearing of, say, honey on the clitoris. The male then, one might suppose, is responding to some unusual stimulant, some substance which is not simple honey, and cannot help himself. He must continue to lick the clitoris until it is clean. The female may then, if she wishes, laughingly, scornfully, again apply the compelling, sweet stimulant to her body, and simply lie there, waiting for the irresistible effect to dominate the male, luring him helplessly to her intimate pleasure. Wherever it is placed on her body, her breasts, her clitoris, or lips, he must kiss and lick until it is gone.

Another variant of the dominant female role here is that the woman is capable of physically intimidating and abusing the male into compliance. She may, accordingly, order him to serve her in any way she pleases. His rape is the least he has to fear at her hands. It is nothing for her to hold his head, by the hair, between her legs for hours, until she is satisfied, not releasing him perhaps until she has been carried through a lengthy and indefinite series of delicious, fantastic orgasms. Then, at last, perhaps weary, she may, if it be her pleasure, rape him and order him back to his kennel for the night.

52. The Animal-Shop Fantasy.

This fantasy is laid in the period of faster-than-light space travel, galactic empires, many forms of rational life, hundreds of thousands of inhabited planets.

On a given planet we find the headquarters of an important company, manned by aliens, which specializes in what is, in effect, a display and pet industry. For example, we, rational creatures, after our fashion, are fond of such things as dogs and cats, and various forms of life, and, say, exotic flora and aquaria of tropical fish, etc. We like to have such things in our home, perhaps as one might enjoy pets or plants, or pictures or furnishings of one sort or another. We may well suppose other forms of rational life might have similar interest in such enhancements to their living. A high-order form of alien life, for example, might find it decorative for its residence to be adorned with certain forms of life, a certain form of pet, say. Perhaps some of these forms of alien life are several feet tall, or weigh in the tons, so that their physical relation to humans would be approximately that of ours to puppies and kittens.

In these great shops then, various plants and pets might be available, perhaps a terrarium of Martian lichens, tinted with purple, illuminated; perhaps a tiny ice skittler from Titan, with appropriate gases for its tank; perhaps a small, egg-laying, mammalian creature, large eared and well dispositioned, six legged, from Hephaestus II; perhaps a flowering leatherpod, in bloom, from four-ringed Dara; perhaps a large slothlike phleme from the equatorial high-lands of frozen Mina IV; perhaps, from the land regions of the temperate zones of the planet Earth, an interesting, bluish, watery planet on the borders of civilization, a young, shapely, two-legged, long-haired Earth female, skin color white, eyes blue, pelted blond.

Such specimens are caught (trapped, netted, hooded) with no more thought than the snaring of any other sort of animal, for which there is a price. The alien hunters, or human hunters, hired by aliens, are organized and efficient. Earth, a backward nation, lies much at the mercy of these depredations. The females are treated with the same efficiency and care as any other form of desired commercial animal. They are caught, rounded up, herded, stripped, kept in holding areas, fed and watered, examined as to condition and health, graded and sorted, etc. If found acceptable for return to the alien's planet, they might be branded on the ass with the company's mark; each is doubtless provided with a locked collar, perhaps with ring for leash attachment, coded to inform purchasers of her approximate age, place and time of capture, grade, health data, diet, etc. The age is estimated primarily by size, development of female contours, general appearance, dryness of hair and condition of teeth. In examining the teeth, the head is forced back and the mouth opened rudely with two hands, holding the jaws apart. This serves to open the mouth widely and, as a precautionary measure, prevents biting. Captured Earth females, on the other hand, to the interest of the hunters, almost never bite. Only one in ten thousand attempts to bite. She, of course, is promptly punished, usually by a severe whipping. She will not attempt to bite again. She has learned obedience under the lash, and well. She will now be even more eager to please than the others. The rest are too terrified. They wish only to obey and be pleasing. Earth females are prize slave stock, highly valued in the galaxy. A touch of the whip turns any one of them into a superb slave. If the female is too young or does not meet certain specifications, she is released. Only choice specimens are accepted. The company is competitive, and it is determined to maintain its reputation.

On the alien planet, and where the company maintains its outlets, the girls may be purchased, by various forms of rational life, including Earthlings. For example, one beauty might find herself purchased by a large, sluglike creature, who keeps her in his globe, as an olfactory ornament, pleased by her smells; another might be kept as a portion of a collection of interesting fauna, one among diverse specimens, used primarily as conversation pieces; another might find herself introduced into a house as a lovely pet, perhaps desired by two childless stalklike aliens; the bottoms of the doors are twenty feet high; she is taken outdoors only on a leash; perhaps others are purchased, in large groups, for scientific experiments, which the aliens would regard as immoral to inflict on individuals of their own type; such specimens are kept in heavy wired cages, with metal plates.

We are now, thousands of light years in space, on an alien world, examing such a shop. Earthlings, those rich enough and well enough placed in the commercial unions of the galaxy, may, like other rational creatures, frequent such shops. Perhaps we make a purchase. Perhaps we buy a beautiful blond, or a stunning, naked brunet. Perhaps they beg us to buy them. They do not mean much to us, of course. They are only simple women, from the primitive, backward planet, Earth, the home planet, long ago decisively superseded as a significant world in the galaxy. Or, perhaps you are a trader, with your own small ship, and have sold a cargo of furs, and are now interested in picking up a female of your own kind. You smell, you are rough; and the beauty in the cage, we shall suppose, is highly intelligent, sensitive, well-educated, a most aristocratic woman; to you, of course, she is only a stunning, naked brunet; you look at her; your eyes meet; you can tell from her gaze that she is a proud, spolled beauty, that she has never, even, been whipped; moreover you see that she has lost the initial fears of the captive girl, the terror and shock commonly attendant on their taking by the slavers; she has now regained something of her pride and insolence; perhaps she dares to tell you, "Do not look at me!"; perhaps she comes, arrogantly, to the bars and poses before you, "Do you like what you see?"; you can tell that she despises you, that she loathes you as an ill-educated boor, a ruffian; you buy her. You put her in steel animal restraints, approaching from the rear. You snap the metal device about her belly, putting your arms about her, closing it in front. Then, behind, you thrust her wrists into the attached metal claspers, snapping them shut, locking them. She glares at you in fury. You then take her in your arms, raping her lips with a kiss. You have been in space. She is the first woman you have kissed in six months. She, similarly sex starved since her capture, is visibly shaken, as a female. "I hate you!" she says. You hook your leash, a light metal one, through which the animal cannot chew, on her collar, and lead her on this tether, your purchased pet, to your ship.

The following variation might also be of interest:

She is the first woman you have kissed in six months. She, on Earth, had been an aloof, intellectual, man-hating virgin, in her late twenties, but now, in her months of captivity, stripped, collared, treated as an animal, forced, as in feeding and excreting, to become intimately aware of her body and its most basic needs, she has, in her lonliness and degradation, found herself to her horror almost constantly fantasizing herself as being possessed and penetrated by a male. She had even dreamed of being mated by her alien masters. But she was never sent to the stud cage. She is extremely attracted physically to the rough trapper (why else did she challenge him and pose before him?) but, of course, will not admit this to herself. She sees him as "beneath her," as ignorant, simple and boorish, as dirty, loathesome, contemptible, but, too, frightened, she sees him as a powerful male in whose very presence she feels, fighting the feeling, hating herself for it, weak and submissive. By your kiss she is visibly shaken, as a female. She straightens. Her eyes flash. "I hate you!" she cries. "I hate you!" You smile. You have had this experience with other women. You know this beauty will yield to you in the end, tears in her eyes, crying out to you her slavery.

"You will never tame me," she says.

You hook your leash, a light metal one, through which the animal cannot chew, on her collar, and lead her on this tether, your purchased pet, to your ship.

She knows, as she follows you, on the chain leash, that it is only a matter of time until she is tamed by her powerful master.

To herself she fantasizes yielding to you, as a helpless slave girl. She feels very receptive, very feminine, very weak. When he reaches the ship he puts his hand on her. She is already wet, loose, liquid and hot. He holds his hand before her face. "I know," she says. She turns her head away, refusing to look at him. He locks her leash to a steel step of the ship, and climbs the stairs. He is leaving her.

"Wait!" she cries.

He looks down at her.

She kneels.

"Please, Master," she says.

"What is it, Linda?" he asks.

She realizes that is now her name.

"Do not make me say it!" she begs.

He turns away.

"Please, Master!" she cries.

He looks down at her.

"I want to be fucked," she says.

He detaches the leash and sends her up the stairs before him. Inside the ship she turns, her eyes piteous, pleading, and faces him. She kneels before him, on the steel plates of the ship's floor. She looks up at him. There are tears in her eyes. "Linda begs on her knees to be fucked," she whispers, "—Master."

He touches the door switch and the two steel doors, forming the lock, slide shut, closing him inside with her.

Another variant here is that you are both animals and find yourself in the same alien household, or perhaps nearby households. You escape. You have adventures, etc.

The most delicious variation though, I think, is for you to purchase her, and then, with her, working out the human

relationships in detail, initiate a series of adventures in the
galaxy, for example as the trapper and his purchased "pet,"
the beautiful, intelligent, sensitive, aristocratic Earth girl, the
stunning, naked brunet.

Such a variation permits exquisite developments and
elaborations.

It may well be supposed that she does not soon yield to him,
though perhaps, once in a while, summarily, perhaps when drunk,
he rapes her. Even though, we suppose, she serves him from
time to time as a rape slave, she has not been truly conquered.
As a slave she knows she must expect rape. After a time, it no
longer disturbs her. She even learns to read his moods and to
anticipate when she will be raped. Aside from this she performs
her slave duties in the ship for him, washing, cooking, cleaning,
polishing his boots, and such. Their relationship becomes almost
that of a man and a wife. She talks to him, and he listens to her.
Doubtless there would be conflicts for dominance between them.
On the other hand, the trapper, rough and masculine, isolated
for months in remote regions of space, on strange worlds, where
women are scarce, will not, unlike the weak men on Earth, be
made miserable by his female.

One night he looks at her. "Why are you sitting at the table?"
he asks her.

She looks at him, angrily, and rises, stepping away from the
table.

She fingers her collar. He has never taken it from her.

"Remove your clothing and kneel," he tells her.

She does so, and kneels beside the table, naked, in the collar.

"Your ass bears a brand," he tells her.

It is the company mark, placed long ago on her, shortly after
her capture, and the decision by the company hunters that she
would be kept.

"Say your ass is branded," he commands.

"My ass is branded," she says, sullenly.

"Say, I wear a collar and my ass is branded," he says.

"I wear a collar and my ass is branded," she says.

He walks about her, regarding her. Then he sits down again.
They look at one another.

She is suddenly frightened. She realizes now that he will no longer be content with his casual rapes, but that he intends to make her a complete slave girl; he intends to conquer her.

She looks at him, defiantly, proudly.

It will be an excellent fight.

For the first time he will set about taming her, turning her into an abject, adoring love slave, not only physically but emotionally at his mercy.

"I will resist you!" she cries.

"Splendid," he says. "It will be excellent sport."

The game is on.

How will he tame her? Obviously in taming a woman he will subject her to both physical and mental coercions. Restraints can be desirable, chains, bonds and small cages. Food can be important, rewarding her when she does well, denying her when she fails to please. Uncertainty can be useful, too, keeping her off balance and unsettled. Is she to be struck or commended? When you approach her is it to strike her or to caress her clitoris? She doesn't know. She is confused, frightened. She is dependent on your whim, your mercy. You make her, further, do many small tasks, degrading and menial, for example, putting on and tieing your shoes in the morning, untieing and removing them at night with her teeth, bringing you coffee and drinks when you wish, running meaningless errands hurriedly, etc. Then you may use other psychological techniques; for example, you may have her repeat, standing, lying or kneeling naked before a mirror, being registered by a computer, "I love being his slave," "I love him to fuck me," etc. for hours a day for weeks. She is also forced to do exercises, and to pose and perform slave dances, and serve food and drink as a slave. She is made, over a period of months, to think and act completely as a slave. Somewhere in this regime, she discovers, to her horror, that she is, internally, psychologically, a slave. Her slavery has been imprinted on her unconscious. She is now a slave, a delight to her master.

Consider an example?

Does he tame her without the whip, or is she the sort of woman who cannot be tamed, except under the lash. Is her pride such that she needs the leather for its shattering? On the steel plates on his ship does she look up at him? "Don't whip me again. Caress me, Master. I am your slave."

Variations are at the wish of the players.

The woman, incidentally, may prefer to play this fantasy in such a way that she can resist even the whip. It is only, after her whipping, to his touch that at last she yields. His lips, his maleness, his hands, do to her body what the leather could not. It is in his arms, not at the whipping shackles, or elsewhere, that she learns, lovingly, her true and total slavery. This is perhaps the best variation.

Experimentation is important; mutual delight and sensuous "rightness" will mark the successful experiments. Neither partner will be in doubt as to which are the successful experiments.

Comment:

An intricate fantasy, requiring attention and characterization. This is the sort of fantasy which, from the first establishing of the female's character, as she acts "herself" in, say, shopping, conversation, relations with inferiors and superiors, dressing and undressing, etc., through her capture, processing, transportation and purchase, to her forced surrender on her master's ship, could consume several nights. Indeed, if an indefinite series of adventures is initiated, with perils, captures, etc., the fantasy could be prolonged for months. It could, for its duration, constitute a sexual fantasy life for the partners, a most pleasurable and imaginative hobby. If concluded, of course, it could then, sometime, again be initiated. Sex is one pastime in which men and women are ideally combined. It beats bridge. Fantasies, of course, can be carried on simultaneously, just as one can read new chapters in different books on different evenings, having several in process at one time.[1] On different evenings the players might have different feelings. On some evenings they might not wish sex at all. On another night the wife might say, "Tonight I feel like Linda," or, say, "Tonight, I am Vonda," etc. Perhaps one night a week is set aside for imaginative sex; and other nights, if sex is enjoyed, it is sweet, less exotic, familiar sex, loving and warm, reassuring, intimate, beautiful and marvelous.

[1]*It is not a bad idea to prepare "books" on the fantasies you develop, with notes, reminders, etc. The prototype here, though more extensive and developed, would be the "director's play book," in which the director has not only the script, but his notes, stage directions, sketches of scenery, costumes, etc. A sketch of scenery does not mean you have to build it, of course. The imagination is important. Your wife can imagine, for example, that she lies on a bed in a certain sort of room. If it is not sketched, it can be described in prose in the "book." (A loose-leaf notebook is excellent, in which pages may be entered and removed, as the fantasy is expanded and revised. Typing, too, is superior to longhand, as it is more attractive, more professional and easier for both partners to read. Punched, unruled paper is to be used. Typing looks better on such paper, and sketches may be more aesthetically included.) She, and you, can then imagine the room as actually being like the description. Entering fully and imaginatively into these fantasies is a sine qua non of success. If one cannot, from the inside out, play a role or imagine an environment, one will probably not make much sense out of imaginative sex. It would just seem, I suppose, strange or silly. If one can imagine things, it could be a discovery of a new and joyful dimension of life.*

53. The Slave-Farm Fantasy.

For many hundreds of years, men dived for pearls, often in dangerous waters. In our own century, pearl farms have been developed. Oysters are gathered, a grain of sand is inserted, which will be the nucleus of the pearl, and then they are placed in ponds, where they live until the pearl is ready, which may then be removed. The pearl farm, though it takes time to produce the first crop, is, eventually, a revolutionary advance in the pearling industry. Once the farm is functional, of course, new crops are yielded regularly; new oysters are constantly being gathered, new grains of sand being inserted, etc. The farm, once operational, and once the first crop is in, becomes a gold mine. Not only is it lucrative, but it also beats dodging sharks. Ask any pearl diver.

If we suppose a future time in the galaxy, in which we

are only one form of rational life, and perhaps not the most powerful or technologically advanced, we might also suppose a time in which the human animal, with its rudimentary rational capabilities, might have value as a slave of alien beings. Perhaps there are several differing "slave stocks" in the galaxy, of which the human is only one. If this is the case, we might then imagine an enterprising alien, one with imagination and sound business sense, establishing a series of slave farms. After the initial investment, which might be considerable, both in time and money, a slave crop would be annually yielded. How long does it take to raise a beautiful human slave, seventeen years, eighteen? Think of the control that would be possible in breeding, and also in training. Doubtless the aliens would attempt to anticipate the market and breed and trade their stocks accordingly. Perhaps they would even attempt to influence the market and manipulate it. But perhaps they sometimes make mistakes, and would be left with a crop for which there is little market, one then to be disposed of in out-of-the-way places at bottom prices. It is all possible. Suppose, for example, that the aliens, putting their tentacles and antennae together, decide that in seventeen years there will be a market for slender-ankled, beautifully figured, blond-pelted Earth females. They then breed accordingly, perhaps even attending to such details as seeing that a bit of pride and rebelliousness is bred into the crop, to make their taming and defeat more delicious to a master, alien or otherwise. Perhaps orders are placed, which are, to the best of the farm's ability, filled. For example, do they have in their current inventory a female with long black hair, to the small of her back, height approximately five feet six inches, age twenty-two to twenty-three years, high intelligence, blue eyes, bust approximately 32, waist approximately 24, hips approximately 34, vitality and health superb, extra-high female hormone index? Perhaps the farm has several hundred such specimens. One might be crated and sent out on approval, or, if the customer wishes, he may visit the farm and survey the stock personally, examining and interviewing them. Prices, he is assured, are competitive, and the merchandise, if not found satisfactory, may be returned in thirty days. Girls are seldom returned; they are anxious to please their masters. It is not pleasant to be returned to the farm. A girl who is twice returned is placed in a special lot, to be disposed of in bulk at unimportant markets for what usually amounts to chained gang labor in the shallow farel fields, under the whips of spiderlike overseers.

From these hills now one can see a portion of such a farm, in the valley. It is a breeding facility. One can make out the high, steel-wire fence from here, beyond which lies the force field, set to torture and stun, and the guards' occasional patrol vehicles. Within the fence one can see the long dormitory sheds, and the mating sheds, with their chains and mating stalls, and the commissary, and the water tanks, the food troughs, the examination, administration and medical facilities, etc. On a farm such as that are kept several thousand young, beautiful slave females, used for breeding. When they attain twenty-five years of age they are transferred to other facilities to be disposed of on the market. These women are kept as simple breeding stock, to be regularly inseminated by a selected stock of handsome, strong stud males. Perhaps, we might suppose, through the aliens' science, the reproductive cycle is considerably shortened, and, perhaps also, the maturation parameters of offspring are steepened and forced, to permit a greater yield of the slave crop. We leave this detail undecided; resolve it as you will. For certain, the aliens would prefer for the time from conception to market to be as short as possible. But we may suppose it still takes seventeen or eighteen years to ready a specimen. It does not matter.

Many of the girls at the breeding facility are bred slaves, and have known only the farms. They were among the most beautiful and servile perhaps, bred from the most beautiful and servile before them, and so on. But some of the girls at the breeding unit are captures, fresh wenches snared and hooded on Earth, to be brought here as slaves.

Our heroine is one such, a beautiful, excitingly bodied wench who has had the misfortune to fall to alien slavers. Perhaps her entire sorority was taken, the aliens striking suddenly, sealing off the entire building with a force field, surprising the girls in their sleep, quickly stripping and chaining them and taking them to their ship, to disappear again in a matter of minutes.

The other girls have been distributed elsewhere. This girl, our heroine, was selected for breeding. Unknown to her, a proud, intellectual girl, she has an abnormally high percentage of female hormones. Unknown to her, and horrifingly to her, if she knew, she is not simply a neuter person, given the identity-of-the-sexes theory then popular on Earth, but, latently, a fully *female* person, psychologically as well as physically. This terrible information was never revealed to her, in her own best interest. It might have produced depression, and neurotic attempts to overcompensate, to prove her lack of femininity. The aliens, of course, immediately determine her unusual femininity, and consign her to the breeding farms. She, biologically, latently, a true woman, requires only the proper stimulus situation to release her deliberately and painfully suppressed instincts. Sex on Earth, at this time, is unimportant. Adult minds are not supposed to consider it seriously. Some breeding takes place, but commonly to fill certain quotas, and much impregnating is by artificial insemination. The child conceived is then, often, after the first week, removed from the womb and, if desired, raised in solution. Only animals continue to bear their own young. Sex was taken as the great argument in favor of the division of the sexes. Accordingly, visionary feminists, with large male hormone indices, realized that sex must be suppressed. Their political programs as their organizations became large and powerful, became successful. Their slogan was "There is only one sex— the human sex!" This was carried by the media, reflecting the *ethos* of the dominant establishment, and programmed into the young in education. Quotas for occupations were established; jobs, paradoxically in a putatively sexless society, now began, in many cases, to specify female genitalia as a necessary condition for employment; superior qualifications, whether of a male or female, were no longer of particular importance; female certifying institutions, closed to males, were established, a diploma from which certified the female as fully qualified to fill any societal position; accordingly, there could never be question of the female's qualifications; the genitalia remained crucial.

In accord with the triumph of feminism, or "personism" as it was now called, men and women began to dress identically.

Difference in garments was now regarded as discriminatory. Masculinity in men was discouraged, and cartooned in the press. It was equated, by a brilliant, if puzzling, feminist ploy with nonmasculinity, or homosexuality. The only "true men" became those who fulfilled feminist criteria. So, too, femininity was an object of contempt. The only "true women" became those who were least female. There were only "persons." Men were encouraged to be gentle, submissive, docile, ingratiating, kind, and to smile often and be pleasant; women were encouraged, whether they felt it natural or not, to be outspoken, hostile, obnoxious, vicious and aggressive. The idea was to produce a person, something which would be a neuter compromise. Men, encouraged to imitate a foolish stereotype of woman, and women, trying to imitate a foolish stereotype of man, were supposed, by these hopefully convergent efforts, to produce in themselves a sexual nothing, the much-desired "person." Neurosis, of course, became rampant in society. Biology, dwarfed and warped by conditionings, as it may be, took its vengeance in illness, anxiety and disease. The aliens, accordingly, have little difficulty in raiding the Earth for slaves. The population of Earth is largely helpless. Masculine pursuits like defense, armament, and weaponry were abolished as immoral. Technology was turned into channels which took men's eyes from the stars, and turned them to the improvement of labor-saving devices, the beautification of parks, and the multiplication and improvement of vast public nurseries, etc., on earth. As technology deteriorated the Earth fell to the status of a tenth-rate planet, becoming, in effect, a source of slaves for more advanced, more vigorous peoples, still expanding imperialistically, adventurously, in the galaxy. The aliens are invulnerable. The feminized Earthlings lack even space travel. They managed to do little more than touch, once or twice, their own moon, and that long ago. They now, thus, for all practical purposes, lie at the mercy of stronger, more effective species.

Let us suppose that the captured Earth female, taken to the breeding farm, somehow, manages to escape, managing to pass the fence, the force field, the patrol vehicles. Perhaps, desperate, she effected her escape on the evening prior to her being chained for insemination in one of the numbered mating stalls.

In being herded, running, with some two hundred other
naked girls, her herd, to the feeding troughs, under the whips
and slave goads of the aliens, she noted a patrol vehicle, within
the fence. Lifting her face from the feeding trough, itself a
punishable offense, she notes its driver is engaged in conversation
with one of the guards. She works her way down the feeding
trough, beneath it, between the girls on either side, her herd
and another herd, and manages, crawling, to slip beneath the
vehicle; she then rests her body on the bars of its substructure.
Girls so seldom escape; no one notices her. Even her fellow slave
females do not notice her; they fear to lift their faces from the
feeding trough; the whistle has not yet blown; they do not
wish a whipping.[1] That night the vehicle goes on its patrol and,
when the alien leaves it, perhaps to chew mim weed, a mildly
intoxicating plant, she slips free and runs.

[1]*If one of them did see her, she would doubtless have shrieked
the alarm, to a guard. The slaves, utterly at the mercy of the guards,
are eager to please them. Many of them are little more than bred
properties, domesticated animals. Some of them have not even
been taught to speak. They run panting to the mating stalls, eagerly
placing their wrists and ankles in the shackles. Some of the stud
slaves are similarly bred. Most girls, however, and men, are taught
a slave version (limited vocabulary, simplified grammar, distinctive
pronounciation) of Heisa, a language important on rocky Telnaris
(Telos II) of the Telian system. In the preceding century, Telnaris
was a significant power. Heisa, one of its major languages, followed
its conquering ships. Today, following the decline of the Telnarian
hegemony, their ships departed, Heisa remains behind, a suitable*
lingua franca, *common on several systems, one of the subtle traces,
like ruins and rusted armaments, of a vanished Telnarian glory.
Slave Heisa, incidentally, is the butt of many jokes. These jokes are
usually told in dialect. One of the advantages of Heisa, it should
be noted, making it suitable as a* lingua franca, *is that most of
its sounds are feasible to a large variety of vocal and near-vocal
mechanisms. There are only a few sounds in Heisa, for example,
which are anatomically impossible for a human to imitate.*

She has not gone far. She is perhaps only to these hills, from which we now look down at the breeding facility, when the lights of the camp go on, and the sirens whine. A breeder is missing. (It is girl 187 of herd 40, series 117, camp 9, i.e., Girl 9-117-40-187. This number appears on a small metal plate, dangling, punched into her left ear lobe.) She, naked in the hills, barefoot, sees the patrol cars leaving the farm. She notes small air cars, with search-lights, lifting from the farm. She sees a pack of six-legged, howling creatures released from a van, dragging on chain leashes held by attendants.

She runs helplessly, a vulnerable female. Never before had she been so conscious of her slightness, her breasts, the width of her hips. She knows she cannot escape her hunters. She hides in brush as an air car glides swiftly overhead, its light a rapid disk scuttling across the ground. She emerges and runs again. The howling grows closer. She is exhausted. Her feet and legs are bleeding. She can run no more. She falls. Will the jaws of the beasts tear her to pieces? She struggles to her feet, stumbles on, and then falls again.

Suddenly, about her neck, a rope draws tight. The slave has been caught. She cannot cry out. She turns and looks up. It is not an alien. It is a human male. He is rough. He is an outlaw. Long ago he himself escaped from aliens. He has been living in the brush, usually far from the camp.

She looks at him, her eyes wild.

"Greetings, Slave," he says. He speaks in English.

She cannot speak.

He loosens the rope, slightly.

Mindful of her Earth training, though overjoyed that he speaks English, she knows that she must be outspoken, that she must take the initiative. He is, after all, only a man.

"I am not a slave," she says, as irritably as she can.

His hand lashes out, snapping her head viciously to one side. There is a hot, sticky smear of blood at the side of her mouth, at the side of her face and over her chin. Her lip has been split. She is bleeding. She tastes blood in her mouth. She feels it on her left breast. She looks at him with horror. She can scarcely comprehend. No man of Earth would have done that.

"Be silent, Slave," says the man.

The rope tightens, choking her, then loosens.

"Yes," she says.

"Yes, what?" he demands.

"Yes—Master," she whispers.

He holds her to the ground as another air car passes overhead.

When it passes, disappearing, low over the brush, he gags her. Then, his fist in the rope at her throat he drags her to a concealment of vegetation, in which his mount waits, a gigantic, swift, shaggy animal, which frightens her. The howling of the hunting beasts grows nearer. He binds her, hand and foot, gagged, belly up, over the saddle. Then he speeds from the concealment, making good his escape.

She has escaped from one slavery, to that of another, to that of a man.

At first he merely despises her, as any wench from the slave farms, and treats her with cruelty, keeping her "as what she is," an animal slave, making her do servile work, using her for his rude pleasures, tieing her at night to prevent her escape. Perhaps, once, during the day, she attempts to escape from him. He trails her, recaptures her, brings her back bound to his cave. There with a switch, she bound, he beats her, severely. He then throws her to her stomach and, kneeling across her body, from behind, roughly fastens a metal slave collar on her throat, his own. He then turns her on her back, and takes her. She, brutalized, intimidated, responds to him; she well realizes now that he is truly her master. He rises, stepping away from her beaten, collared, fucked body. She, the ex-sorority girl, now only a nude, collared slave girl, piteous, punished, looks up at him. She now understands, truly, that she belongs to this man. She realizes that he will take no nonsense from her; he is not weak; he is not like the soft, manipulable men of Earth; if he is displeased with her, he will simply beat her and, if it pleases him, use her. Her will has no choice, to her horror, but to break beneath his; they are mammals; she is a female; he is a male, her master. "I am your slave," she tells him, "please be kind to your slave, Master." She a woman, soft, vulnerable, beautiful, forced to submit, subdued, exhausted, breathless, from the numerous lengthy orgasms he has imperiously induced in her, lies at his feet, looking up at him, helpless, pity and vulnerability in her eyes. The ancient blood in her beautiful body leaves no doubt in her mind that she has encountered the rare, true male. Following an irresistible impulse, which she scarcely understands, before which she is helpless, she kneels before him and, hair falling about his sandals, kisses his feet. As her lips press upon his feet she understands suddenly that she is acknowledging that he is her blood master. She weeps and again and again kisses his feet. It is the only act of submission she knows. She, a woman, to her misery, her horror, and joy, has, for the first time in her life, encountered a truly dominant male. No longer does she wish to flee him. She fears now only that she might not sufficiently please him. She loves him, completely, helplessly. Gradually, in time, he softens toward her, but still he keeps her always, completely and perfectly, in her place. From time to time he uses the switch on her. Her femaleness must, from time to time, test his strength, challenge him, but, to her joy, it is never found wanting, and it is she who is always, to her joy, defeated, dominated. Gone from her now are the tensions of male/female conflict, the neuroses induced in women by weak men, neuroses which come of spiteful striving for psychological dominance over men, or for a meaningless, verbal equality, unnatural between such diverse animals, one made for bearing young and obedience, the other for hunting and mastering. As she lies in his arms she does not know whether to pity or envy unmastered women; she envies them their freedom but pities them that they have not known a man such as hers; in his arms she knows that the freedom which is theirs her master will not even think of permitting her; she envies them, in her way, but then she snuggles against her master, hoping that he will permit her to do so. He is lenient; he does. Their freedom is not hers; she herself, she knows, is a mastered woman. "I love you," she whispers, "—Master." Who has been forced to be the true woman? In his arms she knows that it is she. Womanhood is a hard lesson; she has learned it well; it can be taught only by a strong man.

She touches her collar, and kisses her master.

They have many adventures together.

Comment:
None.

EPILOGUE

Well, this has indeed been an unusual book.

It is now finished.

Doubtless to many it has been quite a shocker, or, at least, eye opener. Perhaps to others it has merely articulated principles and love games with which, in substance or nature, they were familiar. I hope that it will not scandalize so much as stimulate. There was a time, of course, when the sight of a girl's ankle might bring a blush to the matron's cheek and a bumptious sputtering to the jowls of the bewhiskered squire. Those times are gone. Girls are no longer arrested for exhibiting their knees on public beaches. The outrage at their shamelessness, of course, was real. Those were genuine motions of indignation and horror. We have become inured or accustomed to the publicity of the body, perhaps too much so. But we tend, still, to conceal the mind, the imagination. They tend to remain, still, as once did the ankles and knees of the girl, delights of dark, pleasurable hours. I do not know whether this should be proclaimed right or wrong, but it is surely irrational. Hopefully irrational things are not right. Sex is too marvelous a potentiality of the total human organism, mind and body, to be restricted by irrational value limitations to the body, as though it were primarily a matter of manipulations and hygiene, of pinches and rubbings, towels and toilets. Sex, like love and music and chess, and coin collecting and gardening, and poetry and painting, can be a source of intricate delight. All that is required is the determined intrusion of intelligence and imagination into its sphere. Let those who can break their chains, break them. Let those who cannot, keep them.

APPENDIX 1. Garments.

Pants, pants suits, etc., on a woman can be very sexy. They appeal to the homosexual in a man, and each male has certain homosexual elements. For some men, doubtless a woman in pants combines the best of two worlds. Also, of course, pants, from the woman's point of view, appeal to the Lesbian in her. Every female, of course, possesses some Lesbian inclinations. It is natural, to some extent, for a woman to occasionally feel attraction toward other women, and for a man to feel it toward another man. Indulging these inclinations, of course, is quite a different matter, one likely to lead to frustration and incompleteness. It is no accident that there are two sexes, which have been, by sexual selection, designing one another for hundreds of generations for the mutual pleasure of the other. Men have chosen attractive women, and women, to the extent permitted, have chosen attractive men. After hundreds of centuries of this sort of thing it is no wonder that human males and females are sexy, attractive creatures. Men and women are for one another; anything else is second best. Another significance of the pants suit, etc., is that it taunts the man, in a very female fashion, challenging him. It is the assumption of what, culturally, is still regarded primarily as a male prerogative. It is a tacit sexual challenge to the male to remove them from her, to make her again a female. What man does not, or would not, enjoy removing such a garment from a woman? They can be removed rudely and swiftly, of course, only if the woman is on her back. (In certain sex games, one might suppose, the woman begins them in pants; she is not, however, permitted to finish them that way.) Incidentally, it is doubtless a cultural matter that pants have been identified as a male garment and dresses as female garments. If men wore dresses and women pants, many of the same observations such as those above would retain their validity. Substantially the same challenge, for example, in a world in which dresses were primarily male clothing, would be symbolically uttered by a woman who refused to wear pants and donned a dress. In our culture, of course, the dress is predominantly a female garment. This may change, but, as of now, it is substantially true. It is perhaps worth remarking on why women have been placed in dresses. Simply because something is cultural does not mean that it is random, or might as simply have been another way. The reasons would appear to be twofold. Pants permit great freedom of movement; dresses, particularly long dresses, prohibit it. The dress is a hobbling device, which reflects the bondage of the female. It is as useful as chaining her ankles together. She cannot run. She is confined. She is captive. She is owned. The second reason is an extremely sexy one. It is, briefly, that she, at least throughout most periods of history, is not permitted protection or shielding for her genitals. Petticoats, for example, do not shield the genitals. They cover the hips and legs. Most men, throughout history, have had the exquisite knowledge that, beneath those long dresses, the genitals of those gracious beauties were exposed, even those of a queen. The hand can easily creep up an ankle; it can knife up a dress; a dress can be, simply and aesthetically, lifted and thrown back. The dress, historically, is a tantalizing garment. It also makes the woman more available. The current miniskirt, incidentally, is a marvelous garment symbolically. Long may it wave! First it incorporates a clear rejection of the role of woman as hobbled prisoner. The miniskirt permits great freedom. Secondly, it exhibits an admirable pagan acceptance and pride of a girl in her body. In this sense it is very healthy and very feminine. She is female, and she shamelessly and joyously exhibits her beauty. Thirdly, it is a tantalizing garment, because it suggests the openness of her, her availability, the ease with which a male hand is invited to touch her. It says she is beautiful and sexy, and wants to be a good lay. In the light of such considerations the panties or pantyhose commonly worn under such a garment are almost irrelevant. The one difficulty

with the miniskirt is that it, like other skirts, does not exhibit
the sweetness of her ass as well as it might. This difficulty is
remedied, of course, by levis, bikinis, and such. Women must
understand, it seems, that their asses, like the rest of them, are
very attractive to men. The flanks of a filly drive stallions wild.

It is interesting that, throughout many periods of history,
women would have been ashamed not to wear dresses; this is
an indication of how social pressures can be effective in the self-
subjugation of human beings; it is rather as if a woman should
be raised in such a way as to be ashamed if she did not wear
her ankle chains; she might, of course, compete with other
women, to see that her ankle chains were prettier than theirs; it
is interesting that women put up with dresses for so many years,
long, hobbling dresses; perhaps this is some evidence of their
masochism; today, however, whatever may be the case with their
natural masochisms, or those of men, it is glorious to note that
women are becoming more inventive, more complex, prouder,
perhaps even more beautiful creatures. The dress, today, however,
seems to remain a masochistic garment, an invitation to men to
sexually subjugate them, if only for the hour, but it is mixed
today with other elements as well, elements of freedom and self-
assertiveness, and self-pride; this can only be good; on the other
hand, the dress remains a symbolic declaration by woman that
she is determined to remain vulnerable quarry, masochistically
the object of the male's hunt. It is her nature to be hunted, and
she knows it, and loves it. She wishes to be pursued, and then
caught and, by the man of her choice, and no other, raped. That
is something important the husband in imaginative sex has
working for him. He is, presumably, hopefully, the man of her
choice, or at least one of the men of her choice. By him she is
willing, perhaps eager, to be raped.

A word is perhaps in order here on the subject of the return
of the long, ankle-length dress. We note, incidentally, it has not
"caught on" with women at large. But, with those women who
are attracted to it, what might be their motivations? Presumably
it is not simply a mindless reflex response to fashion dictates.
The women who wear them are presumably no more simplistic
than those who do not. Similarly, although there is a theory that

men are more interested in what they cannot see than in what they can see (a theory perhaps invented by a sexually nervous woman with bad legs or a distracted homosexual dress designer attempting to justify fashion change), it seems probable that the reasons lie elsewhere. For example, if it were really true that men were more interested in what they could not see than in what they could see, one supposes they would go about wearing blinkers and sunglasses, or else that the girls, catching on, would bundle themselves up in large black sacks with periscopes. This is not the case, of course. Men can, and do, like long, lovely dresses on girls, but this is not so much because it conceals the girl from them as it is because it enhances her loveliness. Girls can be beautiful so adorned. The advantage of the dress is not that it conceals an ankle, thus driving a male mad with curiosity, but that it makes her appear beautiful. Evening dresses, for example, are often beautiful. No one claims they are attractive because they conceal girls. They are attractive because they look beautiful on them.

That a long dress could make a girl look beautiful is surely a sufficient justification for her desiring to wear it. We might ask ourselves, however, if there may not be additional reasons why a girl might care for such a dress. I suspect there may be two. We live in a rushy, litter-strewn, chrome-plated world. In this world there seems little time for leisure, paying attention to one another and love. The longer dress speaks of a more refined, slower time, a time of gentleness, of romance, of pressed flowers, of speaking tenderly to one another. It is not reprehensible, then, for a girl to make, by means of a garment, a plea for these values. It is interesting, in this respect, to note that the girl who owns such a dress or dresses, usually also owns several miniskirts. Consistency is no more to be required of women than men. We all, from day to day, from time to time, have different moods and desire different things. The long dress also, it seems to me, has its lovely masochistic aspects. They may be reasonably clear by now. It identifies the girl, symbolically, with the women of an earlier time, when women were shackled as ladies, and were, in effect, the love prisoners of their husbands. It says, in effect, see, I am as they were. I, too, am a captive. I, too, cannot move freely.

I accept the confinements of the role of lady. You will give me no alternative to do otherwise. You make me like this! Yes, I am now vulnerable. I am now as they were. I am now pretty; I am now helpless; I am now trivial; I am now a charming sex object. What are you going to do with me now? I know. You are going to treat me as such a woman. You are going to send me to the bedroom and teach me what it was to be such a woman. You are going to dare to use me as such a woman! On the other hand, it is well to remember that this same girl probably owns two dozen miniskirts. She is attracted to many roles. Woman is superb. She requires and deserves a man who can give her a hundred lives, a thousand personalities. She is fortunate indeed if she finds a man who can understand, and satisfy and love the many of her.

APPENDIX 2. Ties

There are hundreds of ways to tie women. Many are obvious. It is interesting that the sight of a naked, bound woman is extremely sexually provocative to a male. This probably has to do with evolution, with capture and rape, etc. Every man, from time to time, fantasizes complete power over a woman. In his blood he wants it. This doubtless goes back to the caves. Those who were less possessive, less commanding and lustful failed, in large numbers, to propagate their kind. Any man who senses the sexuality of the bound, naked woman is responding to the heritage of the hunter and captor. If such thoughts are not "sexy" to him, he is a very unusual male. Indeed, such males may not exist. It is important for a woman, too, to realize that there is a predator in any male. This either worries her or scandalizes her, or stimulates her sexually. Perhaps it does all three. In female sexual fantasy, of course, she commonly fantasizes herself as the helpless object of such predation. We are not the only ones who date back to primeval hunting packs. It might be useful for a woman to understand not only that her body is stimulating to a male, but her body in certain contexts, attitudes and postures. I do not know whether she will like this or not, but her body lying naked and bound at his feet is often several hundred percent more sexually exciting to him than it is in her tweed suit critically examining pictures at the Museum of Modern Art. (It is exciting there, too, of course, particularly if she seems to know what she is doing. Intelligence is extremely sexy in a woman. Stupid women are bores, not worth the trouble of capturing. Imagine a highly intelligent woman lying naked and bound at your feet, like any other slave. (What a prize!) Even something like a rope tied about her ankle and knotted in bed can be sexually stimulating. The reasons for this seem fairly obvious. They suggest the female as captive, as being in the male's power. This, for better or worse, but as a fact, is extremely provocative, sexually, to most males. In their heat, they commonly wish to own their women, to literally possess them. When one speaks of "having" a woman there is a symbolic undertone here that is more honest than, say, "engaging in intercourse" with her. A brief experiment, to test this sort of thing out, on the woman's part, would be to ask her husband, one night, to tie her hands behind her back, when he makes love to her. He will probably demur. But, be persistent. And note how he looks at you, as his excitement mounts. Have you seen him look at you in years in this fashion? And, you, how long does it take you to become warm and wet to him, how long does it take you, this time, to attain orgasm?

Experimentation and mutual discussion is helpful with deciding on ties. For example, your wife will probably have ideas of certain ways that she might be bound which would be felt as "sexy" by her. Find out about these things. Her ideas will be illuminating. Take advantage of her ingenuity; she has plenty of it. You, too, of course, will have ideas. You have doubtless fantasized naked women, bound or chained in certain attitudes. Now, in your enacted fantasies, you can have these delicious erotic dreams as reality. There she is, as you have dreamed her, at your mercy. You approach her. You do with her what you please.

The following are some suggestions in connection with ties. Others have been mentioned here and there in the book. Obviously those mentioned in the book, and those following are not exhaustive.

Imagination and experimentation are desirable.

Split-legged ties.

The bedposts are useful here. When a woman has her legs tied apart she feels vulnerable. Tie her hands as you wish, together behind her back, together over her head, behind her head, apart to the upper bedposts, etc. You may even leave her hands free.

The chained-body tie.

The simplest is a chained ankle, say, with about five feet of chain, fastened, say, to the leg of the bed. You have her, say, on a comforter, on the floor. She may also be chained by the throat. Another possibility is to chain a wrist, preferably the left, if she is right handed; her right hand, as she becomes excited, must be free to love your body.

Combination-leash-wrist ties.

The hands are bound behind the back, at the end of a long length of rope. The rope is then looped several times about her belly and knotted, the knot at her navel; she may then be led by this. Another such tie is to loop the rope, or strap, about her throat three or four times, and use that as the leash. (The free end, in its last turn, must pass under the rope lifting to the neck from the wrists. This way she cannot, by turning her body or dipping her head free herself of the leash. More security, of course, is provided, particularly if one wishes to leave her tethered, untended, for a time, by knotting the rope about her neck.)

Stick-behind-the-back tie.

A stick, drilled or notched, is thrust behind her back, and her arms are brought forward under the stick. Her wrists are then lifted and tied, the cords against her belly. Her arms, near the elbows, are fastened to the stick. This keeps the hands tight to the body.

Handcuff ties.

(With remarks on chaining.)

Cheap handcuffs may be purchased even in department stores. The variety with keys are desirable. A naked, handcuffed woman is stimulating. The handcuffs simulate slave hardware. A short length of chain, with two padlocks will also serve. Chains and padlocks, of course, available at any hardware store, permit great latitude in securing prisoners. A chain, for example, which is fastened about the neck and dangles to the floor, to which other chains, for hands and ankles are attached, is very beautiful on a woman. I personally prefer light, gleaming chains for a woman. They enhance her beauty. Others might prefer blunter, heavier chains, contrasting their obduracy with her helpless, imprisoned loveliness.

Stocks.

The simplest stock I know dates back to Egypt. It is an oval board, about an inch thick. It has one rectangular opening, half cut from each board. The captive's wrists are placed in the opening and the stock is closed. It is then tied shut. It hangs about the neck on a strap. Ankle stocks, or wrist stocks, with two openings, are not difficult to make. The captive should be able to walk somewhat or move in these stocks. They are analogous to chains, not posts to which one might be tied. A simple metal and wood stock can be made by finding a board and two large "U" bolts. The board is drilled. The captive's wrists or ankles are then placed against the board, the "U" bolts inserted over the wrists or ankles, pushed through the board, and, on the other side, behind the board, secured. A small wrench is useful.

The slave hobble.

The girl's right wrist is chained to her left ankle, with about a foot of chain. She is thus hobbled. Do with her what you wish. (This tie is interesting because it permits her some movement, some resistance, but, frustratingly, teasingly, never enough for her resistance to be effective. It seems she is not completely at your mercy, and this stimulates her, but she soon learns, as you knew all the time, that her apparent opportunity to resist is actually illusory. Crushed, she yields to her master.

The ankle leash.

The metal ankle leash is snapped about the female's left ankle. The leash is about five feet long, terminating at the captor's end with a ring, to which are attached five slender straps, which may be used for slave discipline. The captive must follow perfectly, and gracefully, in such a leash, or be thrown from her feet. She may then be dragged, if the leash is attached to a mount or vehicle; if not, her clumsiness, at least, is likely to earn her a taste of the straps. A clumsy slave is an embarrassment to her master. She is accordingly punished. Another advantage of the ankle leash is that it makes it possible, at the master's pleasure, say, at a sign of rebellion, insubordination, hesitance, etc., to throw the slave from her feet. In an instant she can be on the ground, under the straps. Too, the slave cannot well reach the leash without bending down, thus placing herself in a position where she is vulnerable to his blows. The straps, too, may be used to bind the slave, while the master rests, or attends to his other duties. The leash is placed on, and removed from, the slave in the following manner. The master approaches from the rear and, taking her left ankle in his left hand, lifts it, until her heel is tight against her lovely ass; and then couples it on her with his right hand; thus she cannot, helpless on one foot, in any way, kick or resist.

The mind-control tie.

No physical restraint whatsoever is used. The woman is merely instructed to place her limbs in certain positions, say, to cross her hands behind her back. She then discovers, to her horror, that she cannot move them at all. Her mind is controlled. In this matter it is supposed that her will is helpless. Imagine her frustration, her despair, as he abuses her, making her yield to him as a sex slave, she confined by her own helpless will.

The magnetic shackle tie.

It is supposed that captives wear, on their wrists and ankles, some form of metal rings, perhaps with facing flat plates. They can normally move freely. At a signal, however, from an instrument, these devices snap together, confining them. This permits immediate immobilization of a slave population.

Electronic control devices.

Pain collars, implants in neural pain centers, etc., which can be actuated on signals, are doubtless pertinent here. Some such devices, implanted perhaps in male infants, would be useful in a technologically advanced, woman-dominated society.

Slave chain ties.

Here the woman is one of a set of slaves. She might be bound, or chained, to them by the neck, by the wrist, by the ankle, etc. She imagines herself one of several. Here it is important for the tie to be extended on each side of her, and fastened on each side of her. This is useful when she is being "picked out" from others, perhaps as the most desirable for acquisition, etc.

Love bows.

For binding over the saddle, the "love bow" is a possibility. There are two, standard love-bow ties, one in which the ankles are bound together, the other in which they are not; in both the wrists are bound together, generally palms exposed, over and behind the head. Let us suppose that she is bound, belly up, over a saddle. The saddle, let's suppose, is three cushions from the sofa, over which she is arched. The ankles, in the first tie, are fastened together and the bond passed under the cushions and then used to fasten her wrists together and back. The principle of the love-bow ties is that her movements, as she struggles, are transmitted by the rope tensions through her body. If she moves her feet, it pulls against her wrists; if she tries to free her hands, it more cruelly pins back her ankles. The love bow exposes her body, gracefully, helplessly, for your touch. As she writhes, bound, the tie makes her the center of a pleasure loop, her stimulated clitoris the center for a radiation of sensation. In the "open love bow" the wrists are fastened, as before, but each ankle, separately, is bound to the two wrists. (Tie the wrists at the center of the rope and then run the two ends to the ankles, tieing them.) The point of this, of course, is that it allows the male to penetrate the female. In this variation, of course, it is not pretended she is bound over a saddle, but, say, some other object. What about a pleasure rack?

Circle ties.

The circle tie is useful. In it the wrists are tied behind the back and bound to the ankles, which are pulled back and fastened in proximity to the wrists. This is primarily a holding tie. The captive, thus secured, cannot rise to her feet. She may be, thus, on her side, fastened about a tree or stanchion.

Ties behind the neck.

A woman's hair, if sufficiently long, may be used to fasten her hands behind her neck. It may also be useful, incidentally, in keeping her in place. Let us say she is kneeling, bound hand and foot. Her hair then, lifted, looped about a low-hanging branch, knotted about it, will hold her for you. Another device is to have her cross her wrists, palms up. They are then tied together. With the loose ends of the strap then her hands are pulled back over her head and the strap looped twice and fastened about her neck. In exhibiting a woman, naked, for a casual sale this is an old slaver's trick. It lifts and accentuates the beauty of her breasts. (Only a fool, of course, buys a woman clothed.)

Whipping ties.

The female is usually whipped on the back (the legs, calves and back of the neck may be included), the stomach or the soles of the feet. Broad, soft leather straps are used, that her back not be cut to pieces, that she be only punished, and not marked. Switches are also acceptable. Slave girls in coffle, incidentally, are normally herded by switch.[1] There are numerous ties. A simple one puts her on her knees at the foot of the bed, her wrists bound before her to the bed post. She may also be spreadeagled on the bed, stomach down. Other ties fasten her hands over her head, either together or tied, or chained, apart. She is usually nude to the whip; she must be, at least, stripped to the waist. (She is not actually beaten, of course. That would hurt her. The pillow trick has been mentioned twice; it provides clitoral and labial stimulation. The difficulty with tieing her on her feet, of course, is that this mode of stimulation is impractical. You may, of course, hold her sweetness, and let her, as she is "struck" press into your hand. Another variant is the "stimulation post." In this her hands are tied together, high above her head. She is utterly nude, except perhaps for a collar. Your finger is inserted into her beauty and she, as she is "struck" writhes upon it. The stimulation post, of course, can also be used as a "training device" to teach the slave the belly dance. Music is played and she moves, hands over head, bound, on and about your finger, hips rotating, grinding sensuously, to the music. This gives her pleasure. She is also very beautiful. Also, it teaches her sensuous movement, and its meaning. In the belly-dance variation of the stimulation post, I would recommend that the girl's hands be tied lower than in the whipping-post variation; she need not be untied; the rope need only be slackened a bit; this is to allow her more room for her pelvic explosions. Needless to say, a woman, properly handled on the stimulation post, can be literally brought to orgasm, on her feet, to the music. It is a fantastic experience, both for her and, visually, emotionally and sexually, for you. If she should beg for the stimulation post, do not deny it to her. A well-aroused slave will have plenty left for her master. The whipping-post variation and the belly-dance variation, incidentally, can follow one another quite nicely; the whipping-post variation warms her for the belly-dance variation. The fantasy sequence too, is natural. The whip has taught her that she has no choice now but to learn, against her will, sensuous dance, in its full erotic implications. (If she kneels across your body, incidentally, commanded there by you, and the music plays, of course, you, too, can experience the belly dance; you can experience the movements from within as her love and heat, that of a commanded slave girl, writhes obediently, impaled on your manhood. This is an exciting experience; it is, however, difficult to withhold ejaculation in this situation; it is, accordingly, recommended that one have had at least one orgasm earlier in the game. Do not worry; you will have another. (An advantage of fantasy, of course, is that it gives partners time to ready themselves, psychologically and physiologically, for second and third orgasms.)

[1]*For the soles of her feet a light, springy board is used; her ankles are tied about six inches to a foot apart; if there is a rail at the bottom of your bed, they may be bound to this; also good is to put her on her back, bound, on the floor, and tie her ankles over a chair, placed on its side; in both cases it is desirable if her head is lower than her feet; this induces a feeling of helplessness and makes the beating seem more painful; this mode of punishment, incidentally,*

is mild slave discipline, sharp and humiliating enough to be effective, yet not as serious as a full-scale application of the slave whip; it is excellent for punishing small, unintentional infractions, such as, say, stumbling in the master's presence, spilling wine, etc. This punishment, incidentally, is normally administered by one slave girl to another; they hate one another and enjoy striking one another; pettiness, jealousy, mutual distrust, etc., is encouraged in slave girls; it makes them easier to control; the master, after having given his orders, leaves the room; he does not even watch. This is a further insult to the punished girl. When he returns, she looks up at him, then looks away. She cannot look into his eyes. She has been beaten. He unties her. She finds it difficult to walk. He forces her to do so. She falls to her knees, crawling to him for mercy. He carries her to his bed and rapes her. She is a truly punished slave. (Slave rape is, of course, common. Slaves are unimportant; commonly the master inflicts slave rape on his girl, but, if she should be caught in the street, or in the alleys, by ruffians, they too might, almost with impunity, rape her. Furthermore, even on errands, she is not out of danger. A shopkeeper may even order her to his back room; similarly she is much at the mercy of soldiers and magistrates; the penalty for raping a slave is nothing or negligible, sometimes the tiniest coin given to the master. Many masters send their girls forth only if they are fastened in the steel belt, preventing their penetration. The extremely short garment of the female slave, and the fact absolutely nothing is permitted to be worn under it, invite her rape. It distracts attention from free women, who are thus relatively safe from assault. Interestingly, many slave girls respond excitingly to their rapes; being an owned girl, helpless, locked in a collar, no reputation to protect, fully aware of the power and beauty of male animals, they sometimes, it is claimed, provoke their own rapes, particularly in the presence of a male that excites them. No one thinks the less of a slave girl for begging to be raped; that is all they are, slaves. They are not permitted pride or inhibitions; they must be complete, willing, eager female animals. Once they are broken to the collar, they become eager for sex; indeed, they wish it frequently and are miserable when denied; in selling a girl she is often, prior to her sale, deprived of sex for several days; then, when sent to the block, she is often whimpering and moaning for *a master; this is very different from the "free woman," but, it is noted that the "free woman," once reduced to absolute bondage, becomes, almost overnight, as eager and wanton as the most despicable of bred slaves.)*

The short-leash hold.

Hands tied behind her back, the girl, nude, kneels beside the bed. her neck fastened to it by a short leash. This holds her on her knees, preventing her from rising. It also prevents her from lying down. It keeps her in a kneeling position at the foot of your bed. Excellent discipline for a proud woman.

The kneeling-short-wrist-hold tie.

She kneels, her back against some object. Her wrists, tied behind her back, are fastened to the object, about a foot above the floor. This keeps her in a kneeling position, belly facing you, hands unable to protect her body from your touch. This is excellent for caressing her, until she pleads to be used. The fact that she is on her knees contributes, considerably, to her sense of being in bondage, at your mercy. Excellent for swiftly warming a woman.

The four-limb-open tie.

The girl's wrists and ankles are tied separately. She has quite a bit of play but cannot bring her hands together or her legs. Accordingly, in spite of the play she has, she cannot defend herself from your touch or penetration. This is a psychologically interesting tie, making her feel very helpless.

The four-limb-closed tie.

The girl's wrists and ankles are tied separately, but she has little or no play. The wrists and ankles may be spread widely. She is "staked out" at your mercy. Enjoy her.

The she-is-waiting-for-your-pleasure tie.

Your "servants" or "retainers" strip her. She is backed, kneeling, against the bed post. Her ankles are tied behind the bed post; her hands are crossed, similarly, and, behind her head, about the bed post, are fastened. She is left this way for fifteen minutes or so, and then, when you come in, you notice her. Perhaps she was an enemy female, or one who was insolent with you. It is a pleasant surprise to come into your bedroom and find her there, awaiting your pleasure.

Slave-post ties.

For these, one needs a pole, stanchion or tree. She is then tied to the post. This can be done any number of ways, standing, kneeling, hands behind the post, hands over the head behind the post, etc. Her belly and neck, and ankles, can also be bound at the post. This tie can be excellent for displaying her, jeering her, exhibiting her in a market, etc. Useful tie for slave abuse. (Avoid hot pipes; be careful that stanchions are solid.)

Hands-to-belly tie.

Her hands, possibly in handcuffs, are tied or strapped against her belly. (The belt buckle would be turned to the back; the rope knot would be in back.) She cannot reach high enough to protect her breasts from your touch; she cannot reach low enough to protect her clitoris and vagina from your touch. This is most effective when she is also, say, chained by the neck. The futility of her hand movements; clenched fists, etc., add to her impression, and yours, of her helplessness. Before she yields in orgasm, it would be kind on your part to release her hands (she is still secured by the neck) so that she may hold to you, tightly, helplessly, riding out the storm of her passion. (If she is in handcuffs merely remove the belt or rope and unlock one of the cuffs, the one on her left hand if she is right handed; both cuffs may then be locked about her right wrist or, if you wish, the decision being yours, she being your captive, one permitted to dangle from her right wrist, it either open or closed. As she yields in orgasm it will not interfere with her pleasure to know that she still wears slave steel, it locked on her body. After her orgasm whether you put her in cuffs again is up to you. "Please continue to hold me, to caress me!" A woman's orgasm can be as wild and jagged as a man's, but it takes time to build to it, and, once it is attained, her body still begs for attention; her

excitements more gradually subside than those of the male; it is
cruel to abandon her once she has attained the orgasm; remember
that her sexual need is rather different from yours, and take this
into account in your loving; after orgasm, she will desire to be
kissed and held, to be warm and close and loving in your arms,
probably for several minutes; after this time of coming down the
slopes of her pleasure, it would be up to her whether she wants
to be thrust again to those heights; she needs recovery time, of
course, just as a male; there is a difference between the ascending
series of orgasms which culminates in the master orgasm, and
the master orgasm itself; the above remarks are pertinent to
the "master" orgasm. Time and rhythm are important. "Love
spacing," of course, is easy in fantasy. (In the above situation,
you leave the woman immediately after her orgasm, after putting
her back in cuffs. She, nude, helpless on the bed, lying or sitting,
handcuffed, still desiring your touch, whimpers and moans
for you to return to her. After a time, you do so. "A slave is
grateful, Master!" "Be silent." "Yes, Master." And you bring her
down gently, beautifully. In her eyes you read her gratitude to
her master. In time, if you sense the wanting of her body (or,
perhaps she begs anew for slave rape), you may, if you wish,
again, before your pleasure, thrust her to ecstasy. (Do as you
please; she is only a slave.)[1]

[1]*"Please rape me, Master." She dares not, of course, beg for
the respectful attention, the solicitude, the deference, that would
be accorded to a free woman, that exalted creature, in bed; she
is only a slave; secretly, of course, she prefers slave rape; in bed
she does not wish to be treated as a "lady," but as a naked slave
girl, completely at her master's disposal; she wants him to do to
her, and masterfully, what he pleases; she wants to belong to him,
completely; if she were truly his "equal," in some sense, how could
she submit to him; every woman, in her heart, desires to find a
man before whom she has no choice but to submit herself sexually;
every woman, in her secret dreams, searches for her master; the
slave girl, of course, must wantonly and eagerly, submit to men; she
is forced to be true to her deepest instincts; accordingly, mastered,
their sexual experiences are fantastic, far other than those possible*

among "equals." Similarly a man who has had a slave girl is then likely to understand the smugness, the sexual poverty, the competitiveness, the vanity, of the "free woman." Free women, of course, fail to understand why a strong, intelligent, attractive man prefers a sensuous little slut of a slave girl, hot and loving, eager and lascivious, in his bed to one of them. The fact that they cannot understand this tells us much about the free woman. They have little recourse but to castigate men, call them names, etc., because they have in them the blood of hunters and masters. No answer need be given to them but to look at them, as a man may look at a woman whose understanding of him is irrelevant and foolish. Undress them with a glance, and perhaps they will understand. Remarks addressed to a free woman (if, as is unlikely, she wishes to satisfy the sexual needs of both herself and her husband): Your freedom ends at the edge of the mattress. When you crawl nude into bed with your husband, be his slave girl.

Sack ties.

She is placed in a sack, bound or not, and the sack is tied, or belted, or snapped, or padlocked, shut. She may be entered into the sack either feet or head first. Make certain that there is adequate air. Make certain, too, that if the sack is moved, she is not injured. Be particularly careful to avoid stresses to the neck. A sack may be dragged along the floor; it may be lifted in the arms; it may be, under no circumstances, dropped on the floor; it may, however, be thrown on a bed. A rug may also be used, tied at four places. A variation, of course, would be to shut her in a trunk, padlocking it shut at both ends. (Holes should be drilled, for adequate ventilation.) It may also be pretended that under the bed is a low-ceilinged, flat slave cell, perhaps even under your bed. When she is released, she perhaps dances, and then, when permitted, crawls humbly into the bed. Perhaps she kneels first at the foot of the bed and lifts the sheet, kissing it, and only then, with your permission, is, head down, given the privilege of your couch. An interesting version of the sack tie has the sack drawn over her head and about her hips, which is as far as it goes. Then the stout cords of the sack are tied under her body, holding the sack on her. (Her hands may be bound behind her back before the sack is drawn over her head.) She is thus much at your mercy. A blanket, similarly, may be thrown over her head and, by means of a belt, tied about her belly. (This variation is based on an American Indian technique for keeping a white slave woman quiet. When the slave cannot see, she tends to become docile. This technique is also effective, I gather, with horses.)

The ankles-up ties
    She lies on her back, on the floor, at the foot of your bed. Her hands are bound either in front of her or behind her. But her ankles are crossed and bound, perhaps to the lower bed post. They are fastened, say, two feet above the floor level. She, thus, cannot rise to her feet. She must lie on her back, under your scrutiny, when you care to look upon her. This tie makes a girl feel helpless. A general point of ties, incidentally, aside from making the girl seem captive, enhancing her beauty, etc., is that they induce this feeling of helplessness, which makes a female feel more sexually vulnerable, more in peril. Along these lines, a blindfold is excellent, too, for people become frightened when they cannot see. Bind your girl's hands behind her back and then blindfold her. She is already stripped. (The sort of mask without eyes used by women to keep the sun out of their eyes in the morning when they wish to sleep late is all right. Perhaps when she went to bed that night she had worn it. When she awakens, she still wears it, but she is now stripped and bound, and perhaps the bed is strange. What has happened to her? "Is there anyone there?" she cries. Perhaps her only answer is the stroke of a whip.) Then, lead her about, by the arm. She will not fall. Perhaps she is being led to the "slaving chamber." Bound, blindfolded, stripped, led about, this can be exciting to her. Be in no hurry to reach the "slaving chamber." Another variant here is not to hold her arm but to direct her by voice command. Since she cannot see, this will be even more frightening to her. Care must be taken, of course, to see that she does not fall. Stay close to her, or be sure to stay between her and any possible danger, such as, say, a coffee table. When she is where you want her tell her to kneel. She then has the blindfold removed. She

looks about herself, in terror. She is in the "slaving chamber." She imagines it to be as you, together, have worked it out in planning the fantasy. Are there other females there, chained to the wall? In cages? Are girls branded there, or whipped? Is that where they may be tortured, if they are not pleasing? Will her head be placed on an anvil, and a metal collar curved about her neck? Will a lock collar be fastened on her throat? When she emerges from the chamber will she be a complete slave, even to having been, perhaps, subjected in her processing to the indignities of slave rape? Or, is her virginity guarded, even to a steel belt locked about her, it removed only when she ascends the great block, nude, to be auctioned to the highest bidder on one of the great slave festivals?

Loose chains.

Here there is little confinement. The hands, for example, might be separated by as much as two or three feet of chain. These can be delightful ornaments to the dance of a slave girl. (She might, of course, be nude, save for bangles, bracelets, necklaces, bells, etc. She might wear only jewelry, and perhaps a chain.)

Humiliation ties.

You might or might not be interested in these. I have mixed feelings about some of them. In them the woman is not always displayed at her most beautiful. Generally a tie should enhance a woman's beauty, not abuse it. One that I do find beautiful is the following. The girl kneels, her head to the floor, her ankles under her. Her neck is tied to her ankles; her wrists are then bound behind her back. This holds her head to the floor, in a beautiful submission posture. Also her whole body, with its delicious curvatures, is "packaged neatly," confined into a lovely, vulnerable area. This is useful in "slave discipline." I would not keep her this way, however, more than a minute or two, or it will become uncomfortable. One can always pretend she has been bound in this disciplining position for hours. If she really were, of course, she would be one wench eager to please her master when released. Another tie, which might or might not be regarded as a humiliation tie, is to throw the woman over the back of a low, heavy armchair or sofa, her wrists tied together before her and, by the same rope, running under the chair or sofa, tieing her ankles together. Her ass, then, is lifted into the air for your pleasure and penetration. A humiliation tie I would not recommend has the woman's hands bound behind her back, and she lies on her back, her ankles tied together and fastened, on a strap about twenty inches long, about her neck. This lifts her cunt to you, most helplessly. This seems to me a bit rough.

The above ideas will perhaps suggest other possibilities to the reader.

It is perhaps important to remind ourselves, though it should be unnecessary, that love games are meant to be performed only between lovers, usually men and their wives. Without love there is not even fantasy, there is only exploitation and degradation. One objective of this book is to bring some of the less common but authentic pleasures of sex within the ambit of love. For many people, they have been there a long time. For others, there is no reason they should not be.

The important thing is to care for women, and love them.

The man who truly abuses a woman is not a man. He is no more than the freak who abuses animals or children. Fantasy can be delicious; but reality must, on the whole, be where we live.

APPENDIX 3. Apparel in Fantasy.

We are concerned here with remarks on costumes for the female in the fantasies. She is, in my opinion, the star of these enactments. Women can be endlessly inventive in these matters, and details are best left to them. They can design costumes that are sensuous dreams.

A few observations are, however, perhaps in order.

There are many items commercially available, which are fantastically sensuous. Consider, for example, the range of female nightwear, from white, classic garments which, with barbaric armlets, etc., will transform her into a pagan queen, to brief, sleeveless gowns of red silk that might have been designed by male chauvinists to set off their harems of captured women's libbers, now their slave girls. With the short gowns, of course, the woman is not permitted to wear the panties. They are a cop-out, making the shortness of the gown meaningless. I like to see plenty of leg in my own slave girl. Moreover, she must move with exquisite care or she will expose more than her lovely legs.

Belly dancer and slave girl costumes are commercially available. Veils, too; bells, finger cymbals, etc.

Female undergarments are also possibilities. Brassieres and panties are obvious choices. It is assumed, of course, that they constitute, normally, the entire costume. Such items come in colors and patterns. Some have animal patterns, e.g., leopard. If you are capturing a "Sheena of the Jungle," or something, and turning her into a harem slave, she might, orginally, be so clad. On the other hand, if you are capturing an English lady aristocrat, circa 1840, and taking her to the jungle as your slave, you might give her such garments to wear. (Presumably you have killed the

animals, etc.) Dyes can alter colors, of course. A white brassiere
dyed slave scarlet can be exciting. Perhaps you do not immediately
strip your capture but permit her, behind a screen, to exchange
her civilized apparel for that of a barbarian's slave girl. She then
steps forth, in fury, proud, for your inspection. Wow! (There
are varieties of foundation garments with possibilities. Also, of
course, they may be altered, e.g., beaded, fringed, etc. (Ankle
bells, incidentally, can be sexy; the master knows where his
wench is; she cannot surprise him; and, as she moves in love,
the bells are exciting.)

Swim wear is less appropriate, though a bikini that ties, and
is easily removable, is good. A brief terry cloth cover-up, with
absolutely nothing under it, is delightful. Generally, however,
swim wear is less easy to remove, and the girl is less available in it
than in other garments. It, too, is usually too heavy. Diaphanous
silk, half parted, brief, clinging, beats a bathing suit any day.

Rags can be good; for example, the shreds of an old house
dress, suitably ripped short and torn from the shoulder, etc., can
be splendid. Such a rag, of course, must be her only garment.
(Panties, incidentally, are never worn, unless they are all that is
worn.) "Of all these beautiful garments, Master, which will you
give me to wear?" "None. You will wear the rag of a slave." An
old slip or nightgown, suitably altered and shortened, can make
an excellent slave garment. It is silk. It can be ripped here and
there, half split, torn, etc. Slips, incidentally, if nothing else is
worn, are quite sexy, particularly if "doctored" a bit, with the
display of the prize in mind. I think both white and red slips are
very suitable.

Sometimes a surprise is good, or something a bit different,
unexpected, for example, only colored pantyhose and a collar.

I am fond of most of a woman; indeed, all of her. Do not forget
maximum leg display. A cord may be tied about her waist. It
should be tied in such a way that it can be casually yanked
loose. It supports, say, a rectangle of silk in the front and rear,
thrust over and behind the cord. If it is desired a long piece of
silk can be passed over the front cord, between her legs, and
then up and under, and over, the cord in the back. It should
then be made snug to her body. Separate pieces of silk are even

sexier. These may be wider or narrower. They may be only a few inches in length, or they might reach below her knees, or even to her ankles. (There might be only one such rectangle. Perhaps it is cultural on a certain planet that a slave girl's ass is bared, perhaps the better to be switched. The woman, if a captured Earth wench, of course, must find this acutely, breathtakingly, scandalously shameful. It is nothing, of course, to the barbarians of the other planet. We might also suppose, as I think would generally be the case, that in many cultures supporting slavery important differences would exist between the dress of free women and girls in bondage. Perhaps, commonly, the slave girl is not permitted to conceal her breasts. They must be bared. Imagine a wench wearing only a narrow rectangle of red silk and a matching scarlet collar approaching you, to serve you wine. Women's breasts are beautiful, and they mark her so excitingly, vulnerably, as a female, it is a shame that our culture recommends their concealment. They are nothing to be ashamed of. I think we may suppose that, in many cultures supporting slavery, the slave girls would be forced, willing or not, to display their beauty for the pleasure of free men. Who knows; perhaps in some cultures they would not even be permitted clothing, save for their brands and collars.)

Costume changes in these fantasies can be stimulating. They also give the male a minute or two to cool off.

A man's shirt, and that is all, can be sexy, too. I am not sure why this is. It may be a flirtation with homosexuality, but that seems oversimple, particularly considering that it is a *woman* in the shirt, and not a man. Men just look silly in men's shirts, until they get their pants on. Women don't. They look exciting. Perhaps what makes it exciting on a woman is that it is kicky on her part, challenging, stimulating, different, surprising. In the context of a fantasy, of course, it could be pretended that all her clothing was burned, and there is only male attire for her to wear. She must, against her will, wear the shirt. (Women find it fun, incidentally, to wear a man's shirt like this. I do not know why that would be. Perhaps they know they look sexy in such a garment, and that turns them on. Perhaps it has to do with a Lesbian flirtation on their part. Perhaps they regard it as issuing a delicious challenge to the male, by donning one of his garments. I do not know. I think they may like it because it calls real attention to themselves; it makes the man sit up and take notice; and it stimulates him to address himself to their pleasures. "Take it from me if you can!" So you catch her, open the shirt, and convince her, over the period of an hour or so, that she is really a female. Why should a female look incredibly *female* in a *man's* shirt? Perhaps because of the contrasts. She is *so different* in that shirt than a man, that her essential femaleness screams its difference at you.)

Do not forget evening gowns, cocktail dresses, severe "business suits," etc. Women look lovely in them, and they are pleasures to remove, before putting her in, if anything, something more comfortable, more "suitable." An aristocratically dressed woman is a delight to strip. Perhaps the last things you remove are her pearls and earrings. Or perhaps you permit her to retain them, and then command her, still wearing them, to kneel before you and, with lips and tongue, lick and suck your genitals. (Are her hands handcuffed or bound behind her back? It is up to the players.)

What about a scarlet halter, and she bare otherwise, saving perhaps a matching strip of fabric, or ribbon, tied about her left ankle? It should be, perhaps, two inches wide. (If she is nude, a man's wrist strap, with double buckles, fastened about her left ankle can be a lovely slave marking device. A small link chain, with padlock, can be another. A chain and padlock collar, too, is lovely.)

The following two suggestions can produce exciting slave garments. (1) A rectangle of cloth is used, with a hole cut out for the head, poncho fashion. It is then thrown over her head. The sides are open. It is belted, perhaps, with a rawhide thong. Its length is up to the players. My own feeling is the shorter the better. (2) The woman makes an "inverted T garment." It fastens behind her neck, falls before her, is gathered and drawn between her legs and behind, and then the bars of the "T" (beveled) are wrapped around and tied in front. It may also be tied across the back, this drawing it in such a way as to accentuate her breasts.

Don't forget leotards. Perhaps you have nabbed some ten

beauties at their ballet practice. Body suits are also terrific. They were clearly designed by someone interested in displaying the beauty of females. Leotards and body suits might, in many cultures, particularly of the future, in relatively automated futures, make excellent slave garments. Can't you imagine the beauty, so clad, moving about among complicated machinery, computers and such, bringing the engineers their coffee? (Perhaps one of the computer technicians or electronics experts is a female. Perhaps her male colleagues, this being a relatively permissive planet, enslave her and force her to wear such garments while attending to her duties. It gives them pleasure to see her body; even in the future they are men. She also, of course, at a word from them, must run for their coffee, serve their pleasure, etc. Perhaps aliens attack and carry her, and others, off. Then she is, of course, only another beautiful slave girl. Doubtless she is sold, escapes, has adventures, etc.)

A common slave garment would be the brief slave tunic. Any woman can make one of these. They are sleeveless, terribly short, may be belted or not. They might have patterns or be plain. They should be, however, simple. Their very simplicity will be quite sexy.

Notice the broad hair ribbon holding back the hair of that slave girl. It can be drawn forward, and used as a blindfold. Moreover the rawhide thongs looped about her throat and loosely knotted, collarlike, or those belting her tunic, can be used for binding her, hand and foot. She carries bonds with her.

Do you like scarlet garters? Perhaps a prim Victorian girl, one of a high family, is kidnapped by young rakes and carried to their private club, near the wharves of London. Chained by the neck in her great heart-shaped bed, at their pleasure, the girl, scandalized, is given only a scarlet garter to wear. They put it on her, high on her left thigh. They then, over a period of several nights, teach her the pleasures of the senses. She becomes their wanton slave. When, the next month, they capture another wench, perhaps a rigid, but beautiful, young governess, the first girl is bound and gagged, placed in a trunk or sack, and taken, at night, to a packet, bound for the Middle East. She will be sold in an Arab slave market. The following month, of course, as a new girl is brought in, the young governess, body, mind and senses now fully readied for abject and total slavery, will follow her predecessor to an Arabian market. This is the Nineteenth Century. Lovely young white slave girls, shapely infidels, fit only to serve the faithful, do not escape the Arab world.

Brief, wrap-around skirts are excellent ideas. What can be wrapped in one direction can be unwrapped in the other. Such garments can be removed in a very sexy fashion. They need not be climbed out of. The female can remove it gracefully, teasingly; humbly, obediently; in tears, in despair; insolently, whipping it from her, thrusting forward her cunt, tauntingly; "I know I belong to you. I strip myself before you, your slave. You own me. Use me!" And so on.

It is important, too, not to neglect the hair. An obvious consideration here, applicable in some fantasies, is the transition from a severe, intellectual hair-do, appropriate to a man-hating blue stocking, to the wild, loose pelt of an untamed slave girl, perhaps on her hands and knees, stripped, looking up at you, in hatred, in fury, determined to resist. But she fears the whip in your hand. I personally like long, loose hair in a slave girl, exciting, uninhibited, sexy, wild, barbaric, uncivilized. I also like the feel of it on my body. Doubtless an aware slave girl uses her hair to please and stimulate her master. There could, of course, be different hair styles for different girls, and different hair styles for different statures or types of women, and in different cultures, etc. Linda, for example, might wear her hair quite differently from Vonda. Perhaps a certain kind of hair ribbon or metal barrette signifies slavery. Perhaps a house slave must braid her hair in a certain way, whereas a sex slave must wear her hair in a different fashion. Hair can be used, too, for signals. Perhaps when a slave girl wears her hair in a certain fashion, or, say, wears a certain pin in it, that is a wordless signal that she is begging for attention. The "bondage knot" might be of interest here, used in some slave cultures. Some strands of her hair, say, about a half inch, or an inch's worth, are separated from the rest and, loosely, knotted. The knot falls at her right cheekbone. This can be used as a general mark that the female is a slave, say, in lieu of collar, or as a special mark that she, fearing to speak, desires to be used as what she is, her master's girl. The master also, of course, could approach her, and tie this knot in her hair, she then understanding that she is to prepare herself for love, and love as a slave girl. (A certain pin or hair-do, of course, can serve as a signal between husband and wife that she desires imaginative sex that night; seeing a certain pin in her hair the husband knows then that, as their secret, perhaps even in the presence of her mother, his mother-in-law, she is telling him that she is truly, say, "Linda" or "Vonda" and is, thusly, asking him, silently, even in the presence of her mother, to serve him that night as a slave girl. I would not, incidentally, use the bondage knot for this purpose; it will provoke curiosity; it is too obvious.)

Candlelight, incidentally, can be very lovely. It gives a warm, loving glow, soft and intimate. Do not hesitate to make love by candlelight. It can also, of course, have value in imaginative sex. A girl seen in candlelight need not, as usual, be wearing an evening dress and sipping champagne. She might be dancing, nude, in chains, before a barbaric master. He, cross-legged, sits on cushions, observing her. She dances, desperate to please him. He assesses her casually, determining in his own mind whether it will be she or another whom he will have sent to him for the evening. What man has lived, who has not, by candlelight, witnessed the dance of a nude slave girl? When her dance ends, she kneels before him, head down.

"What is her name?" he asks his chamberlain. Perhaps he does not even remember, months before, having captured her.

He is told.

"Send her to me tonight, after I have finished my work," he tells the chamberlain.

It will be done.

That night she arrives, her hands confined in slave chains behind her back, the key tied about her neck, to her collar.

She has been kept in the slave quarters for months. This is the first opportunity she has had to please her master. For all she knows it may be her last.

He looks her over. She stands beautifully. "Master," she whispers, acknowledging his dominance over her. He scrutinizes

casually, expertly, for he has owned many women, every turn
of her body, both those gross and obvious, such as the marvels
of her breasts and ass, and those intimate and subtle, such as the
turn of the instep, the tilt of her head, the flexions of a wrist, the
tendons behind a knee, the sweet turn of a hip, the melodies of
her thighs and delta. He likes what he sees. She has passed the
first test. He removes her chains.

"Linda is grateful that her master is not displeased with her,"
she whispers.

"Get in bed," he tells her.

"Yes, Master," she whispers.

Starved for sex, owned, only one lovely property among many
others, she crawls into his bed. She must make him remember
her. She does not wish to spend perhaps several years of her life
locked, imprisoned, in the slave quarters, neglected, overlooked,
forgotten. She remembers how the other girls looked at her with
envy and hatred as she was chained to be taken to the master's
chamber.

She looks at him. She knows he may even order her slain, if
she is not sufficiently pleasing to him. She trembles. He is not
displeased to see her fear. But she tries to overcome her fear.
She wishes to become one of his favorites. In the first weeks,
and months, after her capture she hated him, and feared that he
might summon her; then, for months, accustoming herself to the
indolence, the disciplines and routines of the slave quarters, his
harem, she became indifferent; but then she noticed that the other
women did not respect her, and rejected her as an unattractive
freak, an oddity in the lofty, ornate, perfumed halls; she became
skeptical of her womanhood and attractiveness, and miserable;
enemies in the harem, resenting her beauty and intelligence,
made her life miserable, demeaning her loveliness, insulting her,
playing tricks on her, such as spoiling her food, and stealing
her garments or ornaments. Once they tied her, naked, on the
tiles all night. Her standing in the harem, she understood, would
depend on her standing with the master. Also, she is becoming
desperate for sex. Insolently then, she asked the chief eunuch
to be brought to her master's attention. "There are other slaves,"
he told her. She suddenly realized then that she would have to

await his pleasure, completely. At last, in the past two months, she has lived on the hope that her master would summon her to his chamber. Then, she was given the opportunity to dance for him.

Now she lies, frightened, in his bed.

She, before her dance tonight, had seen him only once, and that briefly, when he, in the helmet of a warrior, had struck her down from horseback with the flat of his sword on her neck. Stunned she had fallen, and he had leapt from his horse, dragging her to her feet and tethering her to his stirrup. She remembered then a nightmare of being dragged through burning streets, with fighting about her, and crashing walls. When he came to his camp there were two other women, too, tethered to his stirrup. He turned all three over to his men, for herding into the compound of captured women. He then disappeared again, toward the city. She had not seen him since then, until her dance before him. Then, observing her, he seemed not the rough warrior, blood on his helmet, in torn tunic, with great shield, but a man, adorned in noble robes, of power and riches, one significant in the state, one who could own many girls such as she.

She wishes to become one of his favorites. It will make such a difference in her life in the slave quarters. All the girls vie eagerly to be a favorite. But, suddenly, looking at him she realizes he can make her love him, literally, and that she will. She had not counted on that. She turns her head to one side.

"Regard me, Slave," he says.

"Yes, Master," she whispers.

He slips into the bed beside her. Suddenly she resolves to try to resist him.

But his hand touches her. It is on her breast, not harshly but with a tenderness and power that alarms her. It seems such a strong hand, so large and rough.

"Your breasts are beautiful, Slave," he tells her.

"Thank you, Master," she says.

His hand then slips to her delta, gently but as something he owns and would touch.

She feels a subtle, incredible pleasure.

She lifts her lips to his. "I love you, Master," she whispers.

I do not think the master will forget this girl. I think it possible she will become one of his favorites.

The light from an open hearth is also very beautiful, of course, and barbaric. It can suggest a cave fire or the blaze in the hall of a Viking chieftain. You need, of course, a heavy rug before the fire, on which you may lie. It should be simple and deeply piled. It may be, if you wish, an animal rug. On this rug, the slave, naked save for her collar and chains, responds helplessly, eagerly, to her master. She makes marvelous love to him. (If she is a captured cave woman, she might begin the game with her hands thonged behind her; when she becomes fully aroused, she is released to roll, to kiss, to laugh and squirm with her captor, to lick and caress and such, one of a pair of deliciously mating animals.) Viking chieftains often kept slave girls. Girls were prize plunder. Heavy collars might be put on their thralls. There could even be a "Viking feast," at which the prizes, stripped, serve their new masters. Roast meat. What about trying to whip up some mead? Perhaps better stick with warm whiskey.[1]

[1]*Torchlight, doubtless, is sexy, too; but most houses and apartments do not come equipped with torches; also, there is no point in smoking up the ceiling or burning down a residence; torches, legally, I would suppose, would count as "friendly fires," and, accordingly, would not be covered by fire insurance policies; furthermore, most people unfortunately use torches for burning down buildings, not illuminating beautiful women; accordingly, there would be a presumption, I expect, not of imaginative sex, but arson; if you have a private patio, of course, torches on a summer's night might be lovely. (Various patio "torches" would seem suitable.)*

Slave dances, incidentally, can be invented. There can be dances to the whip, dances in chains, dances of sexual desire, dances of pretended fear and despair, dances of insolence, dances of rebellion, etc. Combinations, too, are appropriate. Many dances, one supposes, end with a physically expressed, wordless, plea for the touch of the master, the rape of the slave. An interesting dance is a tether dance, in which she performs in a tether. Needless to say, any woman who has studied expressive dance has a head start in these matters. All expressive dances need not be the representation of the growth of a bean plant. Dance, incidentally, is an excellent way for a woman to express her feelings. If she, for example, has a chip on her shoulder for men, let her dance it off. She will feel much the better for it. Similarly, a woman can erotically stimulate herself by dance. It is hard to dance sexual passion before a man and not become eager for his touch. Here is a standard, five-phase slave dance. Phase I. The woman clothed lightly, but as a free woman, dances her scorn and hatred for men. This is a proud dance, haughty, decorous, stylized. Phase II. She has been caught. She dances her attempt to escape, her fury, pulling, say, against a rope looped about her. Phase III. She has been stripped. She wears short chains on her wrists. She is in bondage. In her "cell" she dances her misery, her fear, but then, as though confronted by the captor, she dances her determination to resist him; but he will have none of this, and she dances as though struck by the whip, as though fearing him, as though attempting to shield herself; this phase ends with her on her knees, head down. Phase IV. She now wears the garments of a slave girl. Her wrists are no longer confined. She is, however, collared. She dances her resignation to her slavery, a beautiful phase, in which she expresses her longing for freedom, but her realization, too, that she is in bondage; this phase contains many submission gestures, sitting, lying, rising, reclining, etc., as a slave girl, but with resignation. She knows that she is not free, that she is now truly slave. There can be a wistful-ness to this phase. She is slave, but she does not yet understand the true meaning of her slavery. Phase V. She awakens. She touches her collar. She feels her slave beauty. She lifts her head. She is becoming aroused. She looks at the master, with bitterness, but with desire. He claps his hands once, sharply. She is immediately alert. Every fiber in her body is alive. She awaits her signal. He claps his hands once more, fiercely, sharply. She springs to her feet and, thus commanded, begins to perform the desire dance of the slave female. From her lovely ankles to her small, beautiful hands, over her head, she is a helpless, wild, sexually maddened slave. She now *wants* her master, and, from the bottom of her luscious slave ass, dances the beauty of her body for him, begging him to subdue it. In its climax, tearing away her clothing, she dances before him nude, his aroused, piteous slave girl, begging him for his touch, for her penetration and conquest. At the end of the dance, she is frightened and submissive; her master terrifies her. She is sent to his bed. She trembles with fear and desire. He then uses her, at length. In the end, she is completely conquered. She has become the helpless love slave of her dominator, her master. "I love you, Master," she whispers. "Be kind to your slave. I love you, my master!"

No longer does she think of freedom. She thinks now only to please her master. She fears that he might sell her. She wants now only to be a superb slave. Even if he should sell her, she is not, now, too discontent. She would still have a collar. She would then belong to another man, perhaps even stronger, more attractive. She no longer wants to be a free woman. She now wants the incredible and fantastic fulfillment of the owned slave; she has now, in a collar, writhing under the touch of her master, found an incredible fulfillment as a woman denied to the lofty ladies so prizing their freedom. She envies them their freedom, and fears them, of course; but, in her heart, she would not, for anything, trade her lowly, degraded status for theirs. In her heart she now knows that men are masters, women slaves. "Yes," she tells herself, "I am a natural slave girl. I am not unhappy." She snuggles against her master. She is fulfilled, completely. She is a helpless female slave, an owned woman, but, for the first time in her life, content in her femaleness, happy. No longer does she, like many women, wish she was a man. Now, a conquered slave girl, she rejoices in her womanhood. A woman is not a mistaken, or an incomplete man; she is different; she is a marvel, a jewel, a joy; in bondage she has learned her womanhood; she will refuse to surrender it; she would not now exchange her sex, nor her collar; she is now a woman, a loving slave; she is happy.

Do not forget perfumes and lipsticks. Both are sexually stimulating. Lipstick, of course, in the sweet games, can be smeared, get on pillows, etc. Perfume doesn't smear. Perhaps, by agreement among the players, certain perfumes and shades of lipstick have certain significances. Is a certain perfume, for example, slave perfume? Similarly, different characters might have different tastes. For example, a given perfume might suit Linda's personality, but not Vonda's, etc.

Good luck with imaginative sex!

APPENDIX 4. Notes on How to Buy a Slave Girl

You always buy a woman naked, of course. Only a fool buys a clothed woman. If she stands before you in a behind-the-neck restraint, order her freed of it, that you may better assess her. You can always have her turn before you, slowly, head back, hands clasped behind her head. If you are alone with the slave and her seller, you have an excellent opportunity to examine her, better than if she stood some distance from you, on the block. Order her to walk and move before you, and to lie down, and rise, and kneel, and look over her shoulder, etc. You can tell a great deal from such simple things. Also, stand before her, hold her by the arm, and look down into her eyes. You will then sense the chemistry between you. Look carefully into her eyes, she in your grip. Do her eyes tell you that she fears you, or that you excite her, against her will, or that she will try, desperately, to resist you? Feel her body, her ankles, her calves, the ass of her, her belly, her breasts, her throat. Do you like the feel of her? What is the length and condition of her hair? Long hair, other things being equal, is desirable. There is more that can be done with it. Open her mouth and examine her teeth. You can tell much of the slave's condition from her teeth. Be rough with her; she expects it; she is property; if she senses the least weakness in you she will attempt to exploit it, to dominate you; she cannot help herself; she is a woman. Examine her candidly; is she young enough to have a good resale value? How many masters has she had? Why did her last master sell her? Was she a bred slave or a capture? If she was bred, what is the reputation of the house that bred her? What sort of training do they give her? If she is a capture, what sort of training, if any, has she received? What is her general background, if of free birth? What, roughly, is her intelligence? Can she cook, iron, clean, wash, sew, etc.? Has she been taught to serve foods and wines? (You might wish to use her as a table slave, as well as a sex slave.) You are not rich, and perhaps you can afford only one girl. Accordingly you wish to make a sound purchase, and, considering possible resale, a good investment. You can also see if she can dance. Not all girls can. You should also, while holding her arm, gently move your finger on her clitoris. This is to test her responsiveness. If the merchant, in a private sale, does not permit this, he is not a *bona fide* dealer. Lastly, if the merchant is willing (this varies from merchant to merchant), try her out, to see if she is any good. If the girl seems, on the whole, acceptable, you may purchase her. Be sure to receive a bill of sale, and her registration papers, suitably endorsed. Little then remains but to lock her in slave cuffs, hood her, put her on a leash, and take her home. At your threshold you unhood her and remove the leash. You leave the cuffs on her; then you throw her to your shoulder and carry her into your home. This is a symbolic act, indicative that she is captive; it is done even though she was purchased. The first thing you do with her inside is to beat her, and then use her. Later she may be set about her work. She must learn from the first instant that you are her master; and that she is complete slave.

Some men prefer to buy from the block; it is very exciting to do so, and the girl, stimulated by the buyers, almost always presents herself well; private sales, of course, allow more intimate inspection of the merchandise (some auction sales, though, it should be noted, maintain exhibition cages with lot numbers, in which the slaves may be observed closely before bid upon. These exhibits take place in the afternoon of the sale; the actual sale takes place at night; naked women on the block, under torchlight, are very beautiful. Some men, incidentally, like to buy from friends or private owners; sometimes exchanging slaves for a trial period. A purchase from a private owner is sometimes less expensive; the slaver's commission is avoided.

That night, as your new girl serves you, you regard her.

She is not bad. You congratulate yourself. You have made a good buy. She knows that she is your slave; you have taught her that; within moments of entering your house you initiated her to her servitude with the whip; and then, brutally, forced the lesson home with the pounding hammer of your manhood, her abdomen struck, shocked, again and again, reeling under the blows of your weight and power, she holding to you, fingernails unconsciously digging your shoulders, in terror and joy, eyes closed, crying out, surrendering, moaning, gasping, struck, in the helpless submission of the slave female.

You now regard her. She serves you. Women are beautiful beasts. Either you or she will be the master. When she looks at you you see in her eyes that it is you, and will be you, who are the master.

"Kneel beside the table," you tell her.

She does.

You give her food. She feeds delicately, turning her head to eat from your hand. Her teeth are small and white; her head is very beautiful, and her hair.

You wonder about her. She seems, somehow, different from the others.

You fear that you might begin to care for her. Only a fool, it is said, cares for a slave girl. It is dangerous to do so.

But she seems somehow different, so vulnerable, so fine, so beautiful.

Perhaps later you and she will fall in love. But first she must be slave. No woman understands the meaning of love unless she has first been a conquered slave girl.

Remember, even if you should be fool enough to free her, she may be, promptly and completely, re-enslaved, even sold if you wish. This is a culture in which women are expected to be pleasing to men, not men pleasing to women, as in our own culture.

She looks up at you. Timidly she ties a bondage knot in her hair.

You smile at her. "You will be well used later, Slave," you tell her.

She smiles. "Thank you, Master," she whispers.

APPENDIX 5. Notes on Investments, Documents and Conception.

The price of slave girls, like that of any commodity, varies with supply and demand.

If a city has recently fallen, the market may be glutted with women; in times of relative peace, when they are scarce, their prices may be outrageously high. We may assume, however, that with a well organized slaving industry, a regular number of property females will commonly be available, the fruit not only of professional slave raids but of the breeding pens. Speculation in slave girls is risky, as the market tends, aside from the stabilities provided by the slaving industry, to be uncertain. The price of a girl is usually lowest in the winter, however, and highest in the spring. Accordingly some houses lay in large stocks in the winter months, and then dispose of them in the spring and early summer. Investors may purchase stock in such houses, and receive dividends. These stock shares, too, of course, vary in price and speculation in such shares is not uncommon.

Women are not always cheap to obtain, of course. It takes time and money to organize an intelligent, efficient slave raid. A young slaver, skilled with rope and iron, a master of weapons, commands high wages, both in gold and women. Furthermore, many times one must travel far to obtain women, to outlying villages and islands, less protected. Even after her capture, the woman must be returned to the pens, and processed, and trained and fed, until she is sold. All this costs money.

For an individual, however, a single slave girl, or two or three such, can constitute a small investment and pleasant hobby. If you sell a girl for more than you bought her for, in a relatively

stable economy, she will have cost you little more than the food
you have given her. With an initial investment, that way, one
can manage, serially, buying and selling, to have a succession
of lovely female slaves, at little or no cost beyond their food.
You might, of course, assuming you are keeping one at a time,
find one, eventually, perhaps the seventeenth or twentieth, that
you are fond of. You may then, if you wish, keep her. (If you
need money, of course, you will presumably sell her. When your
fortunes improve you could then buy another, or perhaps she
again, if convenient. Another way to make money on her, of
course, would be to rent her. This way you retain legal ownership.
(The rentee has complete slave rights, of course, including the
application of discipline and body use. If he should, however,
mutilate or slay the slave, compensation must be paid to the
owner. Compensation is figured according to a flexible scale,
applied by judges; if the slave is slain or rendered useless, as in
being hamstrung, the owner is entitled to his original purchase
price plus ten percent. Hamstrung slaves are usually disposed
of; sometimes, nude, they are used for begging.) The difficulty
with renting is that one makes only a bit of money at a time,
over a long period of time. If money is needed, it is doubtless
preferable to sell the girl outright. When your fortunes improve,
as mentioned, you could always buy another, or, if convenient,
buy her back again. (Does she, in the market, chained to the wall
with the other girls, seeing you, beg you to purchase her again,
promising to serve you even better this time, more abjectly,
more imaginatively, more sensuously? You may then either buy
her again or not. It is up to you. Perhaps there is another wench,
chained at the wall, who looks at you, lips parted, eyes pleading,
as a slave girl, who might be of even more interest. Perhaps you
let them compete, each trying to please you more? Perhaps you
buy both and bring them home, playing them off, one against
the other. Each, then, tries to be your favorite. A most pleasant
situation for a male! (Your wife, of course, plays both roles, being
catty about the other, trying to serve you best, etc. Let her act
the dual role of two slave girls, competing for the attentions
of their master. If she does not please you best, the other girl
will, of course. She will then be the favorite. Not only, in such a

case, would the wife, at least temporarily, have been bested as a female, but she would then be, in many respects, at the ungentle mercies of the other girl. The most troublesome and menial of slave tasks would then, doubtless, fall to her. "Let Linda do it, Master." "Very well." "Please, Master!" "Be silent, Slave." "Yes, Master." One girl looks with superiority at the other, the ordered slave. There is hatred between them. The master is master. He enjoys the attentions of his two women.)

It can be great fun to prepare a bill of sale and registration papers on your wife. Such papers might include biographical data, including capture report, date of branding, processing, training, etc., with appropriate stamps and signatures. Her medical condition, similarly, certified, should appear in these papers, with perhaps a categorization of her sexual responsiveness, for example, is she an "A" female, a "B," or a "C," etc.? (As she learns sex, of course, these ratings might be updated; if she should become complacent, they might be reduced. A high sex rating is much in a girl's interest, incidentally; it raises her price and tends to assure her a richer master, and a comparatively easier life). These papers should include, too, measurements, for example, height, weight, hips, waist and bust; and, perhaps, left ankle and throat, the former for slave-anklet size, if wished, the latter, of course, for steel-collar size (it can be a delight to measure the body of a naked woman; and there is no reason that alien cultures might not be interested in measurements that we do not customarily make; for example, what does she measure from the right armpit to the right hip, from the back of the knee to the back of the ankle, etc.; perhaps there are blanks on the forms for these measurements to be entered, and others; in measuring her, of course, treat her roughly; she is only an animal, a slave; the measurements, too, should perhaps not be in inches but in a similar, small unit, on a suitably marked tape, appropriate to another culture; for example, how many Telnarian slave increments gives your wife's waist size, her bust size? It seems appropriate that slaves, animals, would not be measured as human beings, or high-order rational creatures. They would have their own measures; this distinguishes them from free persons and confirms, in their own mind and that of others, their essential differences from free individuals; a girl, for example, might only know her weight and sizes in slave measures; she could not even give her bust size, except in slave increments, as the bust of a slave; the sex ratings mentioned previously, as well as other measures and categories, might be "alienized"; this helps the female to think of herself as a slave and gives an exciting "alien reality" to the fantasy; for example, sex ratings in Telnarian might be based not on "A's" and "B's," etc., but on a popular analog to, say, a Telnarian 100-point temperature scale; the sex rating would be a function perhaps of the rapidity with which the slave can be brought to orgasm, combined with the frequency of the orgasms and their intensity; any girl who has a rating of over, say, ninety degrees, might be quite good; she might be the sort of woman who, under a man's touch, in spite of herself, is spontaneously and helplessly responsive, a "hot" girl. This is not entirely genetic, incidentally, though the capacity would be. Apparently almost any woman, under proper slave disciplines, can be forced to become a ninety-degree girl. Slavery itself immediately, startlingly, effects a considerable improvement in a female's sexual performance; it is not unusual for a 20-degree free woman, struck and collared, hurled to her master's bed, not permitted inhibitions, to give performances in terror in the seventies and eighties, sometimes in the nineties, sometimes, in unusual cases, in the high nineties. These physiological facts have led some physicians, in male-dominated cultures, to hypothesize that the female is a natural slave. Whatever be the likelihood or unlikelihood, the truth or falsity, of this, it is established, clearly, that the female responds sexually to a master far more organically, profoundly and excitingly than to a putative equal. She talks one game; her orgasms, in spite of herself, play another. The female with her mouth tells us one story; her heaving haunches and moans, once she is enslaved, tell us another; perhaps, too, the papers include fingerprints; these are useful, with measurements, in slave identification; the girl kneels, incidentally, while her prints are taken; if the fingerprints should be defaced or altered, the other measurements may serve for identification, they being fed into a computer; certain measurements might change, e.g., waist size, but others, such as height and ankle circumference, would remain relatively stable; each approximate measurement of the identification set fed into the computer would eliminate thousands of possibilities; each set of two would eliminate thousands upon thousands of possibilities; and so on, geometrically; no two human females, for example, are built exactly alike; and the differences are precise and measurable; each measurement, of course, would give a certain range of error, to minimize tiny alterations; further, we might suppose that the slave measurements, by law, are kept reasonably up to date; further, we might suppose that slaves, under discipline, are forced to keep, as well as they can, their original or optimum set of measurements, e.g., the "block" measurements, those imposed on her by steam bath, exercise and diet, before she was certified acceptable merchandise to be sold; consider the case of the girl caught last night by two magistrates in the Salarian Swamps, with net and swamp sled, who claimed to be a free swamp girl; her stripping revealed the brand; she was put in slave steel; she had tried to burn her fingertips; prints were imperfect; her measurements, communicated to a computer station, revealed her, within minutes, to be Sylvia, a slave escaped more than fifty rotations ago from Pron of the city of Prius, more than a thousand laks from the Salarian swamp; she is being returned in chains to her master, a slave whip knotted about her neck; brands, of course, stay on the girl; it is a serious offense to attempt to remove one surgically, punishable by enslaving the physician; furthermore, slave women do not have moneys for the operation; slaves have nothing; they do not even own their own rags, collars or eating utensils; they own nothing; it is they, rather, who are owned; tissue studies can determine whether or not a brand has been removed; girls, under slave interrogation, become swiftly glib; accordingly, no physician who removes a brand is safe; accordingly, few physicians dare to remove brands; the girl, apprehended, is rebranded and returned to slavery, usually gang labor on a remote agricultural planet; even if a woman is freed, incidentally, she retains the brand, which she then wears under the clothing of a free woman; it is thought to be an excellent reminder to her that if she is not pleasing to her lover she may be, at his decision, swiftly and completely re-enslaved, thence to be, should he please, placed on the market, not differently from any other girl; photos, too, of course, might be fed into the computer and scanned electronically; in addition to fingerprints, if one wishes, one might also take a print of, say, the large toe of the right foot; this indignity, for some reason, outrages Earth women of free birth, but it is also thought useful, on certain planets, populated by aggressive, imperialistic peoples, in effecting the organism's transition to slavery; many animals, of course, have toe prints taken, the Telian lelp, for example; this print is taken, normally, with the slave either on her stomach or back, not kneeling, as when fingerprints are taken; more sophisticated slave identification, and tracing, devices, of course, might be supposed; perhaps, painlessly, through the scalp, a beam inscribes a slave registration number literally on the bones of the skull, which number can then be read by a suitable scanning device; another possibility would be to insert a tiny plate or pellet (perhaps only as wide as a few molecules) in, say, the base of the brain, which, being detected by a given electronic device, will result in a specific number produced on the device's screen; the papers, too, which one is preparing on one's wife, might contain pasted-in slave photos; if you do your own developing, these may be as sexy as you wish; if you do not do your own developing, there are various possibilities; she might be stripped, kneeling and chained, and you take pictures, front and sideview, of her head only; when the pictures are developed you know the full story; others do not; it might be assumed that slave females always have head photos taken in this fashion; also, if she wears a brief slave garment, perhaps narrowly parted to the waist, revealing little, and a handful of thongs about her neck, and is photographed at the beach, or in your home, say, against a backdrop (what about a plain, or striped, or animal-patterned sheet or bedspread?), carrying a vase, reclining, watching you; kneeling, head to one side, etc., no one but you and she need know she is a slave; the fellow developing the pictures will only see a briefly clad, exciting female, with an unusual neck adornment; he will want to fuck her, but then, one supposes, so would anyone who sees her so clad; if he knows anything about imaginative sex, of course, and many people will, some months after this book is published, he may understand the picture very well; in such a case he might, regarding the picture, turn bright green; he might well envy the master of such a wench; but then, if he *really* knows anything about imaginative sex, he will doubtless have one of his own at home, similarly startling and desirable; if anything, ignorant or not, the picture should make him happy; it is hard to look at a good-looking woman without having one's pupils dilate; indeed, the entire chemistry is cheered up by such an event; the reason so many men look at women is that it gives them great pleasure to do so; pleasure is morally permissible; girl getting, of course, is better than girl watching; but then, it is included in girl getting; it is difficult to get a girl without seeing what you are doing; one of the great advantages of imaginative sex, incidently, is that turns men toward their own wives; they tend, hopefully, to be the girl one gets; imaginative sex, as a supplement to the sexual diet, is excellent at revitalizing tired marriages; no longer is your wife familier, routinized meat; she now becomes a partner in joint, mutually planned, delicious adventures; she now becomes, imaginative sex, a succession of desirable and lovely creatures, yours, and yet, beneath it all, as you and she well know, happily remains the girl, now the woman, you loved and married. She is now many woman to you, and yet, always, herself, whom you love. And that one wench, to whom you always return, in imaginative sex is now revealed as having new and exciting dimensions; she is now something it is a pleasure, in her thousand countries, to discover. You will never grow tired of her. No one yet has succeeded in mapping the continents of the imagination.

There should be, too, in her papers, a leaf, or leaves, for endorsements, indicating her changes of hand, with dates and stamps. The new owner's signature, seller's with stamp, and counter-signature, goes on the last blank line. (This helps to build up the characterization of the female, giving her a "slave history," etc. It tends to improve her performance; she *is* a slave. On a hundred nights, if you wish, you could be a hundred masters. Her papers, of course, reflect her changes of master, and, one supposes, any details felt pertinent.)

In thinking about bills of sale and registration papers, etc., keep in mind that there might be other documents of interest as well. Perhaps there is a form for reporting the escape of a slave, which is, say, finished off when she is apprehended. What about a form for leasing a slave, or renting her? What about, say, "want lists," submitted to dealers, when you are looking for a given type female. What about a purchase order sent to a slave house for a hundred beauties (among these, unknown to you at the time, is there a girl, now fallen to slavery, who was once, behind the protection of her freedom, unpleasant to you? If so, finding her at your mercy could be quite a delight.) A natural document here, of course, could be a capture order, or slave requisition. You might then capture this wench, and see if she fills the requirements of the order. If she does not, she is released. If she does, she is whisked away, to be the property of masters. A capture order, or requisition, of course, could be quite specific. It might be a specification of a given individual, say, Linda E. Rogers, of such-and-such an address, for reduction to bondage. Perhaps a down payment is made to the slaver, in a sort of contract, the balance to be paid when the wench is delivered, stripped, now nameless, chained and branded, ready for your collar.

Conception, of course, is not permitted in a slave, unless one wishes to mate her. On the papers there doubtless appears the last date the slave was forced, in the presence of a master, to drink the "slave wine," a bitter, prophylactic drink which prevents conception for at least four months after being drunk. Each four months, of course, the master may, if he wishes, have her drink it again in his presence. If he wishes to mate her, there is a counter-drink, delicious, though horrifying to the girl, who knows its meaning, which counteracts the effect of the slave wine. She may, thus, be mated at any time that is convenient to the master. Slaves, incidentally, are commonly hooded while being mated, that no possibility of love or affection enter into the relationship, which is a mere animal breeding. The mating, similarly, takes place under the supervision of both masters, to satisfy each that penetration and ejaculation has taken place. Maximum probability of conception, of course, occurs some twelve to sixteen days following the return of the menstrual flow. It is a miserable wench, say, Linda, indeed who is hooded and taken to her stud, whom she never sees, on such a day. She knows that, against her will, she will conceive. Her master will have it so.

About the Author

John Norman, born in Chicago, Illinois, in 1931, is the creator of the Gorean Saga, the longest running series of adventure novels in science fiction history. Starting in December 1966 with *Tarnsman of Gor*, the series was put on hold after its twenty-fifth installment, *Magicians of Gor*, in 1988, when DAW refused to publish its successor, *Witness of Gor*. After several unsuccessful attempts to find a trade publishing outlet, the series was brought back into print in 2001, and after *Witness of Gor* (2002), *Prize of Gor* (2008), *Kur of Gor* (2009), *Swordsmen of Gor* (2010) and *Mariners of Gor* (2011), they are now preparing the 2012 release of *Conspirators of Gor*. Norman has also produced a separate, three installment science fiction series, the Telnarian Histories, plus two other fiction works (*Ghost Dance* and *Time Slave*), a nonfiction paperback (*Imaginative Sex*), and a collection of thirty short stories, entitled Norman *Invasions*. The *Totems of Abydos* was published in spring 2012.

All of Norman's work is available both in print and as ebooks. The Internet has proven to be a fertile ground for the imagination of Norman's ever-growing fan base, and at Gor Chronicles (www.gorchronicles.com), a website specially created for his tremendous fan following, one may read everything there is to know about this unique fictional culture.

Norman is married and has three children.